Recent America:

1933 to the Present

The Structure of *American History*

DAVIS R. B. ROSS, ALDEN T. VAUGHAN,
AND JOHN B. DUFF, EDITORS

Recent
America:
1933 to the Present

edited by Davis R. B. Ross
COLUMBIA UNIVERSITY
Alden T. Vaughan
COLUMBIA UNIVERSITY
John B. Duff
SETON HALL UNIVERSITY

THOMAS Y. CROWELL COMPANY
NEW YORK · ESTABLISHED 1834

L C Card 78-101951

ISBN 0-690-69137-8

Series design by Barbara Kohn Isaac

Manufactured in the United States of America

Preface

The Structure of American History is designed to introduce
undergraduate students of United States history and interested
general readers to the variety and richness of our historical
literature. The six volumes in the series offer selections from
the writings of major historians whose books have stood the
test of time or whose work, though recent, has met with unusual acclaim. Some of the selections deal with political history, some with diplomatic, some with economic, and others
with social; all, however, offer thoughtful and provocative
interpretations of the American past.

The volumes, with seven substantial selections in each,
cover the following chronological periods:

    I. Colonial America: 1607–1763
   II. Forging the Nation: 1763–1828
  III. The Nation in Crisis: 1828–1865
  IV. The Emergence of Modern America: 1865–1900
   V. Progress, War, and Reaction: 1900–1933
 VI. Recent America: 1933 to the Present

Each volume opens with a general introduction to the period
as a whole, in which we have suggested major themes that
give coherence to the era and have outlined briefly the direction of past and recent scholarship. An editors' introduction
precedes each selection; in these we have not sought to tell
the reader what he is about to encounter but rather to identify
the selection's author, establish its historical setting, and pro-

vide its historiographical context. Finally, a short bibliographical essay follows each selection, in which the reader is
introduced to a wide range of related literature.

Several criteria guided us in our choice of readings: the distinction of the author, the significance of his interpretation,
the high literary quality of his style. Because we conceived of
the series as a supplement to, rather than a substitute for, the
reading usually assigned in college-level survey courses, we
have tried to avoid material that merely expands in detail the
coverage offered in the traditional textbooks; we have sought,
instead, selections from works that shed new light and raise
new questions, or at the very least provide a kind of reading
experience not customarily encountered in traditional assignments. For at bottom, *The Structure of American History*
stems from the editors' conviction that the great works of historical writing should not be reserved for the graduate student
or the professional scholar but should be laid before those
readers who can perhaps best benefit from an early encounter
with Francis Parkman, Samuel Eliot Morison, Allan Nevins,
Oscar Handlin, and their peers. We want college students to
know from the outset that the stuff of history is neither the
textbook nor the latest article in a scholarly journal. What has
often inspired us, as teachers and writers of history, and what
we hope will inspire students and lay readers, is history written by the great practitioners of the art: men who have written with vigor and grace the results of their own meticulous
research and meditation.

In order to make our selections as extensive as possible, we
have, with reluctance, omitted all footnotes. We urge readers
to remember that the authority of each historian rests largely
in the documentation he offers in support of his statements,
and that readers who wish to investigate the evidence on which
a historian has based his argument should refer to the original published version—cited on the first page of each selection. Readers are also reminded that many of the books
recommended in the bibliographical notes appended to each
selection are obtainable in paperback editions. We have refrained from indicating which volumes are currently in paper

for the list of paperbacks grows too rapidly. We refer those interested to R. R. Bowker Company, *Paperbound Books in Print,* available at the counter of most bookstores.

D.R.B.R.

A.T.V.

J.B.D.

Contents

Introduction

*F*ew intellectual tasks are more imposing than attempting to chart lines of historical continuity and change. Like a vessel at sea whose destination is unknown but departure point fixed, a society easily can log the factual story of how it got to its ever-moving present; the distance and route traversed are known. But to unravel the tangled wind currents, to sort out those that are but Poseidon's quirks from those that ceaselessly and purposively blow, is more difficult. Harder still is it to identify those main currents that both billow sail today and bend mast tomorrow.

The historian of the recent American past has an easy reference point of departure. The Great Depression and the subsequent (and consequent) election of Franklin D. Roosevelt seem impeccably qualified as a "turning point." The economic and political reconstruction affected millions in economic, political, and social ways, as a glance at unemployment, voting, and birth rate statistics attest. The importance of the symbolic year 1933 is heightened by the awareness that we are almost exactly a generation removed from it. Although some thirty-seven years have passed, in 1970 about 30 per cent of the population is old enough (at least eight years old in 1933) to remember personally these events, while another 23 per cent (born between 1926 and 1945) have mixed first- and second-hand experiences. The first two selections in this volume accordingly deal with aspects of the Great Depression and with the Roosevelt Administration's responses.

Younger readers will join with their elders in attesting to the notion that foreign affairs have dominated American life since

1933. For over thirty years many Americans have accepted as
just the United States' unceasing struggle, first with Germany,
then with the Soviet Union, over who shall win the allegiance
of the world's minds, hearts, and pocketbooks. Only in the past
half decade has there grown up at home a serious, neo-iso-
lationist challenge to that consensus. Still, even if the United
States is able to extricate itself from current armed involve-
ments throughout the world, its presence internationally will
remain. In fact, the dynamic post-1945 economic surge in the
United States, occasioned in large part by the cumulative im-
pacts of hot and cold war spending, has brought with it an
expansion of supranational American-based business corporations. Thus, American military forces, although very visible
and important, may well play a subordinate role in the United
States' enduring internationalism. Whether militarily, economically, or ideologically, the United States seems to be in
the world arena to stay. The third and fourth selections reflect the increased importance of world affairs in American
history.

Politically, the post-1933 period has marked one of the
greatest compositional changes in parties. The Republican
Party, holding a slim edge from the 1860's to 1896 and en-
joying hegemony from 1896 to 1932, found itself the minority
party following the Great Depression. Franklin D. Roosevelt,
if he did nothing else, turned a majority of Americans into
Democrats. In the process he altered deeply engrained notions
about the public welfare and the legitimacy of interest group
politics. The fifth and sixth selections cover parts of the continuing story of that "Rooseveltian" shift.

As in any era of American history, there have been many
other developments since 1933 that merit notice. Politics and
great men should not preempt all our attention. Among
others, space exploration, Black Power, urban growth, student
unrest, violence, and environmental concerns are topics that
have increasingly attracted scholarly as well as popular attention. We have chosen as our last selection a treatment of
a phenomenon that affects all the preceding: economic abun-

dance. Ultimately many of the problems and possibilities of our culture flow from that source. And, as navigators peering ahead toward uncharted waters, we suspect that this current will continue to affect our lives.

The New Deal Relief Program

Robert E. Sherwood

Quite apart from the story of the New Deal—which is dealt with more directly in another part of this volume—the Franklin Delano Roosevelt story is fascinating. The man left his indelible mark on modern America: some have regarded him as a savior, others as a dictator. With the exception of a seven year interlude in the 1920's, FDR had a prominent place in American public life for over thirty years—a long time to make enemies and, as the tear-stained faces of thousands attested in 1945 when he died, a sufficient time to make friends.

It is clear today that the election of Roosevelt to the presidency in 1932 brought the end to an era. The victor's campaign speeches, to be sure, did not differ radically from those of the incumbent, Herbert Hoover. In fact, little in Roosevelt's past foreshadowed later events. He had been born in 1882 of Hudson River valley "aristocrats," educated first by private tutors and subsequently at the exclusive Groton Academy, Harvard College, and Columbia Law School. His early career paralleled—quite consciously—that of his distant and

Source: Abridged from Robert E. Sherwood, *Roosevelt and Hopkins: An Intimate History.* (New York: Harper & Brothers, 1948), pp. 38–75. Copyright © 1948, 1950 by Robert E. Sherwood. Reprinted by permission of Harper & Row, Publishers.

distinguished cousin, Theodore Roosevelt. But in one significant aspect the two Roosevelts differed: Franklin tied his political fortune to the Democratic Party. After a term as a New York State senator, he served during World War I as assistant secretary of the navy in Woodrow Wilson's Administration; in 1920 he ran as vice-presidential candidate with his party's choice for chief executive, James M. Cox. Although the ticket was overwhelmingly defeated in America's return to normalcy, Roosevelt's career still seemed very promising. But in August 1921, he was stricken with poliomyelitis, cut down and partially paralyzed in the prime of life.

This personal misfortune, however, may well have stood him in good stead in later years; some commentators have speculated that the illness made the future President more sensitive to the sufferings of Americans during the Depression. He did not let the illness interfere with his sense of humor. Once while being wheeled into the White House's map room by a naval lieutenant, the chair became wedged between a map and a cabinet. After several entanglements FDR looked up at the lieutenant and asked, "Young man, are you trying to file me?" On the serious side, it is likely that his enforced withdrawal from active politics for the bulk of the Republican decade of the 1920's helped him in the post-1928 period. He could, through correspondence and trusted friends, serve the role of a party mediator and fence mender, while other Democratic leaders—like William Gibbs McAdoo and Al Smith—engaged in internecine strife.

Roosevelt's courage and the quiet support of his wife, Eleanor, brought him back into public life. At the 1924 and 1928 party conventions, he nominated Al Smith for President, the former time with his famous "Happy Warrior" speech; then he won the election for New York State governor in 1928. As governor, FDR led the way in some reforms that prefigured the New Deal—in conservation of State lands and forests, in public works planning, in unemployment relief, and in labor legislation. He did not exhibit, however, the boldness and spirit of experimentation that later characterized his activity during the "hundred days." He remained aloof, for example, from pleas to regulate the stock market and from demands that he discipline New York City's mayor, Jimmy Walker.

But, as President, Roosevelt did inject into his new office an enlarged sense of responsibility for the nation's welfare—a sense that transcended the concepts of even his most energetic predecessors. His deep concern for the country and people he served has been explained in several ways. We have already mentioned the suggestion that the new President's physical handicap made him more sensitive to the sufferings of others. To that should be added the social concern and tradition of public service bred into the Hudson River patrician by family and formal education. This principle would also help explain the unstinting devotion to the public welfare of his neighbor and secretary of the treasury, Henry Morgenthau, and of his diplomatic emissary to the Soviet Union in later years, W. Averell Harriman.

Roosevelt breathed life into his office virtually overnight. His was a mind always open to new ideas and theories, however bold and experimental. No intellectual himself, FDR relied upon college professors and social theorists for ideas on how to implement his programs. He drew from the brain power of Columbia and Harvard universities at will: Rexford Guy Tugwell, Adolf A. Berle, Jr., Raymond Moley, Felix Frankfurter, to name only the more prominent. His enemies later sought to attack the New Deal precisely on the grounds of its reliance upon the so-called "brain trust." Such attacks, although sometimes successful in neutralizing an individual's influence (as in Tugwell's case), usually came too late; the novelty and boldness had already been imprinted on the New Deal's programs.

Another source of Roosevelt's strength lay in his own relatively non-ideological approach to the problems of the Depression. He did of course have a central set of values by which he operated: he saw himself as the savior of capitalism. This point is affirmed in Robert E. Sherwood's comment in the following selection that Roosevelt was leading a "revolution of the Right." Still,

FDR was far more open to suggestion than his rigidly principled predecessor, Herbert Hoover. To the astonishment of another ideologue, his adviser Raymond Moley, FDR instructed that a speech on American trade policy include both free trade and high tariff sentiments. When his advisers could not agree, as in the case of drafting the National Industrial Recovery Act, he told them to lock themselves into a room until they had settled differences; apparently few principles seemed uncompromisable to him. Untroubled by the fundamental conflict of ideas, Roosevelt sailed on with other projects. He endorsed governmental spending for relief, but sternly cut back spending for veterans' pensions in the 1934 Economy Act. Though inconsistent, such acts also had their virtues, since they permitted him to try many different problem-solving avenues.

Another strength emerged from his acute sensitivity to political considerations. As with the case of Woodrow Wilson, Roosevelt faced a nominally Republican nation. One of his important partisan tasks involved the molding of a new political majority for the Democratic Party. Appealing to potentially powerful and disaffected blocs, he skillfully constructed a new majority that consisted of farm, labor, ethnic, and Southern votes. This political necessity again made him particularly sensitive to the appeal of hitherto neglected minorities and interest groups.

His administrative techniques may also have contributed to his political effectiveness. This is curious, for critics often damned FDR's staffing methods. Authority was blurred, staff lines unclear, and project assignments vague. Not infrequently several people worked on a project, most not knowing that FDR had entrusted the same tasks to someone else as well. The President's notorious inability to say no to an importunate request created some problems. Despite these flaws and his seemingly loose hold on administrative reins, Roosevelt may well have encouraged a healthy competitive spirit within the various reaches of the federal bureaucracy. Sherwood notes other by-products, chiefly the ability to put two highly ambitious and gifted men, like Ickes and

Hopkins, in harness and extract from both the maximum effort and contribution, when, in other settings they may well have spent their energies fighting one another. Thus, in spite of stories of inefficiency, the administrative techniques of FDR did produce a lean and energetic top-level bureaucracy.

Lastly, his basic humanitarian thrust impelled him to make decisions that went far beyond Hoover's concept of governmental responsibilities. Robert E. Sherwood, in his Pulitzer-prize winning study, lays bare Roosevelt's and Harry Hopkins' humanitarian interests. Sherwood of course is not an unbiased observer. Although not a member of the administration during the period that Hopkins and Roosevelt cut a wide swath in public relief history, he later served FDR as a speechwriter and a wartime propagandist with the Office of War Information. His work remains a durable classic in Rooseveltiana, especially in its extensive coverage of Hopkins' and Roosevelt's relationship in foreign-policy making during World War II.

$\mathcal{A}$dolf Hitler became Chancellor of Germany on January 30, 1933, and some Americans who had read *Mein Kampf* and had taken seriously its implications were frightened as they tried to peer into the heavily clouded future. It was not that there was any immediate prospect of war, for Germany still seemed to be prostrate militarily and faith in the precautionary measures of the Treaty of Versailles still persisted. Far more immediate as a threat was the deeply disquieting suspicion that *it could happen here.* The dragon's teeth of Fascism and Communism were being sown throughout the world and in that winter of closing banks, of "scrip" currency and interminable breadlines, it was all too possible to fear that these destructive seeds might take root in American soil. The people as a whole knew very little of the true character of the new man who was coming into the White House on March 4. What if he should prove to be another Man on Horseback? Under the existing circumstances, it might not have been difficult for him to seize dictatorial power.

The American people were literally starved for leadership. Herbert Hoover, who had appeared to possess exceptional qualifications for the Presidency, had failed lamentably under the stress of major emergency. Although he had been honored as "a Great Humanitarian," his performance as President of a depressed nation was that of one who was pathetically inept in the exercise of common, human understanding. He first coldly assured the people that the depression was an illusion which it was their patriotic duty to ignore; then, when economic collapse occurred in Europe, he angrily denounced the depression as something un-American from which we should isolate and insulate ourselves; and, finally, he truculently scolded the people for blaming the depression on his own Republican party which had taken full credit for the preceding boom. (As a noble Republican, Dwight Morrow, said at the time, "Those who took credit for the rainfall should not complain when they are blamed for the drought.") The unfortunate fact was that Herbert Hoover was, in a word—and the word was applied by that sage Hoosier, George Ade— "clammy." Under his hapless Administration the prestige of the Presidency had dropped to an alarmingly low level and so had popular faith in our whole constitutional system and particularly in what Hoover himself stoutly maintained to be "the American way of life." The temper of the people was fearful and bitterly resentful and ominous.

There is a persistent theory held by those who prate most steadily about "the American way of life" that the average American is a rugged individualist to whom the whole conception of "leadership" is something foreign and distasteful —and this theory would certainly seem to be in accord with our national tradition of lawlessness and disrespect for authority. But it is not entirely consistent with the facts. We Americans are inveterate hero worshipers, to a far greater extent than are the British or the French. We like to personalize our loyalties, our causes. In our political or business or labor organizations, we are comforted by the knowledge that at the top is a Big Boss whom we are free to revere or to hate and upon whom we can depend for quick decisions when the going gets tough. The same is true of our Boy Scout troops and our criminal gangs. It is most conspicuously true of our passion for competitive sport. We are trained from childhood to look to the coach for authority in emergencies. The masterminding coach who can send in substitutes with instructions whenever he feels like it—or even send in an entirely new team—is a purely American phenomenon. In British football the team must play through the game with the same eleven men with which it started and with no orders from the sidelines; if a man is injured and forced to leave the field the team goes on playing with only ten men. In British sport, there are no Knute Rocknes or Connie Macks, whereas in American sport the mastermind is considered as an essential in the relentless pursuit of superiority.

In times of peace and prosperity, it is true, when the American people feel they are doing all right for themselves, they do not give much thought to the character of the man in the White House; they are satisfied to have a President who merely "fits into the picture frame," as Warren G. Harding did, and who will eventually look sufficiently austere on the less frequently used postage stamps. But when adversity sets in and problems become too big for individual solution then the average citizen becomes conscious of the old "team spirit" and he starts looking anxiously toward the sidelines for instructions from the coach. That is when the President of the United States must step out of the picture frame and assert himself as a vital, human need. American faith in the recurrence of that miracle is unlimited. There is deep rooted in our consciousness the conviction that a great President will appear "whenever we really need him," and in the years 1929–33 the question was being asked, constantly and apprehensively, "Where is he *now?*"

No cosmic dramatist could possibly devise a better entrance for a new President—or a new Dictator, or a new Messiah—than that accorded to Franklin Delano Roosevelt. The eternally ironic fact is that the stage was so gloriously set for him

not by his own friends and supporters, who were then relatively obscure people, but by those who were to become his
bitterest enemies. Herbert Hoover was, in the parlance of
vaudeville, "a good act to follow." Roosevelt rode in on a
wheel chair instead of a white horse, but the roll of drums
and the thunderclaps which attended him were positively
Wagnerian as emotional stimuli and also as ugly warnings
of what might happen to American democracy if the new
President should turn out to possess any of the qualities of a
Hitler or even of a Huey Long. The people did not have to
wait long for him to reveal himself, clearly and irrevocably.
As the occasion of his entrance was tremendous, so was the
manner of his rising to it. Harry Hopkins, who was to participate in the preparation of so many of the President's later
speeches, wrote after Roosevelt's death, "For myself I think
his first inaugural address was the best speech he ever made."
It was certainly most thoroughly representative of the character of the man himself. In something under two thousand
words he made it abundantly clear that there was going to be
action on a wide variety of fronts—"and action now." The
most famous phrase, and deservedly so, was "the only thing we
have to fear is fear itself"—and one thinks of these words
over and over again when considering Roosevelt's career and
the well-springs of his philosophy.

. . . . .

Eight days after the spectacular inauguration of the New
Deal—eight days during which all the banks in the country
had been closed—Franklin Roosevelt gave his first Fireside
Chat. "It has been wonderful to me to catch the note of
confidence from all over the country. . . . Confidence and
courage are the essentials of success in carrying out our plan
. . . Together we cannot fail." Here was the first real demonstration of Roosevelt's superb ability to use the first person
plural and bring the people right into the White House with
him. The very fact of a "chat" was in itself surprising and immeasurably stimulating: traditionally, when a President spoke
to the people, it was an "Address," which might be intended

as an exhortation, or an elaborate apologia, or a stern lecture. But Roosevelt spoke simply, casually, as a friend or relative, who had figured out a way to prevent foreclosure of the mortgage, and those of us who heard that speech will never forget the surge of confidence that his buoyant spirit evoked. It was all the more thrilling after the hair-shirted carping and petulance that we had been hearing from Hoover. During the three days following this Fireside Chat, 4,507 national banks and 567 state member banks reopened and Roosevelt sent a Message to the Congress asking for modification of the Volstead Act to permit the manufacture and sale of beer, thus writing the beginning of the end of fourteen years of prohibition and attendant crime. This long-overdue reform was tossed in as a sort of bonus and it was hailed joyfully by the people as proof that the new Administration was not only progressive and dynamic but also essentially cheerful. Happy days were here again! More than eleven years later, when Roosevelt was running for President for the fourth time, he evoked roars of agreement from a crowd in Fenway Park in Boston when he said:

> If there ever was a time in which the spiritual strength of our people was put to the test, that time was in the terrible depression of 1929 to 1933.
> Then our people might have turned to alien ideologies—like communism or fascism.
> But—our democratic faith was too sturdy. What the American people demanded in 1933 was not less democracy—but more democracy—and that is what they got.

The difference of opinion (to use the mildest of expressions) that existed between Roosevelt and his domestic foes was based on the definition of that word "democracy." Indeed, they came to hate the word so vehemently that they claimed it had never been applied to our form of government until Woodrow Wilson dreamed it up. They said that our government, as conceived and established by the Founding Fathers, was a *republic*, not a *democracy*, but they were reluctant to explain just what was the difference; they didn't dare. (It might be noted in this connection that, in his first Message to Congress, more than two years before he spoke at Gettysburg, Abraham Lincoln defined the United States as "a constitutional republic or democracy—a government of the people by the same people.") The political attacks on Roosevelt and the New Deal always resolved themselves into a plea, "Let us get back to the Constitution," but Roosevelt successfully persuaded a majority of the people that what this really meant was, "Let us get back to special privilege," or "Let us get back into the temple from which That Man ejected us."

In *The Roosevelt Revolution,* the authoritative Ernest K. Lindley covered the first six months of the New Deal and it is interesting to note that in this book he considered Hopkins as worth no more than a paragraph of mention as among those present in Washington. The conspicuous figures of that first year of the New Deal were Raymond Moley, Rexford G. Tugwell and Adolf Berle, of the "Brains Trust"; Louis Mac-Henry Howe, Roosevelt's close friend and most intimate adviser; Henry Morgenthau, Jr., another old friend who was at first Governor of the Farm Credit Administration; Lewis Douglas, Director of the Budget; Hugh S. Johnson, of N.R.A.; and, in the Cabinet, William H. Woodin, Harold L. Ickes, Frances Perkins and Henry Wallace. However, well within Roosevelt's first term, Hopkins came to be regarded as the Chief Apostle of the New Deal and the most cordially hated by its enemies. I think it may fairly be said that he earned this distinction. He was brought into the government on May 22 when seventy-nine of Roosevelt's "First Hundred Days" had already passed. He was made Federal Emergency Relief Administrator and it is my understanding that, as in the case of his Albany appointment two years previously, he was not the first choice for the job. Roosevelt later wrote of him:

> The task he faced was stupendous. Little was known at Washington about the efficiency of the various State and local relief organizations throughout the country. There were no such organizations in some of the States and in many of the coun-

ties. There were no immediately available reliable statistics
either about relief needs or relief expenditures.

Action had to be immediate. It was immediate. The day after
he [Hopkins] took office he telegraphed his first communication
to the Governors of the respective States; and before nightfall
he had made grants of money to Colorado, Illinois, Iowa,
Michigan, Mississippi, Ohio and Texas.

From the very beginning two important points of policy were
evident: (1) The operations of the program, aside from certain
basic standards and stipulations, were to be decentralized and
local in character, and (2) work, rather than idleness on a dole,
was preferred.

The original grant of money, in accordance with the statute,
was on the basis of $1.00 of Federal funds for every $3.00 of
local, State and Federal funds spent during the preceding
quarter year. The statute also provided that part of the fund
could be used in states without such matching where the
amount available by matching would be insufficient to meet the
needs for relief in any State.

The day after Hopkins went to work for the Federal Government the *Washington Post* printed a somewhat mournful
headline, "Money Flies," and stated, "The half-billion dollars
for direct relief of States won't last a month if Harry L.
Hopkins, new relief administrator, maintains the pace he set
yesterday in disbursing more than $5,000,000 during his first
two hours in office."

Hopkins was off. He sat down at his desk and started flash-
ing out telegrams even before the men had arrived to move
the desk out of the hallway into his office. He said, "I'm not
going to last six months here, so I'll do as I please." He had
been told by Roosevelt that his job was to get relief to people
who needed it and to have no truck with politicians. Of
course, the Relief Program offered more juicy plums in the
way of political patronage than had ever before been known
in peacetime. But at first, while Hopkins was still an amateur
in Washington politics, he was scornful of these sordid considerations. In the early days of the New Deal he worked, as
he was to work later in war, with regard for nothing but the

interests of the American people and of Franklin D. Roosevelt, which to him meant one and the same thing. In appointing men and women to positions of authority he was concerned only with consideration of their competence and zeal; he did not give a damn whether they were Methodists, Baptists, Catholics or Jews—and he was specifically instructed by the President never to "ask whether a person needing relief is a Republican, Democrat, Socialist or anything else." Hopkins said, "I don't like it when people finagle around the back door." He thus soon found himself involved in controversy with James A. Farley and with various members of Congress and State Governors whose duty it was to look out for the interests of "deserving Democrats." Confident of Roosevelt's support, Hopkins continued for a long time on the principle that relief was entirely nonpartisan. For that was a period of soaring altruism. In the first, triumphant sweep of the New Deal, it was possible to afford the luxury of being nonpolitical—but Hopkins learned better (or perhaps one should say "worse") later on when the opposition began to recover its dissipated strength and elections became less easy to win.

There had been a pretense of a relief program before F.E.R.A. Confronted with the obvious, overwhelming need for some kind of Federal Government aid for the idle and hungry victims of economic collapse, Hoover had found himself in one of the many impossible dilemmas that beset him: the "dole" system was naturally repugnant to him, but the only logical alternative appeared to be a form of government subsidy of public works projects which smacked of State Socialism. Since the dole was traditional, and had been since the institution of the "Old Poor Law" in the reign of Queen Elizabeth, Hoover favored that, however much he hated it, simply because it was traditional. Thus, American citizens who had so recently been given the assurance of two cars in every garage and a chicken in every pot were now given basically the same kind of treatment that was accorded to paupers in sixteenth-century England. Hoover tried to meet this problem, as he tried to meet so many others, by appointing commissions to "study" it. (His principal committee was headed by Walter S. Gifford, of the American Telephone and Telegraph Company.) But this was an emergency which demanded action first and study later. Finally, in the summer of 1932, with an election imminent, Hoover supported legislation which provided for loans, at three per cent interest, of $200 millions from the Reconstruction Finance Corporation to the various States for relief—the Federal Government to assume responsibility for the bookkeeping but not for the actual application of these funds. This was known as the Emergency Relief and Construction Act and it provided a nuclear regional organization which Hopkins took over when he started work; but it provided him with no funds, for the money had run out when he started to minister to the needs of some seventeen million people who were subsisting on the relief rolls. Under the new dispensation of F.E.R.A., the funds appropriated—$500 millions— were in the form of outright grants rather than loans to the States; but, otherwise, there was no essential departure from the principle of the dole. The main burden of cost and of administration was still on the local authorities to whom the needy must go, cap in hand, to accept charity. This is precisely where Hopkins came in and produced a profound change in the whole conception of governmental responsibility and function.

Hopkins inherited from the previous relief organization several key men who were predominantly social workers, like himself, trained to think that local problems should be handled with funds locally raised and administered by local and, to the greatest possible extent, *private* charitable organizations. In other words, the fact of Federal relief must be disguised in all possible ways. This was in deference to the creed that private enterprise must always provide the cure for any and every ill and that anyone who said that it might be unable to do so was a declared enemy of the American way of life. But Roosevelt as Governor had proclaimed the principle of State responsibility to "the humblest citizen" and Hopkins took those words literally. This was the great tenet of the New Deal, which became the number one item in Roosevelt's Economic Bill of Rights of eleven years later: the right to work.

One of the first men that Hopkins brought into F.E.R.A. to advise him was Frank Bane, whom he had met in the First World War when he was working for the Red Cross in the South. In 1931 Bane had organized the American Public Welfare Association and had consulted with Roosevelt and Hopkins on relief problems in New York State and with the Gifford Committee on the problems in the nation as a whole. The Gifford Committee was interested in developing the activities of private charitable agencies, whereas Bane insisted that all levels of government—Federal, State and community —should be directly and openly responsible for the administration of public relief. The Bane slogan was, "Public funds expended by public agencies," which did not find favor under the Hoover Administration but was right in line with Hopkins' thinking.

Bane agreed to work for Hopkins without pay on a temporary basis. He named, as his permanent successor, another social worker, Aubrey Williams, of Alabama, whom Hopkins did not then know but who was to become one of his ablest, most loyal and most smeared aides in the whole New Deal achievement. Williams had been a field representative of the American Public Welfare Association, of which Bane was Director. The long-scorned social workers were coming into their own as figures of national importance.

On June 17—three and a half weeks after he had entered government service—Hopkins went to Detroit to speak at the National Conference of Social Work. Bane and Williams were already there when he arrived. They begged him to take a stand in favor of direct Federal relief—as opposed to relief administered through private agencies. He was in grave doubt as to the practicability of this; but it was the way his natural inclinations tended, and he followed his natural inclinations. He spoke out in favor of relief as an obligation of the Federal Government to the citizens—without any pretense of private agencies interposed—thereby putting into effect the Roosevelt doctrine that this relief was a sacred right rather than an act of charity, an obligation of government to its citizens rather than a mere emergency alleviation of suffering in the form of alms. Hopkins' Detroit speech was given scant notice in the press and such attention as it received overlooked utterly its main import. I do not know if Roosevelt himself or any of his then advisers knew at the time just what it was that Hopkins had said; but the principle had been stated, and it was followed religiously in the administration of F.E.R.A., and Roosevelt supported it and came to admire Hopkins and to give him more and more opportunities to exert his influence in the official family.

There were two other important principles that Hopkins advocated successfully in the beginnings of F.E.R.A. One was the payment of cash instead of grocery slips to those on relief rolls. The other, considered revolutionary and wildly impractical by the more conservative social workers, was the extension of relief to the provision not only of food but of clothing, shelter and medical care to the needy. These principles have continued and have affected the whole concept of social work, particularly in the field of public health.

It may be interposed at this point that I have often wondered about the accuracy of the famous statement, attributed to Thomas Corcoran, that "we planned it that way." Roosevelt had contemplated, in broad outline, the Tennessee Valley power project, the Agricultural Adjustment, Conservation and Public Works programs, the Securities and Exchanges Control and something like the National Industrial Recovery Act, more than a year before he became President, and they were all quickly put into effect. But the vast Relief Program, as Hopkins administered it, certainly did not work out according to any plan. It was a series of remarkable improvisations impelled by the character of the myriad problems that were discovered from day to day. By enforced research and a great deal of shrewd guesswork Hopkins found out what was really going on in the country as a whole and brought the facts home to Roosevelt. He personalized the problems for the President, and also most importantly for Mrs. Roosevelt who made the concerns of helpless individuals her own. Any appraisal of the Roosevelt Administration must begin with the fact that the government in Washington in the years following 1933 achieved an incomparable knowledge of the aspirations and the fears and the needs of the American people and that knowledge became of supreme importance when those same people had to be called upon for unprecedented efforts in the waging of the Second World War. The research needed to get the program started was multiplied by the various, extensive research projects carried out subsequently under the program itself.

Although Hopkins will never be celebrated as a "sound money" man or a champion of the sanctity of the taxpayer's dollar, he was exceptionally economy minded in one respect: he liked to run his own organization on the smallest possible budget. Unlike most bureaucrats, he hated to have a lot of civil servants around. What he wanted and what he obtained was a small staff composed of people of such passionate zeal that they would work killing hours. At the end of the first year Hopkins' relief organization had handled on its rolls the vital problems of some seventeen million people and had spent a billion and a half dollars, but the organization itself consisted of only 121 people with a total payroll of only $22,000 a month. To anyone in any way familiar with the normal workings of government, the lowness of those figures is well nigh incredible. But Hopkins managed to obtain people to whom a sixty-hour work week would be a holiday. Hopkins' own salary was under $8,000 as opposed to $15,000 he had earned before entering the government. He and his wife and baby lived for a considerable time on $250 a month, the remainder of his salary going for the support of the three sons by his first marriage. He told a reporter, "I'd like to be able to forget this $500,000,000 business long enough to make some money for clothes and food. Mrs. Hopkins is yelling for a winter coat. I don't blame her." Hopkins was by no means frugal in his personal tastes. He would like to have had a great deal of money and if he had he would have spent it lavishly, but he never did have it to the end of his days. Now

and then he would supplement his income by writing a magazine article and would feel very flush for a while. In 1944, in
his last year in government service, his salary was raised to
$15,000; so he ended up just where he had been before he
started.

In his perpetual haste, Hopkins was contemptuous of bu-
reaucratic procedure. When inspectors from the Bureau of
the Budget came around asking to see the "organizational
chart" they were told there wasn't any, as Hopkins would not
permit one to be made. He said, "I don't want anybody around
here to waste any time drawing boxes. You'll always find that
the person who drew the chart has his own name in the middle
box." He was also contemptuous of the formality—or "dignity"
—with which a high government official feels it necessary to
surround himself: the wainscoted office with thick carpets and
two flags on standards behind the huge mahogany desk. Hopkins owned no morning coat and striped pants, but he rented
this diplomatic uniform for the visit of King George VI and
Queen Elizabeth to Washington in later years when he was a
member of the Cabinet.

There was a kind of fanaticism in Hopkins' drive toward
the objectives that he had to a large extent established for
himself. This fanaticism was communicated to his co-workers
who felt that they were fighting a holy war against want. But
—lest this analogy be misinterpreted—it is necessary to add
that no fighter in this war who served under Hopkins was
compelled to wear the sackcloth uniform of asceticism. Despite
the rigid Methodism of Hopkins' early training, many of his
most important staff conferences during the New Deal years
were held in automobiles en route to or returning from the
Maryland racetracks around Washington. The organization
which became W.P.A. was first outlined by Hopkins in a suite
in the aristocratic Hotel St. Regis in New York. As Joseph E.
Davies has said of Hopkins, "He had the purity of St. Francis
of Assisi combined with the sharp shrewdness of a racetrack
tout."

Hopkins, in his first few months in office, sloughed off some
of the tradition-bound social workers whom he had inherited

from the previous, halfhearted regime and brought in men and
women who agreed with his own unrestricted conception of
governmental responsibilities. This did not mean that his staff
was composed of yes men and yes women; they were on the
contrary tireless and inveterate needlers, as he was, who would
not hesitate to prod and goad anyone, including their own
boss, who seemed at any instant to show signs of slacking on
the job. Hopkins always thrived in an atmosphere of protest.

. . . . .

In October, 1933, Hopkins knew that with winter coming on
the unemployment problem was bound to become more desperate and he believed that the only decent solution was a
huge work program. Aubrey Williams and other aides were
urging him to propose such a program to the President but
Hopkins felt sure that it would be turned down. He knew that
Roosevelt would be under fire on this not only from the conservatives: organized labor was strongly opposed to a program
of governmentally "made" jobs. This was one of the times
when Hopkins was impatient and irascible with those who
were prodding him to do the very thing that he himself most
wanted to do.

On Saturday, October 28, Hopkins arrived in Chicago to
have lunch with Robert Hutchins, President of the University
of Chicago, and to attend a football game. He was met at the
station by Frank Bane and Louis Brownlow, Director of the
Public Administration Clearing House, who had been talking
to Williams about the work program and who now joined in
hammering at Hopkins to bring it to the President. Both men,
experts in public administration, were able to give Hopkins an
abundance of facts and figures and he was able to absorb
them; but he still did not know how to sell the idea to
Roosevelt who was concerned about the attitude of organized
labor. He went from Chicago to Kansas City to make a speech;
among the people with whom he conferred on relief problems
while there was the Federal Unemployment Director for Missouri, Judge Harry S. Truman. Williams reached Hopkins in
Kansas City by telephone to announce that he had just seen

Dr. John R. Commons in Madison, Wisconsin. Dr. Commons was one of the country's greatest authorities on all matters pertaining to labor and, when he heard what was on Williams' mind, he dug into his voluminous files and came up with a clipping dating from 1898 of a statement by Samuel Gompers in which the father of American organized labor advocated precisely the form of work program then suggested. Gompers called it "The Day Labor Plan." That was just what Hopkins had hoped for. It was his convenient conviction that a precedent can almost always be found for a new idea, however revolutionary it may seem, if you really search for it; the precedent for Lend Lease was found in an unimportant law passed by Congress in 1892, during the Benjamin Harrison Administration. Thus, when Hopkins learned what Gompers had said, he knew he had the persuasive argument that Roosevelt needed to overcome the labor leaders' objections to the work relief program. He telephoned to the White House and was given an appointment for lunch on the day of his return to Washington.

During that lunch, Roosevelt asked how many jobs would have to be provided and Hopkins said about four million.

"Let's see," said Roosevelt. "Four million people—that means roughly four hundred million dollars." He thought this could be provided from the Public Works fund which was under the guardianship of Harold Ickes, who was neither then nor subsequently extravagant in his admiration for Harry Hopkins or for his methods. When Hopkins left the White House after this lunch he "fairly walked on air," as he had when he saw the house in which Keats wrote "Ode to a Nightingale." He put through a telephone call to Williams, who was by then in New Orleans making a speech for the Community Chest Fund, and insisted that Williams interrupt the speech and get to the telephone to hear the news that the work program was going to start with $400 millions. Williams, Brownlow and Bane were summoned immediately to Washington where they assembled Saturday night, one week after the football game in Chicago, together with Hopkins, Howard Hunter, Jacob Baker,

Julius F. Stone, Clarence M. Bookman, Ellen Woodward, Robert S. McClure, Corrington Gill, Pierce Williams and T. S. Edmonds. They worked most of Saturday night and Sunday in the Hotel Powhatan (later named the Roger Smith) and drew the plans for the Civil Works Administration which put the four million people to work in the first thirty days of its existence and, in less than four months, inaugurated 180,000 work projects and spent over $933 millions. It was the parent of W.P.A. and marked the real establishment of the principle of the right to work from which there could be no retreat.

Of the formation of C.W.A. Roosevelt wrote:

> The Public Works Administration (P.W.A.) had not been able by that time to commence a very extensive program of large public works because of the unavoidable time consuming process of planning, designing and reviewing projects, clearing up legal matters, advertising for bids and letting contracts.

This was Roosevelt's tactful means of explaining why he took nearly a billion dollars away from Ickes and entrusted the spending of it to Hopkins at that time (he eventually did the same with many times that sum). Ickes was a very careful, deliberate administrator, who took pains to examine personally every detail of every project and the disposition of every nickel that it cost, whether it be a village post office or a Triborough Bridge. This is hardly to his discredit for it was the approach to each problem of a hardheaded businessman as well as a conscientious public servant. Ickes was concerned about the return on the taxpayers' investment. Hopkins did not give a damn about the return; his approach was that of a social worker who was interested only in getting relief to the miserable and getting it there quickly. His ultimate argument was, "Hunger is not debatable." Ickes thought primarily of the finished job—Hopkins of the numbers of unemployed who could be put on the job immediately. As an instance of Hopkins' impatience: someone came to him with an idea for a project which would take a lot of time to prepare in detail but which, Hopkins was assured, "will work out in the long

run," and his exasperated comment on this was, "People don't
eat in the long run—they eat every day."

To quote further from Roosevelt's review of C.W.A.:

> Its organization and operation were essentially different from
> that of the F.E.R.A. [which was] mostly a State and local pro-
> gram loosely supervised and in part financed by the Federal
> Government but actually administered and exercised locally.
> The C.W.A. was, however, completely operated and 90 per cent
> financed by the Federal Government.

It was, actually, one of the broadest programs ever instituted
by the United States Government. It sought to provide for individuals work as near as possible to their previous employment and to pay the prevailing wage in each category and
region with a minimum of thirty cents an hour. It abolished
the "Means Test" whereby a man who sought government
relief was denied it if a member of his family was already
employed; Hopkins felt that the Means Test was an insult to
the dignity of the individual who, able and anxious to work,
was forced into the status of an idle dependent. The organization of C.W.A. was a clean sweep for the Hopkins theories of
work relief, and keen were the fears and violent the trembling
of those who did not trust him, who suspected him of being
an apostle of State Socialism rather than Jeffersonian Democracy. But Roosevelt had confidence in Hopkins' imagination
and ingenuity and both those qualities were required in abundance on this program.

The charge has often been made that Roosevelt was "so
intoxicated with the pomp and privilege of power that he
could not bear to delegate authority." Much of that came in
later years when the defense effort was mounting and Roosevelt for some eighteen months stubbornly refused to appoint
one man to be head of the huge production program; but,
when he did finally appoint Donald Nelson, he delegated to
him more authority than Nelson was able to handle. The
record in general seems to prove that Roosevelt delegated
authority with a lavish hand when he could find a man willing

to take it—and he certainly found one in Hopkins. When he
told Hopkins to invent jobs for four million men and women
in thirty days he expected him to do it in his own way and
without continually coming back to the White House for
advice on details. The President also told Hopkins to talk
the whole thing over with Harold Ickes and "straighten it
out" with him; but that proved a much more difficult task
than the four million jobs.

Roosevelt was greatly comforted by the fact that he had
his old friend Frank Walker on hand to keep an eye on Hopkins' activities. Walker, as President of the National Emergency Council, exercised a supervisory control over all the
sudden New Deal agencies. Montana born, a graduate of Notre
Dame, he was a quiet, gentle, trustworthy, unquenchably
friendly man who was invaluable to Roosevelt through the
years as spreader of oil on troubled administrative waters. He
later became Chairman of the Democratic National Committee
and Postmaster General after Farley "took a walk." Roosevelt
knew he could trust Walker to report if Hopkins were showing
signs of going crazy and producing dangerous political re-
percussions throughout the country. Indeed, in the early days
of C.W.A., such reports did come into the headquarters of the
National Emergency Council from its State Directors. Some
of them were almost hysterical with alarm at the intimations
of wholesale waste and even corruption in the program.
Walker decided to take a trip through the country and see for
himself. He returned to Washington with the assurance that
C.W.A. was doing more than all the other New Deal measures
to boost morale. He said that in his own home State of Montana, "I saw old friends of mine—men I had been to school
with—digging ditches and laying sewer pipe. They were
wearing their regular business suits as they worked because
they couldn't afford overalls and rubber boots. If I ever
thought, 'There, but for the grace of God—' it was right then."
The sight of these old friends made him feel sick at heart,
but when he talked to individuals he felt very differently, for
they were happy to be working and proud of what they were
doing. One of them pulled some silver coins out of his pocket

and showed them to Walker. "Do you know, Frank," he said, "this is the first money I've had in my pockets in a year and a half? Up to now, I've had nothing but tickets that you exchange for groceries." Another said, "I hate to think what would have happened if this work hadn't come along. The last of my savings had run out. I'd sold or hocked everything I could. And my kids were hungry. I stood in front of the window of the bake-shop down the street and I wondered just how long it would be before I got desperate enough to pick up a rock and heave it through that window and grab some bread to take home." It was not only hunger from which these men suffered; it was the deep sense of indignity and of grave injury to their national pride. The analogy used by President Roosevelt in his Inaugural Address was far from inappropriate: Americans felt as if, at a time when their country was being invaded and ravaged by alien enemies, their government had failed to provide them with any weapons for defense. Now, armed with a shovel, or even a rake, they felt able to fight back. "Leaf raking" became the term of supreme opprobrium for the New Deal, but great numbers of people who did the raking preferred it to breadlines or grocery tickets.

Walker said to Roosevelt: "I'd pay little attention to those who criticize the creation of C.W.A. or its administration. Hopkins and his associates are doing their work well. They've done a magnificent job. It is amazing when you consider that within the short time since C.W.A. was established four million idle have been put to work. During Christmas week many of them were standing in a payroll line for the first time in eighteen months. You have every reason to be proud of C.W.A. and its administration. It is my considered opinion that this has averted one of the most serious crises in our history. Revolution is an ugly word to use, but I think we were dangerously close at least to the threat of it."

Walker was not always so cordial in his approval of Hopkins' administrative methods, but in his reports to the President throughout the New Deal years, he was stanch in supporting Hopkins against the numerous and violent critics. A large part of Hopkins' original prestige with Roosevelt was undoubtedly attributable to Walker. The direct and unmistakable benefits to the jobless and their families were augmented by many evidences of business revival. Within the first weeks of C.W.A. shoe stores all over the country began to report that they were sold out and shoe factories began to reopen to meet the enormously increased demand.

C.W.A. came none too soon. That winter of 1933–34 was a terrible one. The temperature went to 56° below zero in parts of New England and to 6° below even in Washington, D.C., where the legislators could feel it. This was the first of a series of natural calamities—including droughts, floods and hurricanes—which occurred during these years as if to test the Roosevelt Administration in its program for national recovery. Hopkins had to increase his efforts to meet widespread suffering. By mid-January nearly twenty million people were dependent on Federal relief for the essentials of life and the $400 millions granted to C.W.A. was almost gone. Hopkins, with White House approval, went to the Congress for $950 millions more.

The Republican National Committee denounced him and C.W.A. for "gross waste" and "downright corruption" and one Democrat, Congressman George B. Terrell of Texas, arose to say, "The Constitution is being violated here every day because there isn't a line in the Constitution that authorizes the expenditure of Federal money for other than Federal purposes. . . . I think [C.W.A.] is going to start civil war and revolution when we do stop it anyway. . . . The others [in Congress] can go through on these things like dumb driven cattle if they want to, but . . . I won't sacrifice my independence for any office I ever heard of."

But Terrell's was a lone voice on Capitol Hill. The members of Congress were hearing from their constituencies the same kind of reports that Frank Walker had brought back to Washington, and there was an election coming up in 1934. So Hopkins got the money. One lamentably profane Senator was quoted by *Time* magazine as saying, "If Roosevelt ever becomes Jesus Christ, he should have Harry Hopkins as his prophet."

Time ran Hopkins' picture on its cover and, in a long article about him, paid tribute to him for having done "a thoroughly professional job" as administrator. *Time* reported:

> Of the $950,000,000 given him by the new law, Mr. Hopkins said he intended to use $450,000,000 to taper off C.W.A. gradually and $500,000,000 for direct relief. Congress would like him to use more for C.W.A. but he came out strongly against it, declaring that C.W.A. was an emergency measure, should not be permanent, should be gradually demobilized.

Hopkins was not then speaking from the heart. He was, with utmost reluctance and deep disappointment, obeying orders. For, even while he was scoring triumphs on Capitol Hill, C.W.A. was being torpedoed at the other end of Pennsylvania Avenue and this was done not by Republican enemies of the New Deal but by conservative elements within the Democratic party itself. The first crack in it came when Southern influence caused the abandonment of the thirty cents an hour wage minimum—causing wages in some parts of the South to drop to ten cents an hour or worse. Then Roosevelt was persuaded by Lewis Douglas and other economic advisers that there was something in what Terrell of Texas had said. They felt that there was serious potential danger in the work relief program, their argument being that if you got large numbers of people settled in government-made jobs, with guarantees of security that they would not readily obtain from private industry, *you might never be able to get them off the public pay roll.* That argument carried weight with Roosevelt and he told Hopkins that C.W.A. must be liquidated before spring and the former F.E.R.A. program of direct relief resumed.

Although this was a bitter blow to Hopkins, it provided him with his first opportunity to demonstrate his utter loyalty to Roosevelt. He did not afflict the President with a threat to resign. He was harsh in compelling his shocked associates to take this setback without complaint and to get on with the job of relief. Roosevelt was keenly sensitive to this and his personal fondness for as well as confidence in Hopkins increased more than ever at this time. The more he contemplated the C.W.A. record, the less he thought of the advice given him by Douglas, who soon came to the breaking point with his Chief and left the government. (He returned after Pearl Harbor and worked very closely and amicably with Hopkins during the war years.)

The ending of C.W.A. produced protests throughout the country which could not possibly be ignored. In one week upwards of 50,000 letters and 7,000 telegrams came into the White House. There were riots in various parts of the country. The people on the relief rolls made it clear that they agreed with Hopkins in his theory that direct relief had a demoralizing effect: they did not want tickets for baskets of groceries —they wanted *work*. In a review of the whole Relief Program and problem, *Fortune* magazine made the following rather supercilious statement:

> Direct relief is—purely and simply—the Dole. Almost as purely and simply, work relief is the Dole, too, except that it does provide a little more self respect for its recipients: at least it creates for them the fiction that they are still useful citizens and that there is work for them to do.

Yet, in this same article, *Fortune* presented many illuminating instances of work relief which belied the cynical use of the word "fiction." For example: Hopkins took over 250,000 bales of surplus cotton from the A.A.A. for the dual purpose of supplying work relief for women who made the cotton into mattresses and then distributing the mattresses to people who could not otherwise afford them. (This evoked howls of protest from mattress manufacturers but it was pointed out to them that they were not being subjected to unfair competition since the purchasing power of the recipients of the work relief mattresses was zero.)

For another example, as cited by *Fortune*:

> In Bay City, Michigan, an underwear manufacturing concern went bankrupt, and the closing of its plant threw some 250 workers on relief. Whereupon the State Relief Administration rented the plant, reopened it, and put the 250 workers back

at their jobs on a subsistence level to make enough underwear
to give every relief family in the state two sets for the winter.

The C.W.A. was unquestionably an expensive program and
could not have been continued for long on its original scale.
But its achievement in three and a half months was a memorable one. It included: 40,000 schools built or improved;
12,000,000 feet of sewer pipe laid; 469 airports built, 529 more
improved; 255,000 miles of road built or improved; 50,000
teachers employed to teach adults or to keep open rural
schools which must otherwise have been closed; 3,700 playgrounds and athletic fields built or improved.

Among the 4,264,000 for whom work was found were 3,000
writers and artists, the inception of the Federal Arts Program,
to the numerous criticisms of which Hopkins replied, "Hell!
They've got to eat just like other people."

. . . . .

. . . [T]he Federal Arts Projects were subjected to more
derision and more charges of "un-American activities" than
almost any other part of the huge relief program. And, they
were the first to be lopped off by Congress when the revolt
against the program set in. The word "boondoggle" came into
the language to describe the more fantastic projects dreamed
up by Hopkins and other "wild-eyed radicals" for the purpose
of wasting the taxpayers' money. For years the anti-New Deal
press had a great deal of fun digging up new work relief
projects which sounded very comical, particularly those involving jobless white collar workers who could not build
bridges across San Francisco Bay, or dams in the Columbia
or Tennessee Valleys. One of these projects, discovered in
New York City, involved the study of ancient safety pins. This
led to an exchange between Hopkins and reporters at a press
conference, the literal transcript of which provides an excellent example of his explosive method of speech:

Question. Are you contemplating any Federal investigation of
any kind of the general situation in New York City?

Answer (Hopkins). No. You mean apropos of this stuff in the paper a day or two ago?

Q. Apropos of the project for safety pins.

A. Sure, I have something to say about that.

Q. I asked first, have you contemplated making an investigation?

A. Why should I? There is nothing the matter with that. They are damn good projects—excellent projects. That goes for all the projects up there. You know some people make fun of people who speak a foreign language, and dumb people criticize something they do not understand, and that is what is going on up there—God damn it! Here are a lot of people broke and we are putting them to work making researches of one kind or another, running big recreational projects where the whole material costs 3%, and practically all the money goes for relief. As soon as you begin doing anything for white collar people, there is a certain group of people who begin to throw bricks. I have no apologies to make. As a matter of fact, we have not done enough. The plain fact of the matter is that there are people writing and talking about these things in New York who know nothing about research projects. They haven't taken the trouble to really look into it. I have a pile of letters from businessmen, if that is important, saying that these projects are damn good projects. These fellows can make fun and shoot at white collar people, if they want to. I notice somebody says facetiously, "repair all streets." That is all they think about—money to repair streets. I think there are things in life besides that. We have projects up there to make Jewish dictionaries. There are rabbis who are broke and on the relief rolls. One hundred and fifty projects up there deal with pure science. What of it? I think those things are good in life. They are important in life. We are not backing down on any of those projects. They can make fun of these white collar and professional people if they want to. I am not going to do it. They can say, let them use a pick and shovel to repair streets, when the city ought to be doing that. I believe every one of these research projects are good projects. We don't need any apologies!

Q. In that connection, I am not trying to argue with you.

A. I am not really mad. . . .

Q. About this white collar—there are 300 million for white collar relief. Would it be your idea in administering 300 million, that you might just as well continue?

A. The best of them will be continued, sure. Those are research projects they are jumping on.

Q. As a matter of fact, don't you think there are a lot of research projects that would be more valuable to mankind in general than the classic example of ancient safety pins?

A. That is a matter of opinion. You may be interested in washing machines—somebody else in safety pins. Every one of those projects are worked out by technical people. In the field of medical science, we have doctors; in physical, we have physicists; in the social, social economists. Every one of those is under the direction of competent research people. You can make fun of anything; that is easy to do. A lot of people are opposed to the whole business. Let these white collar professional fellows sit home and get a basket of groceries, that is what a lot of people want.

Q. You say that people don't want to work?

A. No, these fellows want to work, but there are a lot of people who don't believe in the work program and want people to go back to direct relief. These people who want direct relief will always kick about these technical projects. Anything that from their point of view isn't utilitarian.

The reports of this conference quoted Hopkins as saying that "people are too damned dumb," and this phrase was given plenty of circulation in the press. Even ten years later in the midst of war, Hopkins was assailed in scathing editorials as the man who believed that "the American people are too damned dumb." The *Washington Post* published a poem by a Virginia lady ending with the verse:

> Though we still pay up our tax,
>   Mr. Hopkins!
> We are sharpening the ax,
>   (Mr. Hopkins)
> Testing it with cautious thumb—
> And we're telling you, by gum,
> We are not quite too damned dumb,
>   Mr. Hopkins!

· · · · ·

A Congressional election was then coming up and this was to be the first real test of the New Deal with the voters. Roosevelt's political opponents, who had been rendered relatively speechless during the "honeymoon" period of 1933, were now regaining the powers of public protest, and violent criticisms of the "spending orgy" and the conversion to "State Socialism" were being heard throughout the land. The Republicans knew that they had no hope of regaining any real power in 1934 but they were energetically starting the counterrevolution which might come to triumph in 1936.

.   .   .   .   .

The Democrats won that election by an overwhelming margin and the Republicans found themselves feebler as a minority in the new Congress than they had been at any time since before the Civil War. This was an emphatic vote of confidence for the New Deal and particularly for the Work Relief Program. Roosevelt immediately started to discuss a formidable expansion of that program along the lines that had been established under C.W.A. The Hopkins star was now definitely in the ascendant.

.   .   .   .   .

When the 74th Congress convened a month later, Roosevelt announced the new Relief Program. He said:

> The Federal Government must and shall quit this business of relief. . . .
> Work must be found for able-bodied but destitute workers. . . .
> I am not willing that the vitality of our people be further sapped by the giving of cash, of market baskets, of a few hours of weekly work cutting grass, raking leaves or picking up papers in the public parks. We must preserve not only the bodies of the unemployed from destruction but also their self-respect, their self-reliance and courage and determination. This decision brings me to the problem of what the Government should do about approximately five million unemployed now on the relief rolls.

It is my thought that with the exception of certain of the normal public building operations of the Government, all emergency public works shall be united in a single new and greatly enlarged plan.

With the establishment of this new system we can supersede the Federal Emergency Relief Administration with a coordinated authority which will be charged with the orderly liquidation of our present relief activities and the substitution of a national chart for the giving of work.

I do not know whether Hopkins helped with the preparation of that message, but it certainly showed his influence. The President laid down six fundamental principles for work relief:

(1) The projects should be useful.

(2) Projects shall be of a nature that a considerable proportion of the money spent will go into wages for labor.

(3) Projects which promise ultimate return to the Federal Treasury of a considerable proportion of the costs will be sought.

(4) Funds allotted for each project should be actually and promptly spent and not held over until later years.

(5) In all cases projects must be of a character to give employment to those on the relief rolls.

(6) Projects will be allocated to localities or relief areas in relation to the number of workers on relief rolls in those areas.

When the Work Relief Bill of nearly five billion dollars was presented to the Congress there were wails of protest from the Republican minority and some signs of revolt by Southern Democrats, but the Bill passed the House of Representatives quickly and overwhelmingly. In the Senate, however, it encountered rough going. The days of legislation by the "rubber stamp" method were unquestionably over. There was much pious talk in the Senate and the Republican press about the Legislative branch maintaining its integrity vis-à-vis the Executive—and the words Fascist and Communist dictatorship were hurled about recklessly then, as later. But the argument had nothing to do with ideology. There was no real dispute over the propriety of spending the taxpayers' money on such a vast scale for work relief. It boiled down simply to the question: why should Capitol Hill yield to the White House absolute control over the spending of these billions which could yield such rich returns in pork barrel patronage? The leading proponents of this question were Democrats rather than Republicans, the latter being glad to go along on anything that was opposed to Roosevelt. The opposition to the Bill was strengthened enormously by the unrefuted claim that Roosevelt was asking for a blank check. As Walter Lippmann wrote:

> The Senators were not told who was going to administer the program. They were not given definite information about the scope or character of the program. They were not even furnished a thorough, cogent, and considered argument in favor of the Bill. . . .
> The Senate was confronted not with a policy but a mystery. This aroused the opposition of Senators who do not believe in work relief, of Senators who conscientiously object to voting money and powers blindly. It was the opportunity of Senators who for partisan reasons were glad to frustrate the President, of Senators who wished to get at the pork barrel.

Hopkins was called before the Senate Appropriations Committee but he evidently did not help much to clarify matters, for the Associated Press subsequently reported so much dissension and confusion in the Committee that one member who did not wish his name used predicted the Bill would be completely redrafted from beginning to end. The truth was that Hopkins himself did not know what was really in Roosevelt's mind. He noted, after a private talk with the President, "We went over the organization of the work program—more charts in pencil—he loves charts—no two of them are ever the same which makes it a bit baffling at times."

The two men most frequently mentioned as Administrators of the Relief Program were, obviously, Hopkins and Ickes.

But it was part of Roosevelt's technique not to let anyone know—including the two men themselves—which one he favored. Thus, neither of them was really in a position to go before the Senate and fight for the Bill. Neither of them knew just exactly where he stood or with what authority he might speak either to the Congress or to the press. There was no definite spearhead of opposition to various amendments proposed and the Administration leaders on the Senate floor could only compromise here and there to safeguard the main interests of the Bill. It was finally passed, after two months, with restrictions which were highly disappointing to Hopkins. . . .

· · · · ·

With the passage of the Work Relief Bill, Roosevelt was brought face to face with some difficult political problems of his own. He left for a Caribbean vacation just as the Bill was assured of passage, at the end of March, and, when it became known that Hopkins was on the Presidential train headed south, the press jumped to the conclusion that the F.E.R.A. Administrator had stolen the inside track. The controversies between Hopkins and Ickes had by that time been widely advertised, and Roosevelt knew that whichever of these men he appointed to the top job would be a prime target for the snipers' fire. Whereas, if he passed over them both and named a new man, it would imply repudiation of the whole Relief Program up to date. He settled the problem in a superbly characteristic manner: he called back to Washington the moderate, reliable Frank Walker—who was everybody's friend and nobody's target—and formed a triumvirate of Walker, Ickes and Hopkins to run the gigantic show.

· · · · ·

Such was the cumbersome high command of the Relief Program: Ickes at the head of an enormous committee and with P.W.A. as an operating agency in his Department; Hopkins with responsibility for the millions of individuals on the relief

rolls and with W.P.A. as the major operating agency; and
Frank Walker squarely in the middle as Chief Accountant,
custodian of facts and figures and keeper of the peace between the two jarring New Dealers. Thus, with this apparently
overelaborate and diffuse set of controls, Roosevelt enforced
at least the semblance of harmony in operations but, more
importantly, established a kind of political insurance for the
relief projects. He certainly did this the hard way for himself,
for he imposed upon himself apparently staggering obligations
in the maintenance of personal relations with all the diverse
elements involved, including organized labor and the American Bankers' Association; but he was supernally confident of
his ability to do this, and events proved that his confidence
was not misplaced. In the first three years of this program
something like a quarter of a million individual projects—
ranging from suspension bridges to sewing circles—passed
through Walker's office to Ickes' committee and thence across
the President's overcrowded desk from which the vast majority of the projects approved were passed to Hopkins who
converted them into actual man hours of work. The operation
of relief was not all directed by Hopkins; there were sixty
different agencies involved, including of course P.W.A. and
the important Farm Resettlement Administration which, to
Hopkins' regret, was moved from his area of authority and
placed in the Department of Agriculture under the direction
of Rexford Tugwell. But Hopkins was the guardian of the
entire relief rolls and it was thus his responsibility to see to it
that the millions of destitute, unemployed individuals were
given work by some agency—and his W.P.A. was by all odds
the biggest of the Federal employers and spenders.

· · · · ·

Roosevelt's methods of administration—typified in his handling of the work relief organization—were, to say the least,
unorthodox. They filled some practical-minded observers with
apprehension and dismay, and some with disgust; they filled
others with awe and wonder. I am sure that no final appraisal

of them can be made for a long time to come; but there is one thing that can be said about these methods—whether they were good or bad, sensible or insane, they *worked*.

While preparing this book I interviewed Harold Smith, who was Director of the Budget from 1939 to 1946. Smith was a modest, methodical, precise man, temperamentally far removed from Roosevelt and Hopkins. But I know of no one whose judgment and integrity and downright common sense the President trusted more completely. In the course of a long conversation, Smith said to me, "A few months ago, on the first anniversary of Roosevelt's death, a magazine asked me to write an article on Roosevelt as an administrator. I thought it over and decided I was not ready to make such an appraisal. I've been thinking about it ever since. When I worked with Roosevelt—for six years—I thought as did many others that he was a very erratic administrator. But now, when I look back, I can really begin to see the size of his programs. They were by far the largest and most complex programs that any President ever put through. People like me who had the responsibility of watching the pennies could only see the five or six or seven per cent of the programs that went wrong, through inefficient organization or direction. But now I can see in perspective the ninety-three or -four or -five per cent that went right—including the winning of the biggest war in history—because of unbelievably skillful organization and direction. And if I were to write that article now, I think I'd say that Roosevelt must have been one of the greatest geniuses as an administrator that ever lived. What we couldn't appreciate at the time was the fact that he was a real *artist* in government."

That word "artist" was happily chosen, for it suggests the quality of Roosevelt's extraordinary creative imagination. I think that he would have resented the application of the word as implying that he was an impractical dreamer; he loved to represent himself as a prestidigitator who could amaze and amuse the audience by "pulling another rabbit out of a hat." But he was an artist and no canvas was too big for him.

He was also, of course, a master politician, and most artists are certainly not that; but, by the same token, you rarely find a professional politician who would make the mistake of being caught in the act of creating an original idea. The combination of the two qualities in Roosevelt can be demonstrated by the fact that it required a soaring imagination to conceive Lend Lease and it required the shrewdest kind of manipulation to get it passed by the Congress.

It was often said by businessmen during the Roosevelt Administration that "What we need in the White House is a good businessman." But in the years of the Second World War there were a great many patriotic, public-spirited businessmen who went to Washington to render important service to their country and they learned that government is a weird world bearing little resemblance to anything they had previously known—a world in which the only competitive struggle was for authority and prestige instead of for profits. The more analytical of these businessmen came to the conclusion that it was no accident that not one of the great or even above-average Presidents in American history had been trained in business. (Abraham Lincoln once tried to run a grocery store and failed dismally. Thereafter, he never tried commerce again but went where he belonged—into politics.)

There were even some businessmen who observed that the New Deal was not what they had feared it to be: the prologue to Communism in America. It was, in fact, as Roosevelt conceived it and conducted it, a revolution of the Right, rising up to fight in its own defense. Although, in one election after another during his Administration, his bitter opponents raised the charge, "If That Man wins—this will be the last free election ever held in this country," free elections somehow managed to continue and more voters than ever went to the polls, giving no evidence whatsoever that they were forced there by bayonet points compelling them to vote in strict obedience to the Democratic (or Communist) party line.

· · · · ·

The nondespairing quality—this quality of effulgent faith in the people—illuminated the New Deal. The critics of the

New Deal, in the face of Roosevelt's tremendous electoral triumphs, could justify themselves only by concluding that the masses of the American people were lazy, shiftless, ne'er-do-well panhandlers who would vote for any demagogue who promised them a handout. The standard cartoon in the conservative press pictured the man on W.P.A. relief as a hopeless derelict leaning on a shovel, and the young man or woman who received aid from the National Youth Administration as a cynical Red and the farmer who benefited from Rural Resettlement as a piece of contemptible white trash; but more than twenty millions of American citizens were at times directly dependent on relief and immeasurably many more— contractors, manufacturers, wholesalers, shopkeepers, landlords, etc.—were indirectly dependent. Thus, Roosevelt's opponents were, in effect, giving mortal insult to a large section of the American people and were thereby helping to identify him as the champion of the people's dignity. As it turned out, this became a great asset to our national security: when war came, the extraordinary prestige and popularity of Franklin D. Roosevelt was the most powerful weapon in our arsenal.

For Further Reading

The best one-volume biography of Roosevelt is James Mac-Gregor Burns, *Roosevelt: The Lion and the Fox* (1956), the title following Machiavelli's rule that a prince must be the former to scare wolves and the latter to scent out traps. Burns, often a critic of FDR, concludes that the President acted the part of the fox during most of his presidency. An ambitious biographical project by Frank Freidel has covered the President's years up through the 1932 election in three volumes: *The Apprenticeship* (1952), *The Ordeal* (1954), and *The Triumph* (1956). Three more volumes are promised for this detailed, yet engrossing, project. The impatient reader wishing to proceed can continue the story through the 1936 election with Arthur M. Schlesinger's *The Age of Roosevelt*, a multivolumed study that, like Freidel's, has three volumes published to date: *The Crisis of the Old Order* (1957), *The Coming of the New Deal* (1959), and *The Politics of Upheaval* (1960).

Among other biographies still useful are John Gunther, *Roosevelt in Retrospect, A Profile in History* (1950), a good piece of journalism; and Ernest K. Lindley, *Franklin D. Roosevelt, A Career in Progressive Democracy* (1931), an unusually good campaign biography. For FDR's performance on the hustings, see Harold F. Gosnell, *Champion Campaigner: Franklin D. Roosevelt* (1952). Alfred B. Rollins, Jr.'s biography of Louis Howe, *Roosevelt and Howe* (1962) is good on FDR's early political career. Richard Hofstadter's marvelous essay on Roosevelt in *The American Political Tradition* (1948) remains one of the best short sketches. Three critiques from the Right, tending to portray FDR with dangerous leftist leanings, are worth consulting for that perspective: John T. Flynn, *Country Squire in the White House* (1940); the same author's *The Roosevelt Myth* (1948); and, the more scholarly, Edgar E. Robinson, *The Roosevelt Leadership, 1933–1945* (1955). Two monographs deal with Roosevelt's prepresidential years: David R. Fusfeld, *The Economic Thought of Franklin D. Roosevelt and the Origins of the New Deal* (1956); and Bernard Bellush, *Franklin D. Roosevelt as Governor of New York* (1955).

The literature on Roosevelt is enriched by many fine published memoirs, journals, diaries, and autobiographies that contain important insights into FDR by individuals who worked closely with him. Books by family members include Eleanor Roosevelt's two volumes, *This Is My Story* (1937), for the pre-1933 years, and *This I Remember* (1949), for the 1933–1945 period. Cabinet level views are: from the Post Office, James A. Farley, *Jim Farley's Story* (1948); from the State Department, Cordell Hull, *Memoirs* (2 vols., 1948); from the Department of the Interior, Harold L. Ickes, *The Secret Diary of Harold L. Ickes* (3 vols., 1953–54); from the Treasury, John M. Blum, *From the Morgenthau Diaries: Years of Crisis, 1928–1938* (1959), and *Years of Urgency, 1938–1941* (1965); and from the Department of Labor, Frances Perkins, *The Roosevelt I Knew* (1946). Other valuable works by associates, in addition to the Sherwood volume, are Rexford Guy Tugwell, *The Democratic Roosevelt* (1957); Raymond Moley, *After Seven Years* (1939), and *The First New Deal* (1966); and Samuel I. Rosenman, *Working with Roosevelt* (1952).

Published collections of Roosevelt's documents are Samuel I. Rosenman, ed., *The Public Papers and Addresses of Franklin D. Roosevelt* (13 vols., 1938–1950); and Elliott Roosevelt, ed., *FDR: His Personal Letters* (2 vols., 1947–1950). Gerald D. Nash, ed., *Franklin D. Roosevelt* (1967) is a fine collection of essays and other writings. Robert D. Graff and Robert Emmett Ginna have put together a collection of photographs in *FDR* (1963).

The New Deal at High Tide

William E. Leuchtenburg

*I*t is difficult to be noncommittal about the New Deal. Even those persons—now well over 40 per cent of all Americans—who were born during or after World War II have well-formed ideas about the Roosevelt years. Basically, three educative forces intersected during the years after 1933 to help implant a highly charged (positive or negative as the case may be) New Deal image. The first was the Great Depression itself, a devastating experience that threw millions out of work and left large numbers of others underemployed. The second was FDR's and his administration's reaction to the problems created by economic collapse: active, imaginative, big with potential, and humane. The third was itself a combination of elements—an affluent post-1945 economy combined with a dramatic revolution in communications, a combination that has kept the New Deal's programs, aspirations, and unfinished business in public consciousness. First radio, then television, and finally a rich flow of audio-visual and published materials have been the carriers of the New Deal story.

Schoolmen have done their part. They have squabbled with each other over such questions as: How "revolutionary" was the New Deal? Was there a shift in its perspectives during 1934–1935 that warrants the labels First and Second New Deal? How successful was the New

Source: William E. Leuchtenburg, *Franklin D. Roosevelt and the New Deal* (New York: Harper & Row, 1963), pp. 167–196. Copyright © 1963 by William E. Leuchtenburg. Reprinted by permission of Harper & Row, Publishers.

Deal; did it "end" the Depression? Obviously these are more than mere academic questions. They reflect the need of a society to probe the nature of its central political experiences. Moreover, willingly or unwillingly, the scholar's answers have often ended up as grist for speechwriters (sometimes the scribe fills both functions) grinding out campaign fare.

The heritage of the New Deal has been so great that few political programs since then can be called novel. Only the civil rights legislation, the Peace Corps, and the foreign assistance programs seem to have significantly augmented the original 1933–1938 reforms. Yet even these may have had their New Deal precursors. Did FDR have black Americans in mind when he spoke of the "forgotten man" and of the nation's one-third ill-housed, ill-clothed, and ill-fed? Are not the Civil Conservation Corps and the National Youth Administration the natural forerunners of the Peace Corps? And does not the logic of virtually all the New Deal programs point to a larger humanitarian and national self-interest in foreign aid?

So thorough and far-reaching is the political acceptance of the New Deal that proposals to dismantle portions of it seem sacrilegious. When the 1964 G.O.P. presidential candidate, Barry Goldwater, suggested that the government divest itself of ownership of the Tennessee Valley Authority (T.V.A.) much of his potential support among conservative residents of the Valley and elsewhere evaporated. Controversial programs in the 1930's have become the norms for the post-1945 period.

The consensus that supports the New Deal, however, may not be immortal. As the 1930's recede (particularly as the memory of the pain of the Great Depression fades) criticism of the New Deal is bound to increase. No doubt this is a natural phenomenon. Where some of Roosevelt's contemporaries may have been willing to view the New Deal's unfinished tasks as testimonies to breadth of heart and vision, a younger group of critics sees these starts as fatal flaws.

In recent years the New Deal's civil rights' record has been cudgeled. This is ironic, for Roosevelt was the

beneficiary of a shift in Negro votes; Roosevelt's open-
ness, his willingness to condemn lynching, and the variety of New Deal welfare projects that percolated down
to Negroes contributed to the shift. Now critics assert
that FDR himself only paid lip service to his ideals; he
really did not care deeply about the black man's plight.
His Administration, despite actions by such leading figures as Harold L. Ickes and Harry Hopkins, also did not
do as much as justice required. Thus in Jacksonville,
Florida, although blacks received 45 per cent of the relief
funds in strict accordance to their population ratio, this
fell far short of their real needs because a dispropor-
tionate number of black families were out of work. In
the distribution of farm acreage allocation checks by the
Agricultural Adjustment Administration, blacks also received second-rate treatment. Southern white landowners
increasingly forced Negroes into a farm laborer status in
order to deprive them of benefits that accrued to owners
only.

Recent trends in New Deal historiography have
sounded a critical note in another exceptionally important matter: New Deal programs were often the cap-
tives of locally dominant interest groups. Roosevelt and
his friends in fact might well be amused by this revisionist tack; during the heyday of its programs the New Deal
was lashed by the Right for its alleged usurpation of the
States' powers. The conservative's keynote was charges
of excessive centralization and bureaucratization. Now
revisionists see key programs in agriculture (AAA), re-
gional resource development (TVA), and industrial code-
making (NRA) as really controlled by the local power
structures most directly affected. Thus big farmers and
big businesses benefit most from the New Deal.

Revisionists also seem to dislike some of the historians
of the New Deal as much as they do its programmatic
failures. Thus, when the author of the best one-volume
New Deal study, William Leuchtenburg, argues with
seeming approval that the New Deal essentially followed
a "broker state" policy—that is, it attempted to mediate
between competing large scale organized economic interest groups—he is attacked for his supposed endorsement

of consensus politics. His stance, one gathers, should have been more critical; it should have emphasized that the New Deal did little to give power or support to the unorganized and weak.

Despite a rising note of revisionism sounded by younger scholars, the nation continues to endorse the New Deal's thrust. Recent political developments, most notably in public welfare proposals, indicate that the New Deal's contribution has had lasting impact. The modern interventionist state is here—and seems durable.

*W*hen Anne O'Hare McCormick returned to the United States in 1936 after interviewing European leaders whose strained, prematurely aged faces revealed the heavy price they had paid for power, she marveled at the serenity of Franklin Roosevelt. "On none of his predecessors has the office left so few marks as on Mr. Roosevelt. He is a little heavier, a shade grayer; otherwise he looks hardier and in better health than on the day of his inauguration. His face is so tanned that his eyes appear lighter, a cool Wedgwood blue; after the four grueling years since the last campaign they are as keen, curious, friendly and impenetrable as ever."

Almost everyone remarked on Roosevelt's inscrutability. Few men claimed they truly knew him. "To describe Roosevelt," reflected William Phillips, Roosevelt's Under Secretary of State, "you would have to describe three or four men for he had at least three or four different personalities. He could turn from one personality to another with such speed that you often never knew where you were or to which personality you were talking. . . ." In depicting Roosevelt, cartoonists frequently used this motif of the multiple image. In one cartoon, he looks into a multisurface mirror at four different images of himself; in others, he smiles back at his own image. Through all runs the conception that a political implication underlay his every move, and that the man could manipulate the different aspects of his own personality for political advantage. Everything about the President—his wife, his chil-

dren, his dog Fala, his stamp collection, his fishing trips—
seemed to have a public quality.

Roosevelt's public face—grinning, confident, but inscrutable
—masked the inner man, and no one knew for certain what
the man, in moments of reflection, really felt. Some doubted
that those moments of personal communion ever came. He
seemed the compleat political man, the public self so merged
with the private self that the President could no longer divorce them. His relentless cheerfulness, his boyish hobbies,
his simple view of God, his distaste for theoretical speculation,
vexed critics who thought him no more than a Rover Boy
who had never grown up. Others believed that beyond that
gay reserve was an infinitely complex man whose detachment
served his political ends, but who had an inner serenity that
came, in unequal parts, from his secure childhood, his early
acquaintance with grief, for he was to be a cripple the rest
of his days, and his private understanding with God.

Both friend and foe marveled at his serenity. Burdened by
the weightiest of responsibilities, he remained high-spirited
and untroubled. "He was like the fairy-story prince who didn't
know how to shudder," [Raymond] Moley has written. "Not
even the realization that he was playing ninepins with the
skulls and thighbones of economic orthodoxy seemed to worry
him." Roosevelt advised Tugwell: "You'll have to learn that
public life takes a lot of sweat; but it doesn't need to worry you.
You won't always be right, but you mustn't suffer from being
wrong. That's what kills people like us." If a truck driver
were doing your job, he told Tugwell, he would probably be
right 50 per cent of the time. "But you aren't a truck driver.
You've had some preparation. Your percentage is bound to be
higher." A man with little formal religious attachment, Roosevelt believed that he walked with God, that he was the instrument of the Lord, and that the Lord would care for him in
moments of trial.

One of the rare breaks in his composure came at the Democratic convention in Philadelphia in 1936. As the President
began his stiff-legged march toward the stage in Franklin
Field, he reached out to shake the hand of the white-bearded

poet Edwin Markham, was thrown off balance, and sprawled to the ground. White-faced and angry, he snapped: "Clean me up." But most of the time he bore his handicap with astonishing good humor. To board a train, he had to be wheeled up special ramps; to go fishing, or to get to the second story of a meeting hall, he had to be carried in men's arms like a helpless child. To walk, he had to be harnessed in leg braces, and endure the strain of dragging, painfully, a cumbersome dead weight of pounds of steel. Yet he carried it all off with a wonderfully nonchalant air, and often made his incapacity the subject of some seemingly carefree jest. He would roar with laughter and say: "Really, it's as funny as a crutch." Or at the end of a conversation, Roosevelt, who had not been able to walk since 1921, would often remark: "Well, I'm sorry, I have to run now!" Indeed, so vigorous did he seem that most Americans never knew he remained a cripple in a wheelchair. Frequently, in fact, writers gave the impression that Roosevelt had fully conquered his infirmity. One "who had summoned from the depths of character the incredible patience to win his battle for health and make himself walk again among men," the President was leading the nation, as he had himself, to full "recovery" from the paralysis that once had afflicted both man and country.

After the lacerating Second Hundred Days, Roosevelt saw 1936 as a time of healing, when he would unite the party by salving the wounds of his opponents and avoid new conflicts with Congress until he had won re-election. On the day the 1935 Congress adjourned, the publisher Roy Howard asked Roosevelt to grant "a breathing spell to industry, and a recess from further experimentation. . . ." A few weeks before, Raymond Moley had written that the public was "developing a terrific thirst for a long, cool swig of political quiescence." Roosevelt asked Moley to frame a response to Howard; his basic program, the President's letter of reply stated, had "now reached substantial completion and the 'breathing spell' of which you speak is here—very decidedly so." When Congress reconvened in 1936, Roosevelt delivered an inflammatory Annual Message in which he spoke of having "earned the hatred of entrenched greed," yet he recommended no new reforms and demonstrated his sensitivity to attacks on his failure to balance the budget by a drive to slash government spending. Throughout the campaign year of 1936, the President stepped up the radicalism of his rhetoric, but accentuated the conservatism of his deeds.

In his plans for a short session, Roosevelt reckoned without the Supreme Court. Early in 1936, in a 6–3 decision, the Court held the AAA's processing tax unconstitutional. Justice Roberts, in a wretchedly argued opinion, found that the levy was not a legitimate use of the taxing power but "the expropriation of money from one group for the benefit of another." In a biting dissent, Justice Stone scolded the majority for this "tortured construction of the Constitution." "Courts," he observed, "are not the only agency of government that must be assumed to have capacity to govern." The Butler decision, which was followed by a sharp decline in farm prices, aroused deep resentment. Senator Bankhead denounced Roberts' opinion as "a political stump speech," Governor Earle of Pennsylvania declared the Court had become a "political body" with "six members committed to the policies of the Liberty League," and in Iowa the six justices who handed down the decision were hanged in effigy.

The Butler decision played hob with Roosevelt's desire to balance the budget. It deprived the government of anticipated receipts from processing taxes, and the Court ordered the return to processors of $200 million already collected. Together with the $2 billion bonus which Congress enacted over Roosevelt's veto, it created an immediate need for new revenue. Keynesians within the administration, who had never liked the regressive processing taxes, rejoiced in the opportunity to agitate for an undistributed-profits tax scaled to penalize size. They hoped the new levy would check the growth of huge personal fortunes, serve as an antitrust weapon, bring corporations within the sphere of regulatory agencies, and, most important, stimulate the economy by draining idle pools of capital. But Senate conservatives had no intention of approving a proposal which Raymond Moley warned would throw businessmen into "paroxysms of fright" and reduce the rich to "rags and tatters." The bill, Senator Pittman observed, was "intended to kill some criminals, but to kill them, it appeared to me that the G-men were ordered to shoot into a crowd." The Revenue Act of 1936 did include a modest graduated tax on undistributed earnings, but this marked a victory in principle rather than in substance for the New Dealers.

No sooner had the Butler decision been handed down than Agriculture officials scurried to throw together a new farm law that would permit the government to disburse funds to the farmer without incurring the wrath of the Court. In a few weeks' time Wallace had won the approval of Congress for a measure which was rammed through over Republican protests that, in an election year, the administration was concerned chiefly with keeping surplus Democrats on the government payroll and not letting the farm vote lie fallow. The Soil Conservation and Domestic Allotment Act offered farmers bounties for not planting soil-depleting commercial crops and for sowing instead soil-enriching grasses and legumes such as clover and soybeans.

The new farm law reflected the intense national concern with soil conservation aroused by the terrible dust storms of the early 1930's. The drought, which began in 1932 and continued each year until 1936, converted a huge area from Texas to the Dakotas into a "Dust Bowl." The dry death scorched pastures and cornfields and turned plowed land into sand dunes. Farmers watched helplessly as cattle fell in their tracks and died. In Vinita, Oklahoma, in 1934, the sun topped 100° for thirty-five straight days; on the thirty-sixth, it climbed to 117°. In the spring of 1935, trains arrived hours late. A conductor on the Santa Fe's Navajo reported: "Noon was like night. There was no sun, and, at times, it was impossible to see a yard. The engineer could not see the signal-lights." As far east as Memphis, people covered their faces with handkerchiefs, a dust cloud seven thousand feet thick darkened the city of Cleveland, yellow grit from Nebraska sifted through the White House doors, and bits of western plains came to

rest on vessels in the Atlantic three hundred miles at sea.
That winter, red snow fell on New England.

While the 1936 farm act was, as Republicans charged,
largely a subterfuge to permit the administration to go on
paying money to farmers to restrict production, it represented
too the long-range commitment of Wallace and his aides to a
greater emphasis on soil conservation. The dust storms were
perceived as a penance Man paid for his "sin" in mistreating
the "wounded land"; if the process were not reversed, the
United States would, like ancient civilizations, disappear into
oblivion. In October, 1933, on Tugwell's recommendation,
Hugh Hammond Bennett, the "father of soil conservation,"
was named to head the newly created Soil Erosion Service of
the Department of the Interior. In 1934, Congress passed the
Taylor Grazing Act, which subjected grazing on the public
domain to national regulation. In 1935, as grit from the
western plains created a copper pall over Washington like
the skies of a smoky steel town, Congress created a permanent
Soil Conservation Service in the Department of Agriculture.
Under the crusading Bennett, the Service taught farmers the
proper way to till their hillsides. The New Deal's conception
of the common man, Alistair Cooke has noted wryly, was one
who could "take up contour plowing late in life." In its
emphasis on soil conservation, the New Deal added a new
dimension to the conservation movement. *Fortune* observed:
"It is conceivable that when the history of our generation
comes to be written in the perspective of a hundred years the
saving of the broken lands will stand out as the great and
most enduring achievement of the time."

The same sense of working against time to save the nation's
resources from "the bastard claims of a bastard acquisitive
culture" permeated much of the rest of the New Deal's conservation program. When President Roosevelt released the
report of the Mississippi Valley Committee, headed by Morris
Cooke, Stuart Chase commented: "Another generation of the
strenuous pursuit of the main chance, and it is safe to say that
Old Man River would roar in lonely majesty, rid of that dirty

animal *homo sapiens,* his waters clean at last." Cooke himself told a reporter that if the country did not adopt the Committee's twenty-year program, "our country as a vital force in human affairs will disappear in, say, three generations." Animated by the conviction that they were racing doom, the conservationists speeded up their timetable: the government established national parks in the Olympic rain forest and in the Shenandoah, new national monuments like Joshua Tree and White Sands, new big-game refuges like the Hart Mountain Antelope Range in southeastern Oregon; demonstrated the feasibility of multipurpose river basin development in the Tennessee Valley; and outlined bold programs of resources development. In the first three years of the New Deal, the government acquired more than twice the acreage in forest lands as had been purchased in the previous history of national forests.

Indispensable to the work of soil conservation and reforestation was the Civilian Conservation Corps. By September, 1935, over five hundred thousand young men lived in CCC camps. In all, more than two and a half million would enlist: boys from the southern pines and the sequoia country of the West, boys from Bayonne and Cicero who had never seen forests or mountains before. They thinned four million acres of trees, stocked almost a billion fish, built more than 30,000 wildlife shelters, dug diversion ditches and canals, and restored Revolutionary and Civil War battlefields. They fought spruce sawflies and Mormon crickets in western forests, grasshoppers in the Midwest, gypsy moths in the East. They built a network of lookout towers and roads and trails so that fires could be detected and reached more easily; when fires broke out, regiments of Roosevelt's "Tree Army" were rushed to the front—forty-nine firefighters lost their lives. Above all, they planted trees—saplings of cedar and hemlock and poplar —in burned-over districts, on eroded hillsides, on bleak mountain slopes ruthlessly stripped of virgin timber. Of all the forest planting, public and private, in the history of the nation, more than half was done by the CCC.

The policies Roosevelt had pursued in his first term had

met with so favorable a response that the Republicans faced
an uphill battle in their campaign to oust him in 1936. To
oppose the President, the G.O.P. named Alf Landon of Kansas,
the only Republican governor elected in 1932 who survived
the Democratic tidal wave of 1934. As his running mate, the
convention chose Colonel Frank Knox, a strongly nationalistic
Chicago publisher who had served as a Rough Rider under
Teddy Roosevelt and boasted a sombrero pierced by two
bullets at San Juan Hill. Landon, dismissed by many as an
Old Guard wheelhorse, was, in fact, a good deal more liberal
than his sponsors. Like Knox a former Bull Mooser, he had
fought the Ku Klux Klan in Kansas, had a superb record on
civil liberties, and had demonstrated that he favored the regulation of business. He had endorsed any number of New Deal
projects in words that were to come back to plague him during
the campaign.

In a race against the dynamic Franklin Roosevelt, Landon
seemed badly mismatched. Chester Rowell, the head of the
California delegation to the Republican convention, thought
Landon "a pretty poor specimen" and even a supporter like
Gifford Pinchot conceded he was no "world-beater." Many
Landon backers were distressed by the Governor's ineffective
delivery on the radio. "For God's sake break your sentences
and make them shorter in your speeches," pleaded one of his
followers. In contrast to the worldly Roosevelt, Landon appeared to be what Jim Farley, in an indiscreet moment, called
him: the governor of a "typical prairie state." Yet it was
precisely Landon's quality of provincialism which appealed to
many Americans. Republican speakers contrasted the steady-
going Landon, with his agreeable smile and comfortable air,
with the sophisticated Roosevelt with his unsettling and
vaguely dishonest charm. Since Landon spoke so wretchedly,
people knew he was sincere. One correspondent, who told
Landon not to change his style, observed: "The people of this
country want exactly what the Pilgrim Fathers wanted, and
exactly what the pioneers who treked to Kansas wanted. . . ."
This nostalgia for the old days permeated the Republican
campaign. The G.O.P., which sought to glorify the horse-and-

buggy days Roosevelt had derided, blanketed the country with
sunflowers, and adopted as its campaign song "Oh, Susanna,"
the ballad of the Oregon Trail.

Landon's modestly liberal record won him few votes. His
appeal lay rather in offering opponents of President Roosevelt
a way to express their displeasure at New Deal policies. Roosevelt's style of politics deeply offended men of conservative
temperament. He refused to be bound by the restraints that
confined other leaders in the past. He abandoned the gold
standard, operated the government with unbalanced budgets,
and moved in a world of "non-Euclidian" economics. The
fixed world of the predepression years—the world where parallel lines never met—had been torpedoed by the commandants
of the alphabet agencies. Roosevelt was seen as the agent of
willful change, a man who expressed the spirit of a decade in
which the swing clarinetist Benny Goodman invaded Carnegie
Hall, a man whose Surgeon General Thomas Parran dared to
speak the forbidden word "syphilis" over the radio, a man
whose defiance of tradition would even permit him to change
the day of the year on which the old New England holiday
of Thanksgiving was celebrated.

Many of the nation's wealthy were almost incoherent with
rage at President Roosevelt. They refused to say his name,
but referred to him as "that man" or "he." One of Roosevelt's
wealthy neighbors, Howland Spencer, hated the President so
much that he exiled himself in the Bahamas and returned
only after the Republicans won the congressional elections in
1946. Terrified by the prospect of confiscatory taxation, the
wealthy viewed Roosevelt as a reckless leveler. Accustomed to
having their authority unchallenged, businessmen resented
the rising empires of government and labor. Many businessmen were openly defiant. Arthur Young, U.S. Steel vice-president in charge of industrial relations, told the American
Management Association that rather than obey the Wagner
bill he would "go to jail or be convicted as a felon." The
Association then gave Young a medal for "outstanding and
creative work in the field of industrial relations." In the fall
of 1935, the American Bankers Association convention re-

jected its own nominating committee's recommendation for second vice-president, because he was a business associate of Marriner Eccles, and chose instead a "Main Street banker," Orval Adams of Salt Lake City. Viewing government as a sovereign power would treat an upstart rival, Adams proposed that bankers "declare an embargo" and "decline to make further purchases." "The Bankers of America," Adams asserted, "should resume negotiations with the Federal Government only under a rigid economy, a balanced budget, and a sane tax program."

Landon won the support of a number of Wilsonian Democrats who believed that Roosevelt had jettisoned virtues like character, thrift, and self-reliance, had forsaken goals like the equality of opportunity to compete for a new emphasis on security and social rights, and had given himself over to a brazen cadre of planners. Like the advance guard of a revolutionary army, these *novi homines* had moved into the Walsh-McLean mansion on Massachusetts Avenue in the summer of 1935. Here, where the Prince of Wales and the King of the Belgians had once been entertained, the New Dealers drafted plans for greenbelt towns, some working at desks in the grand ballroom, some in Mrs. McLean's brocaded boudoir. Most of all, old-time Democrats were discountenanced by policies which they thought fomented class animosity and encouraged minority-bloc politics. Newton Baker protested: "The trouble with this recognition of the class war is that it spreads like a grease stain and every group formed around a special and selfish interest demands the same sort of recognition. As a consequence our Government for the last three years has been the mere tossing of tubs to each whale as it grows bold enough to stick its head out of the water."

For three years, Al Smith had taken a strong stand behind the policies of Grover Cleveland. On January 25, 1936, at a Liberty League banquet at the Mayflower Hotel in Washington before a gathering of two thousand that numbered a dozen du Ponts, business leaders like Winthrop Aldrich, and discontented Democrats like Dean Acheson, Smith charged that the Supreme Court had been forced to work overtime "throwing the alphabet out the window three letters at a time." The Roosevelt administration, he declared, had been turned in a Socialist direction. "It is all right with me if they want to disguise themselves as Norman Thomas or Karl Marx, or Lenin, or any of the rest of that bunch," Smith shouted, "but what I won't stand for is allowing them to march under the banner of Jefferson, Jackson and Cleveland." When the November elections came, Smith warned, he and other Democrats of like mind would probably "take a walk." Together with Smith, men like John W. Davis, another former Democratic presidential nominee, bolted the party, convinced it had been taken over by Republican progressives and hitherto unknown social workers and professors. "Who is Ickes? Who is Wallace? Who is Hopkins, and, in the name of all that is good and holy, who is Tugwell, and where did he blow from?" Smith asked.

Such appeals probably cost Landon more votes than they won him. Infuriated Democrats who had supported Smith in 1928 denounced him as a "Benedict Arnold" who had betrayed his party, and as a turncoat who, unable to resist the blandishments of the rich, had turned in his brown derby for a top hat. "It's a long way from Mamie O'Rourke to the grand dames of Park Avenue, Al," commented the New York *Post*. The Liberty League was so patently an alliance of the wealthy that the Republican National Committee asked it to refrain from endorsing the Landon ticket. Landon himself found it impossible to disassociate himself from conservative party leaders, including its chairman John Hamilton. After the election, Landon wrote: "One of the things that was wrong with the campaign was that I didn't have enough help on the Progressive and Liberal side to pick up the ball and emphasize our really liberal stand on many questions." As the campaign progressed, Landon, who from the outset had favored retrenchment, a balanced budget, and the gold standard, made more and more conservative statements at the same time that he made extravagant promises to farmers and to the aged. By Election Day, many of the disaffected Democrats—Newton Baker, Dean Acheson, James P. Warburg—had returned to

Roosevelt, in part no doubt out of disillusionment with Landon's campaign.

It seemed unlikely that any Republican candidate could outpoll Franklin Roosevelt in 1936; G.O.P. hopes rested on the possibility that a combination of Coughlin, Townsend, and other dissident elements under the leadership of Huey Long would draw enough votes away from the President to allow the Republican challenger to slip through. But all threats from Huey Long in 1936 had ended dramatically at the State House in Baton Rouge on a September night in 1935, when a white-clad figure stepped out of the evening shadows and shot down Louisiana's senator. Dr. Carl Austin Weiss, who had witnessed the dictatorship of Dollfuss in Vienna in his student days, had been outraged by Long's attempt to dislodge an obscure judge, Weiss's father-in-law. As he staggered through the corridors, Huey asked: "I wonder what they shot me for?" Thirty-one hours later, he was dead.

Long's Share the Wealth followers in every part of the country mourned the death of their hero. A New York woman wrote Roosevelt: "God have mercy on poor dead good Huey Long and for give the man who kild him he was a good man Huey Long was. . . ." Alongside paid advertisements to St. Rita and St. Joseph, devout Catholics in southern Louisiana inserted notices that read: "Thanks to Huey P. Long for answers to my prayers." Gerald L. K. Smith, who wired Roosevelt protesting "financing potential assassins with government money," laid claim to the Long mantle, but Louisiana politicians brushed him aside, liquidated the organization, and sought an arrangement with the President. In an accommodation that was jeered as the "Second Louisiana Purchase," the administration was happy to oblige.

As the Long organization disintegrated, the main threats to Roosevelt from the messiah groups came from Dr. Townsend and Father Coughlin. Roosevelt, it has been said, nullified their appeal by reform legislation which wiped out the discontent on which they fed. But Townsend's strength reached its apex after the passage of the Social Security Act; in fact, he gained recruits precisely because of the inadequacy of the

New Deal pension system, which left millions of elderly Americans unprotected. Townsendism, which, as *Today* remarked, was "easily the outstanding political sensation" of 1935, claimed control of two western governors and the legislatures of seven western states. In November, 1935, it threw a bad scare into politicians east of the Mississippi. Verner Main, the only candidate to support the Townsend Plan in a field of five, won the Republican primary in Michigan's Third Congressional District with 13,419 votes; his nearest opponent polled only 4,806 votes. Main went on to defeat his Democratic opponent in the by-election in December. The *Townsend National Weekly* gloated: "As Main Goes, So Goes the Nation."

At the height of its power, the Townsend movement began to collapse. When a former national publicity director of the organization leveled charges of corruption at the doctor and Robert Clements, Republicans and Democrats seized the opportunity to unite to scotch the Townsend menace. A probe by a hostile congressional committee, while unable to prove any wrongdoing by Townsend, revealed that Clements had profited handsomely. In March, 1936, after a political and financial disagreement, Townsend ordered Clements to resign; one week later, the doctor broke with Congressman McGroarty. The Townsend strength had never been as great as western politicians had been scared into believing, and, with the adroit Clements gone, the political organization fell apart. In an Oregon primary, four rival Townsend candidates battled for the same post. Townsend himself headed in a new political direction. After being subjected to severe questioning, Townsend stalked out of the committee room, and the House cited him for contempt. Arm in arm with him as he marched out of the hearings walked Gerald L. K. Smith.

In June, 1936, Smith, Father Coughlin, and some of the Townsendites joined forces to create a new third party. Representative William Lemke of North Dakota, the Union party's presidential candidate, had no hope of victory, but he counted on the battalions of Townsend and Coughlin to roll up a respectable vote. Townsend gave Lemke his personal support, but did not dare try to win official endorsement from his organization. A national Townsendite convention in Cleveland in mid-July shook with dissension. Father Coughlin ripped off his coat and clerical collar, and denounced the President as "the great betrayer and liar" and as "Franklin Double-Crossing Roosevelt." But an Oklahoma Democrat, Gomer Smith, won almost as much applause when he denounced Gerald Smith and defended the President as a "church-going, Bible-reading, God-fearing man," a "golden-hearted patriot who had saved the country from communism."

By the time Coughlin's National Union for Social Justice convened in August, the alliance had been all but shattered. The manager of the National Union convention declared that Townsend and Smith would speak at the meeting "only over his dead body." Coughlin announced he would swing at least nine million votes for Lemke, or he would quit broadcasting. "As I was instrumental in removing Herbert Hoover from the White House so help me God I will be instrumental in taking a Communist from the chair once occupied by Washington," he promised. Yet Coughlin not only scorned Townsend and Smith; he even ignored Lemke. Before the end of the campaign, both Townsend and Lemke had denounced Smith for his fascist sympathies, and Townsend, his own organization in the process of disruption, gave Lemke lukewarm support. Progressives abhorred the Jew-baiting of Coughlin and Smith. Catholic liberals like Frank Walsh, who had once looked with favor on the Radio Priest, now repudiated him.

As Lemke's hopes withered, Coughlin became more violent. On September 25 in Cincinnati, he called the President "anti-God," and advocated using bullets when an "upstart dictator in the United States succeeds in making a one-party government and when the ballot is useless." Increasingly he resorted to the kind of effects Hitler employed in Germany. In Chicago, he walked between an honor guard of 2,500 men who wore armbands and carried flags. When he launched personal diatribes against the duly constituted head of the American government, his own Church intervened to restrain him. The Vatican summoned his bishop, Michael Gallagher, to Rome;

Osservatore Romano upbraided him for creating disrespect for authority; the Papal Secretary of State, Cardinal Pacelli (later Pope Pius XII), embarked for a "vacation" in the United States; and Monsignor John Ryan, on a national radio network, rebuked Coughlin for calling Roosevelt a Communist. Despite all these tribulations, the Union party ticket gave the Democrats no little concern. Reports that the Union party might win 20 per cent of the Irish-Catholic ballots in Massachusetts and Rhode Island indicated that Roosevelt might be in trouble among Catholic voters in industrial states.

The Franklin Roosevelt who campaigned in 1936 had come a long way in four years. He no longer had the same faith in an all-class alliance. In early May, aboard the yacht *Potomac,* he told Moley angrily that businessmen as a class were stupid, that newspapers were just as bad; nothing would win more votes than to have the press and the business community aligned against him. In his opening fusillade of the campaign, on a sticky June night in Philadelphia before over a hundred thousand at Franklin Field, Roosevelt lashed out at "economic royalists" who took "other people's money" to impose a "new industrial dictatorship."

For the next four months, he ignored Landon and campaigned instead against Herbert Hoover and the interests. At the close of the campaign, at Madison Square Garden on October 31, he let out all the stops. The forces of "organized money," he told a roaring crowd, "are unanimous in their hate for me—and I welcome their hatred." "I should like to have it said of my first Administration that in it the forces of selfishness and of lust for power met their match. . . . I should like to have it said—" Another deafening roar from the crowd. "Wait a moment!" the President cried. "I should like to have it said of my second Administration that in it these forces met their master." The Garden was pandemonium.

By 1936, Franklin Roosevelt had forged a new political coalition firmly based on the masses in the great northern cities, and led in Congress by a new political type: the northern urban liberal Democrat typified by New York City's Robert Wagner. Wagner, a true son of the city—he became uneasy

whenever the el train near his apartment ceased to rumble—
spoke for an industrial liberalism considerably more advanced
than that advocated by most traditional Republican farm-state
progressives. While old-stock Americans in the small towns
clung to the G.O.P., the newer ethnic groups in the cities
swung to Roosevelt, mostly out of gratitude for New Deal
welfare measures, but partly out of delight with being granted
"recognition." Under Harding, Coolidge, and Hoover, one out
of every twenty-five judicial appointments went to a Catholic;
under Roosevelt, more than one out of every four. At the 1936
convention, northern cities demonstrated their new power in
the party when delegates wiped out the century-old two-thirds
rule, long one of the chief defenses of southern Democrats. On
Election Day, of the cities of one hundred thousand or more,
Roosevelt would capture 104, Landon two.

Even the depression did little at first to shake the loyalty of
Negroes to the party of Lincoln. In Detroit, Cleveland, Philadelphia, and other cities in 1932, Negroes cast their ballots for
Herbert Hoover. Cincinnati's heavily Negro Ward 16 gave
Roosevelt less than 29 per cent. While Roosevelt won 59 per
cent of the white vote in Chicago, he polled only 23 per cent
of the Negro ballots. The early New Deal provoked sharp
criticism from Negro leaders. They censured the NRA for
displacing Negro industrial workers and raising prices more
than wages: the Blue Eagle, contended one writer, was "a
predatory bird"; the NRA had but one meaning, "Negroes
Ruined Again." They protested AAA policies which drove
Negro tenant farmers and sharecroppers from the land, while
white landowners pocketed government checks. Negroes could
live neither in the TVA's model town of Norris nor in the subsistence homestead community of Arthurdale; the New Deal's
showplace communities were Jim Crow towns. The Negro,
wrote the N.A.A.C.P. organ *Crisis* in 1935, "ought to realize
by now that the powers-that-be in the Roosevelt administration have nothing for them."

Negro leaders also rebuked Roosevelt for the failure of New
Deal Congresses to enact civil rights legislation. After a re-
crudescence of lynching in 1933, the N.A.A.C.P. drafted a

federal antilynching bill, which was introduced in 1934 by
Senators Costigan and Wagner. New lynchings in that year
intensified the plea for federal action. A Georgian wrote Senator Wagner: "In Georgia thay Ar Killing the Colored Woman
and Saturday Night Oct 27th thay mobed a Negro man he is
Not Dead but looking to Die Any Day i Want you to Do your
best to Stop this. . . . i wont Rite my Name fer that it Would
be Publish and thay Will Kill Me as i A Negro." The President
denounced lynching and was willing, after some urging, to
support a vote on an antilynching measure, so long as it did
not tie up other reform legislation. But he refused to make it
"must" legislation, for, if he did, Southern committee chair-
men might kill every economic proposal he asked them to advance. Without the President's help, supporters of the bill
failed to break a filibuster of southern Democrats abetted by
Senator Borah. Not a single piece of civil rights legislation was
adopted in Roosevelt's four terms in the White House. Vexed
at the President's stand, the N.A.A.C.P. broke with him on
April 27, 1935. Vice-Dean Charles Houston of Howard University asked: "Is the Democratic Party determined to make it
impossible for self-respecting Negroes to support it in 1936?"

But there were counterforces pulling the Negro toward the
Roosevelt coalition. Roosevelt appointed Negroes to more
important posts than they had ever held, and New Deal
policies frequently broke the pattern of racial discrimination.
Negroes were especially impressed by the sincerity of Mrs.
Roosevelt and Secretary Ickes. The Democrats took pains to
distribute more than a million photographs of Mrs. Roosevelt
flanked by two young Negro R.O.T.C. officers at Howard University. Harold Ickes, who had been president of the Chicago
N.A.A.C.P., created a new post of director of "Negro economics," made a point of hiring Negroes in the Department
of the Interior, and gave them a large share of the new housing
in his slum-clearance projects. Most of all, Negroes swung to
Roosevelt because they had been granted relief. In many areas,
Negroes, hit harder than any group by the depression, survived
largely because of relief checks. Unlike the CCC, the WPA
imposed no quotas. The NYA, through the noted Negro

leader Mary McLeod Bethune, funneled funds to thousands of young Negroes. Negro intellectuals might fret at the inequities of the New Deal, but the masses of Negroes began to break party lines in gratitude for government bounties and nondiscriminatory treatment.

As early as 1932, G.O.P. politicians had come back with surprising intelligence from Negro wards: "They're getting tired of Lincoln." Disenchanted with the Republican party, Robert Vann, publisher of the Pittsburgh *Courier*, told Negro voters: "My friends, go turn Lincoln's picture to the wall. That debt has been paid in full." In 1934, Negroes began to switch to the Democrats, and by 1936 they were substantially Democratic. That year every Negro ward in Cleveland voted Democratic; Cincinnati's Ward 16 gave the President over 65 per cent of the ballots; Roosevelt ran better than twice as well among Negro voters in Chicago as he had four years before. The President took Pittsburgh's Negro Third Ward by nearly 10–1. By mid-1938, a *Fortune* poll would reveal that 84.7 per cent of Negro respondents counted themselves pro-Roosevelt.

Roosevelt's urban coalition united city leaders like Pittsburgh's Dave Lawrence not only behind the national party program but in support of "little New Deals" in the states. Under Governor George Earle, Pennsylvania passed a stringent child labor law, ended the notorious coal and iron police, adopted a "little Wagner Act," and stepped up taxes on corporations. Under Herbert Lehman, New York extended workmen's compensation, outlawed yellow-dog contracts, and provided unemployment insurance. Michigan boasted a "little New Deal" under Frank Murphy; California waited until 1939 to develop its unique version under Culbert Olson.

In the 1936 campaign, John L. Lewis, a lifelong Republican who had backed Hoover four years before, massed the battalions of the C.I.O. behind Roosevelt. C.I.O. unions contributed the enormous sum of $770,000 to the President's campaign chest; $469,000 of it came from Lewis' United Mine Workers. These contributions marked a historic shift in the financial base of the Democratic party; as business sources dried up, the U.M.W.'s donation made the union the party's largest single benefactor. In 1932, bankers and brokers had subscribed 24 per cent of all sums of $1,000 or more; in 1936, they gave less than 4 per cent. Lewis and Sidney Hillman also persuaded George Berry, leader of the A.F. of L. Printing Pressmen's Union, to join with them to create Labor's Non-Partisan League to help re-elect Roosevelt. Hillman and Dubinsky led a mass exodus of Socialists from the garment unions into the Roosevelt coalition. The defection of Socialist union leaders, and the immense appeal of Franklin Roosevelt's New Deal, all but destroyed the Socialist party.

The creation of Labor's Non-Partisan League appeared to indicate that American unions had decided to adopt the remedy British Labour theoreticians had long prescribed: the creation of a labor party in the United States. In fact, Lewis was doing no more than modifying the Gompers tradition, although modifying it in a significant way. No A.F. of L. walking delegate ever had more concern with protecting the job interest of union members than Lewis, and he regarded his huge contribution to Roosevelt as an offering for which he expected a measurable return. When Lewis sat with the President at a rally in Harrisburg in 1936, he had, one reporter noted, "a slightly possessive air as though this had been a *fête de Versailles* that he had ordered and paid for, as indeed he had." Lewis told a writer later: "The United Mine Workers and the CIO have paid cash on the barrel for every piece of legislation that we have gotten. . . . Is anyone fool enough to believe for one instant that we gave this money to Roosevelt because we were spellbound by his voice?"

In the 1936 elections, Labor's Non-Partisan League was credited with helping swing Ohio, Illinois, and Indiana to Roosevelt and with turning Pennsylvania Democratic. Roosevelt carried traditionally Republican steel towns like Homestead 4–1 and the Jones and Laughlin ward in Pittsburgh 5,870 to 925. In New York, the newly formed American Labor party won 300,000 votes under its emblem. Never before had union leaders done so effective a job of mobilizing the labor vote in a national campaign. Yet the final outcome was less a testimony to their efficiency than of the sense many workers had that the President was their spokesman and, more than that, their friend. As one workingman put it: "Mr. Roosevelt is the only man we ever had in the White House who would understand that my boss is a sonofabitch."

The labor vote indicated the sharpening class cleavage over political issues that marked the Roosevelt years. As early as 1932, the Roosevelt vote divided on class lines. Yet political scientists who analyzed the 1936 returns found to their astonishment that the class division was not as wide as anticipated, in part because Roosevelt received a surprising percentage of votes from the more prosperous. He had no difficulty winning the backing of reformer-businessmen like the Boston merchant Edward Filene. "Why shouldn't the American people take half my money from me?" Filene asked. "I took all of it from them." He held the support of thoughtful financiers like Russell Leffingwell of the House of Morgan, although Leffingwell no longer had his old enthusiasm. "It hurts our feelings to have you go on calling us money changers and economic royalists," he wrote the President. Still more significant was the allegiance of businessmen on the make in the South and West, many of whom had feuded with Wall Street. A. P. Giannini, the powerful California chain banker, urged Roosevelt's re-election and warmly supported the New Deal. Finally, the President drew strength from businessmen in newer industries, typified by Thomas Watson, whose International Business Machines flourished in the 1930's.

Roosevelt campaigned in 1936 as the leader of a liberal crusade which knew no party lines. He mentioned the Democratic party by name no more than three times in the whole campaign. He insisted on an alliance of Democrats and Farmer-Laborites in Minnesota and got the Democratic candidates for governor and senator to withdraw; he encouraged the La Follette Progressives in Wisconsin; he worked with the American Labor party in New York; and he repudiated his own party's nominee in Nebraska when he asked Cornhusker voters to return the independent George Norris, "one of our major prophets," to the Senate.

By 1936, almost all of the progressives had drifted into the

Roosevelt camp, in part because they believed they had no choice save to support the President in order to stave off a return to Hooverism, in part because the New Deal, and especially the Second Hundred Days, seemed to be a fulfillment of the hopes of progressive reformers like Jane Addams and Florence Kelley. When Congress adopted the Social Security bill, Lillian Wald wrote Frances Perkins: "I wish that sister Kelley had been saved to know that. Her life would have been more happily ended." PWA housing projects in Chicago bore the names of Jane Addams and Julia Lathrop. In the Tennessee Valley, Roosevelt was bringing to a brilliant conclusion the battle over Muscle Shoals which had bloodied the progressives for so many years. Some progressive Republican Senators like Charles McNary, Gerald Nye, and William Borah sat out the campaign; others like Hiram Johnson left no doubt they favored the President. Still other progressives like George Norris, James Couzens, and the La Follettes campaigned actively for the President. Norris, who thought Roosevelt's defeat would be "a national calamity," commented: "Not within my recollection has there been a President who has taken the advanced ground which President Roosevelt has taken to free the common man from the domination of monopoly and human greed." In one of the last letters of his life, Lincoln Steffens wrote of Roosevelt: "My trust has grown in him. No one else in sight." By the fall of 1936, the *New Republic* got few takers when it offered five dollars "for the name of an American citizen of either sex, of recognized intellectual distinction and progressive outlook, who is willing to admit publicly that he intends to vote for Landon. . . ."

In less than four years, Eleanor Roosevelt had established herself as the conscience of the administration. In her first year as First Lady, the indefatigable Mrs. Roosevelt traveled forty thousand miles. In one two-week period in the spring of 1933, she unveiled a memorial at Bear Mountain Park, urged the graduating class of Todhunter School to see as many kinds of life as possible, received an honorary degree from the Washington College of Law, told the graduating class of the Malcolm Gordon School to put joy in their lives, received six hundred disabled veterans on the South Grounds of the White House, and flew to Los Angeles. That spring, the *New Yorker* printed its famous cartoon of a bemused coal miner crying: "For gosh sakes, here comes Mrs. Roosevelt!" By June, 1935, the Washington *Star* was running a headline on its society page: MRS. ROOSEVELT SPENDS NIGHT AT WHITE HOUSE.

Sometimes naïve, she had one virtue that more than compensated for her gullibility: a warm, unaffected sympathy with other people. When a second bonus army descended on Washington in 1933, she waded through ankle-deep mire to lead the marchers in singing "There's a long, long trail a-winding." An ardent exponent of Negro rights, the First Lady kept Walter White of the N.A.A.C.P. posted on the President's views, and on occasion secured him an unusual one hour and twenty minutes' conference with Roosevelt. She helped persuade Congress to eliminate the noisome alley dwellings in the District of Columbia; she won White House audiences for reformers; she was the Good Fairy who saw to it that in a world of pressure groups and partisan decisions, the President did not neglect people and causes that had no other voice in places of power.

When Roosevelt toured the country in 1936, thousands of men and women pressed up to railroad tracks for a glimpse of the President. There was something terrible about their response, he told Ickes. He could hear people crying out: "He saved my home," "He gave me a job." In Detroit's Cadillac Square, the cheering was frenzied, almost out of control. In New England, people lined the streets not only in town but well out into the country. A crowd of 150,000 took over Boston Common. In Connecticut, campaign cars could barely maneuver through city streets. In New York City, Roosevelt's party drove for more than thirty miles without passing a block that was not jammed with people.

Roosevelt won loyalty not simply to the New Deal as an abstraction but to particular agencies which acted directly on people as government rarely had before. On an average day, the Farm Credit Administration saved three hundred farms from foreclosure. "I would be without a roof over my head if it

hadn't been for the government loan," wrote one farmer. "God
bless Mr. Roosevelt and the Democratic party who saved thousands of poor people all over this country from starvation."
The HOLC and FHA performed a similar service for distressed
urban homeowners. An FHA loan of $110.12 to Chief Albert
Looking Elk Martinez of the Pueblo tribe in Taos, New
Mexico, enabled him to remodel his ancient house; he replaced
the adobe hearth with a modern gas stove and covered the
earthen floor with bright linoleum. A California real-estate
broker, who had been a lifelong Republican, wrote the President: "Your work saved our humble little home from the
Trust Deed sharks and are we a happy couple in our little
home, and listen too, the Real Estate Business is now over
100% better than in 1932, life is 1000% better since you took
Charge of our United States."

The chief theme of Roosevelt's campaign was "Four Years
Ago and Now." In packed city squares, in jammed open-air
stadiums, to throngs from the rear of train platforms, he
would say: "You look happier today than you did four years
ago." His speeches, noted one reporter, were less campaign
addresses than "friendly sermons of a bishop come to make
his quadrennial diocesan call. Bishop Roosevelt reported on
the excellent state of health enjoyed throughout his vast
diocese, particularly as compared with the miserable state that
had prevailed before he took high office." He could point out
that at least six million jobs had been created in three years,
and that national income was half again as high in 1936 as in
1933. Industrial output had almost doubled since he took
office; by the fall of 1936, Detroit was rolling out more automobiles than in any year save 1929 and three times more than
in 1922, and the electrical industry was selling more current
than at any time in the past. In May, 1936, *The New York
Times* Index of Business Activity climbed to 100 for the first
time since 1930. Corporation profit sheets, which showed a
$2 billion deficit in 1933, ran $5 billion in the black in 1936.
Los Angeles department and specialty stores reported rises in
fur sales of 5 to 50 per cent over an excellent season the year
before, and Montgomery Ward rejoiced in the largest August

sales in its history. From the first quarter of 1933 to the third quarter of 1936, net income of farm operators almost quadrupled. When Alf Landon got word of the latest business indexes and a prognosis of further gains, he gave up the election as lost.

To be sure, there were weak spots. Construction was notoriously sluggish, and some of the recent gains seemed more speculative than sound. Eight million Americans in the seventh year of the depression still had no jobs. Yet there was a smell of prosperity in the air. In the people milling through the exhibits at the Texas Centennial, at ringside at the heavyweight championship fights of the unsmiling, lethal Joe Louis, in the newspaper headlines reporting "U.S. Steel Shows First Net Since '31," there was a heady sense of a nation once more in the money. Not only had gains been made, but Roosevelt's measures had the curious result of driving poverty out of sight. The apple sellers disappeared from the streets, the breadlines from the cities. If you lived in a comfortable neighborhood, you had to look hard to find people on relief.

On November 2, Jim Farley sent the President a detailed report on election prospects. "After looking them all over carefully and discounting everything that has been given in these reports," Farley wrote the President, "I am still definitely of the opinion that you will carry every state but two—Maine and Vermont." On election night, the Roosevelt family and intimates gathered at Hyde Park to sing to Tommy Corcoran's accordion and await the returns. As the night wore on, it became clear that Farley's prediction was being borne out precisely. Roosevelt had been re-elected by the most sweeping electoral margin of any candidate since James Monroe. The stanchly Republican states of Pennsylvania, Delaware, and Connecticut had gone Democratic for the first time since Buchanan's triumph in 1856. Lemke had polled only 882,000 votes in the entire country. Immediately after the election, Father Coughlin, likening his fate to that of the persecuted Christ, announced his retirement from politics.

The President had carried along with him so many Democratic candidates that when the new Congress met in January,

1937, it would be impossible to squeeze all seventy-five Democrats in the customary left side of the Senate chamber, and
twelve freshmen would have to sit with the Republicans. The
Grand Old Party had become the butt of the jokes of politicians and radio comedians. "As Maine goes," Farley gibed, "so
goes Vermont." "The Republican Party," lamented a Pennsylvania judge, "is reduced to the impotency of the Federalist
Party after Thomas Jefferson's sweeping victory in 1800."
Roosevelt no longer had any political liabilities, observed a
writer for *The New York Times*. "If he were to say a kind
word for the man-eating shark, people would look thoughtful
and say perhaps there *are* two sides to the question." Franklin
Roosevelt's fortunes were at high tide.

For Further Reading

The New Deal has bred controversies, hence books. Many of
the works cited in the previous bibliographic note, particularly
those by Burns, Robinson, and Schlesinger, deal with more
than FDR the man, probing as they do into the history of
the New Deal. They also have excellent bibliographies. Two
good bibliographic essays by Richard S. Kirkendall are: "The
Great Depression: Another Watershed in American History?"
in John Braeman et al., eds., *Change and Continuity in
Twentieth-Century America* (1964); and "The New Deal as
Watershed: The Recent Literature," *Journal of American
History* 54 (March 1968), 839–852.

The mood of America during the Depression is captured
vividly by Dixon Wecter, *The Age of the Great Depression,
1929–1941* (1948); by Frederick Lewis Allen, *Since Yesterday*
(1940); and, more recently, by Caroline Bird, *The Invisible
Scar* (1966). Two volumes by Irving Bernstein range far more
widely and authoritatively than their supposed concentration
on the American worker would suggest: *The Lean Years*
(1960), for the 1920–1933 period; and *The Turbulent Years*
(1969), for the 1933–1941 era. Robert and Helen Lynd, *Middle-*

town in Transition (1937) is the best of the community studies; their work is indispensable for an understanding of the 1930's. John Steinbeck's classic, *The Grapes of Wrath* (1939) and James Agee and Walker Evans, *Let Us Now Praise Famous Men* (1939) present in fictionalized form the plight of migrants and sharecroppers in the Southwest and the South.

The culture of the 1930's has fascinated many persons; a fine series of vignettes of individuals who were attracted by Communism is Murray Kempton, *Part of Our Time* (1955). Other valuable studies of literature, drama, and writers of the period are Leo Gurko, *The Angry Decade* (1947); Daniel Aaron, *Writers on the Left* (1961); F. R. Benson, *Writers in Arms* (1967); Harold Clurman, *The Fervent Years* (1957); Maxwell Geismar, *Writers in Crisis* (1942); Malcolm Cowley, *Think Back on Us* (1967); Alfred Kazin, *Starting Out in the Thirties* (1962); James B. Gilbert, *Writers and Partisans* (1968); Frank Warren, III, *Liberals and Communism* (1966); and Jane D. Matthews, *The Federal Theatre, 1935–1939* (1967). Handy collections of essays, contemporary selections, and reminiscences on general social, political, and economic matters are Rita J. Simon, ed., *As We Saw the Thirties* (1967); Harvey Swados, ed., *American Writer and the Great Depression* (1966); Don Congdon, ed., *The Thirties* (1962); Milton Crane, ed., *The Roosevelt Era* (1947); Louis Filler, ed., *The Anxious Years* (1963); Isabel Leighton, ed., *The Aspirin Age* (1941); David A. Shannon, ed., *The Great Depression* (1960); Jack Salzman with Barry Wallerstein, eds., *Years of Protest* (1967); and Daniel Aaron and Robert Bendiner, eds., *The Strenuous Decade* (1970).

The story of the transition from Hoover to Roosevelt is ably recounted by an insider, Herbert Feis, in *1933: Characters in Crisis* (1966); another transitional study of merit is Otis L. Graham, Jr., *An Encore for Reform* (1967), an attempt to see what Progressives thought about the New Deal. Yet another link to the past is stressed by William E. Leuchtenburg in "The New Deal and the Analogue of War," included in the Braeman volume, cited above.

Most of the New Deal's programs have been scrutinized.

The best works on agriculture are: E. G. Nourse, J. S. Davis, and J. D. Black, *Three Years of the AAA* (1937); David E. Conrad, *The Forgotten Farmers* (1965); Christiana M. Campbell, *The Farm Bureau and the New Deal* (1962); Gilbert C. Fite, *George N. Peek and the Fight for Farm Parity* (1954); Richard S. Kirkendall, *Social Scientists and Farm Politics in the Age of Roosevelt* (1966); Van L. Perkins, *Crisis in Agriculture* (1969); Sidney Baldwin, *Poverty and Politics* (1967); (1968). On the TVA, see David E. Lilienthal, *TVA: Democracy on the March* (1953) and *The Journals of David E. Lilienthal*, vol. 1, *The TVA Years, 1939–1945* (1964); C. Herman Pritchett, *The Tennessee Valley Authority* (1943); Wilmon H. Droze, *High Dams and Slack Waters* (1965); and, from a sophisticated critical perspective, Philip Selznick, *TVA and the Grass Roots* (1949).

The National Recovery Administration is part of the focus of a first-rate study by Ellis W. Hawley, *The New Deal and the Problem of Monopoly* (1966). Other works on the NRA and on antitrust are: Hugh Johnson, *The Blue Eagle from Egg to Earth* (1935); Donald Richberg, *The Rainbow* (1936); Leverett Lyon, et al., *The National Recovery Administration* (1935); Sidney Fine, *The Automobile Under the Blue Eagle* (1963); Louis Galambos, *Competition and Cooperation* (1966) on cotton textiles; Gerald Nash, *United States Oil Policy, 1890–1964* (1968); and Thurman Arnold, *The Folklore of Capitalism* (1937). Important works on the New Deal and labor, in addition to the Bernstein volumes cited earlier, are his *The New Deal Collective Bargaining Policy* (1950); Milton Derber and Edwin Young, eds., *Labor and the New Deal* (1957); Walter Galenson, *The CIO Challenge to the AFL* (1960); and Jerold S. Auerbach, *Labor and Liberty* (1966).

Relief, social security, and various community reforms are dealt with by Searle T. Charles, *Minister of Relief: Harry Hopkins and the Depression* (1963); John A. Salmond, *The Civilian Conservation Corps* (1967); Arthur J. Altmeyer, *The Formative Years of Social Security* (1966); and Paul Conkin, *Tomorrow a New World* (1959). The New Deal and the Negro is the subject of Leslie H. Fishel, Jr., "The Negro in the New

Deal Era," an article widely reprinted, as in Barton J. Bernstein and Allen Matusow, eds., *Twentieth Century America* (1969); see also Gunnar Myrdal, *An American Dilemma* (1944), chaps. 12, 15, and 18, and Bernard Sternsher, ed., *The Negro in Depression and War* (1969).

One phase of politics during the 1930's is covered in James T. Patterson, *Congressional Conservatism and the New Deal* (1967); also useful is the fine biography by J. Joseph Huthmacher, *Senator Robert F. Wagner and the Rise of Urban Liberalism* (1968). Donald R. McCoy, *Angry Voices* (1958), deals with left-wing agrarian protesters of the New Deal; while T. Harry Williams, *Huey Long* (1969) details the career of that fascinating demagogue. FDR's third term bid is told by Bernard F. Donahoe, *Prviate Plans and Public Dangers* (1965). Administrative and White House politics have been treated ably by Barry Dean Karl, *Executive Reorganization and Reform in the New Deal* (1963); Bernard Sternsher, *Rexford Guy Tugwell and the New Deal* (1964); and Richard Polenberg, *Reorganizing Roosevelt's Government* (1966).

The best revisionist statements may be found in Paul Conkin's fine interpretative essay, *The New Deal* (1967); Barton J. Bernstein, "The New Deal," in Bernstein, ed., *Towards a New Past* (1968); and Howard Zinn's introduction to Zinn, ed., *New Deal Thought* (1966). Jerold S. Auerbach, "New Deal, Old Deal, or Raw Deal," *Journal of Southern History* 35 (February 1969), rebuts the critics, calling them intemperate, ahistorical, and moralistic.

Two excellent anthologies focus on the New Deal: William E. Leuchtenburg, ed., *The New Deal* (1968); and Frank Freidel, ed., *The New Deal and the American People* (1964). Collections of articles and other pertinent material may be found in the following scholars' edited collections, each of which bears the title, *The New Deal,* but with varying subtitles: Edwin Rozwenc (1949); Morton Keller (1963); Bernard Sternsher (1966); and Alonzo L. Hamby (1969).

The Road to Pearl Harbor

Herbert Feis

Shortly before eight o'clock on the morning of December 7, 1941, Japanese bombers swooped down upon the United States' naval installation at Pearl Harbor, Hawaii. Within two hours, the attackers had completed their task: eighteen ships sunk or damaged and over 2,400 Americans dead. The "organized insanity" of World War II—beginning with Japan's invasion of Manchuria in 1931; Germany's rearmament and reoccupation of the Rhineland in 1935–1936; Italy's aggression in Ethiopia in 1935; civil war in Spain from 1936 to 1939; Japan's invasion of China in 1937; Germany's *Anschluss* in Austria in 1938; Germany's dismemberment of Czechoslovakia in 1938–1939; the Soviet-German Pact in 1939; Germany's invasion of Poland in 1939, and of Norway, Denmark, and France in 1940; Russia's attack on Finland in 1940; and Japan's advance into Indo-China in 1940—had finally reached American shores.

The "unprovoked and dastardly" Pearl Harbor attack marked the "day which will live in infamy"; so spoke Franklin D. Roosevelt to a stunned nation on December 8, 1941. The next day the President pledged the nation to the dual tasks of wiping out "the shame of Japanese treachery" and "absolutely and finally" breaking the sources of international brutality. These two speeches

Source: Herbert Feis, *The Road to Pearl Harbor* (Princeton, N.J.: Princeton University Press, 1950), pp. 307–341. Reprinted by permission of the publisher. All footnotes have been omitted by the editors.

set the tone and cast the first lines of what has developed into a contentious historical debate. Roosevelt viewed the origin of U.S. involvement in World War II as containing several elements. First, the United States had protested the spread of international gangsterism peacefully but firmly for ten years prior to the Pearl Harbor attack. During those years the United States had strived for a "fair and honorable" peace in the Pacific. Second, Japanese aggression was linked to the collaborative efforts of its Axis allies, Germany and Italy, to make all the world's oceans and continents "one gigantic battlefield." Third, during the interlude between the fall of France (May 1940) and Pearl Harbor, the United States had "greatly increased [its] industrial strength and [its] capacity to meet the demands of modern warfare." Supplying countries that had resisted Hitler or Japan gained the United States "precious months." And lastly, Roosevelt spoke of the need to abandon "once and for all the illusion that we can ever isolate ourselves from the rest of humanity."

The "official" version of the origins of World War II was stated as early as December 9, 1941. Documentation for the President's account appeared in 1943 when the Department of State published *Peace and War: United States Foreign Policy, 1931–1941*. This volume included a narrative of events and, more important, many significant documents that presented, in the Department's words, "a record of policies and acts by which the United States sought to promote conditions of peace, and world order and to meet the world-wide dangers resulting from Japanese, German, and Italian aggression."

Rebuttals to the official view appeared quite soon— even before the war had ended. The prewar debate between the "internationalists" (who had increasingly urged Roosevelt to intervene in European affairs after the Italian invasion of Ethiopia in 1935) and the "isolationists" (who believed that American national interests could best be upheld by a position of neutrality, not to say aloofness, towards the European conflicts) burst out once again in 1944 and 1945. The "revisionists" tended to be recruited from the ranks of prewar iso-

lationists who had not held official positions within the
administration during the war itself. Charles A. Beard,
Charles Tansill, George Morgenstern, and William
Henry Chamberlin each had either joined or spoken out
in favor of the American First Movement, the leading
prewar isolationist group.

The revisionists especially attacked the official conten-
tion that collusion among the Axis powers represented
a threat to American security. Hitler, they argued, had
no plans to invade the Western Hemisphere; hence he
was no threat. Revisionists generally explained Japanese
lawlessness by referring to various economic sanctions
imposed by Roosevelt (U.S. negation of its commercial
treaty in 1939; its embargo on all scrap metals to Japan
in 1940 and the addition to the embargo of copper,
brass, bronze, zinc, nickel, potash, phosphate, and uranium in January 1941, and of oil in July 1941; and its
freezing of all Japanese economic assets in the United
States in July 1941) and the administration's "ultimatum" to Japan demanding the latter's withdrawal
from Indo-China and China. It was these actions, revisionists maintained, that had forced the military leaders in Tokyo to take more desperate measures for national survival. The attack on Pearl Harbor, the critics
went on, had not caught the administration by surprise.
Rather, Roosevelt had maneuvered the Japanese to strike
the first blow in order to rally the large majority of
Americans who opposed American entry into the European war. The administration's defense procurement
policies in 1940–1941 were cited as proof of a martial
spirit, rather than of prudence. Revisionists, to sum up,
saw Roosevelt as a misguided internationalist who, failing to gain public support for his policies, carried on
secret preparations for war while he spoke of keeping
the U.S. out of hostilities.

Despite revisionist efforts, the Rooseveltian view has
held sway among historians such as Herbert Feis, Robert
E. Sherwood, William L. Langer, and S. Everett Gleason.
Labeled "Court" historians by revisionists, these writers
held internationalist views during the pre-1941 years
and were close to the Roosevelt Administration during

the war. Their writings emphasize the threat to American security posed by the speed and mobility of the Axis forces. Roosevelt wished to sustain American security by discouraging international aggression, but isolationist sentiment at home hampered him. He strove to shore up European defenses against Hitler by giving material and moral aid to England, France, and to a lesser extent, Finland. In the Pacific, FDR attempted to pursue a course that would not force Japan into the embrace of the Axis on the one hand and not endanger U.S. support of China, Great Britain, France, or the Netherlands in the Pacific on the other. The internationalists interpret FDR's moves as cautious responses to German and Japanese advances. They agree that forces beyond America's control conspired to bring the nation into war. Finally, the attack on Pearl Harbor caught Roosevelt and his administration by surprise, since the first blow was expected to land somewhere in the Southwest Pacific.

Much of the bitterness of the debate relates to postwar events and developments. The seemingly academic questions of historians have taken on deep emotional overtones. Some revisionists, for example, dismayed at what they define as the Soviet Union's expansionist aims after 1945, perceive sinister implications in Roosevelt's wartime diplomacy as well as his pre-1941 policy. His insistence that the Japanese attack was but part of an overall Axis plan of world domination and his consequent strategic emphasis upon defeating Hitler before turning to Japan, permitted the Soviet Union and Chinese Communist forces to consolidate and extend their influence in the Far East. Other critics of Roosevelt have advanced on a different tack. They see the war with Japan as emerging inevitably from the clash between America's historic commitment to an Open Door policy and Japan's equally traditional determination to expand its influence in China. Ironically, the U.S. leaders were sincere in their protestation of peaceful intent in the Pacific; but their very aims to preserve economic access to Far Eastern markets and resources were viewed as "aggressive" moves by Japanese leaders. The failure of

the Roosevelt Administration to perceive this dilemma
kept America on a collision course with Japan, hastening the pace toward war.

Among the historians who have chronicled the tangled
course of events leading to World War II, Herbert Feis
stands out. For many years Feis served as economic adviser in the Department of State; not strangely, his
interpretations fall within the "Court" historians' group.
The selection that follows is taken from his detailed survey of Japanese-American relations over the period 1937–
1941. Although the story is intricate, Feis manages to
recapture the sense of foreboding and drama inherent in
the exchanges of Japanese and American diplomats in
the closing days of November and early December 1941.

Japan's Final Proposal for a Truce
Is Weighed and Found Wanting

Kurusu arrived in Washington. A clipper brought him, and
his flight across the Pacific was watched as though he were a
bird whose coming could bring fair weather or foul. But the
government knew that he was only a trained expositor of
matters already decided.

Hull on the 17th [November] introduced him to the President. The ensuing talk was only a snarled survey of the area of
dissension. The President did not sprinkle his words with geni-
ality, as he usually had with Nomura. There was no liking
either for the man or for his mission. As for the man, Hull
spoke for both when he wrote: "Kurusu seemed to me the anti-
thesis of Nomura. Neither his appearance nor his attitude com-
manded confidence or respect. I felt from the start that he
was deceitful." As for the mission, that was unpromising, even
if not false. His purpose, looked at in the best light, was to
persuade the American government to accept the latest Japanese terms in preference to war. Looked at in the worst light,
it was to engage American interest while the assault plans
were being secretly completed. Just before the meeting, an-

other cable of warning had been received from Grew. Be on guard, he said, against sudden naval and military actions, for Japan would probably exploit every possible tactical advantage, such as surprise and initiative.

On the next day, the 18th, the talk took an unmapped turn. Nomura, speaking as though the idea were his own, asked whether it might not be possible to arrange a type of accord other than that over which the two governments were now so completely at odds. Perhaps, he suggested, a partial agreement which would at least avert immediate trouble. His thought, he said, was that the two governments might restore the situation as it was before July, when Japan moved into Southern Indo-China, and the United States and Britain imposed their embargo.

Hull, up to that point, had been ungiving. But here was a chance, at least, to gain time. Time that would fit us (and our associates) better for war. Time that might enable the Japanese government to persuade the Army to yield more, and the people to accept the thought of retreat. As broached, it was only an idea, incomplete and without authority. Hull said just enough to show he was attracted, no more. He asked Nomura whether, if such an arrangement were made, the talks would continue. Nomura said they would. Hull then observed that he could see how this step might enable the Japanese leaders to hold their position and to organize public opinion in favor of a peaceful course. Therefore he would acquaint the British and Dutch governments with the suggestion and see what they thought.

Nomura and Kurusu stood on tiptoe in the effort to put this idea across. That night (November 18) they hurried off message after message to Tokyo. Togo, the Foreign Minister, had sent them some days before the text of Proposal B—terms for a truce to be offered as a last resort. But its rejection was foreseen by them. The two Japanese diplomats were trying to prevent the final crash by proffering easier and simpler truce terms.

As soon as the Japanese had left, Hull asked Sir Ronald Campbell, British Chargé d'Affaires, to call. He told Campbell of the status of the talks and of the idea of a partial arrangement to allow the Japanese government to direct public opinion. On the next morning he spoke to the Chinese Ambassador and the Australian and Dutch Ministers in the same sense and with a certain show of eagerness.

But "Magic" brought the news that the notions of the two Ambassadors had been rejected in Tokyo. The Foreign Minister frowned on their flow of advice that Japan should accept a loose "give and take" truce rather than a long drawn-out war. They were told that the Japanese government could not agree to withdraw from Indo-China, merely in return for relaxation of trade controls; that it was afraid that the American government would soon bring up other and further conditions. They were ordered to present at once the whole of Proposal B, as stenciled by the Imperial Conference on November 5.

Another snatched message sent on the same date conveyed the fact that a new code was being sent to Nomura. Signals would be given in the daily Japanese language short-wave newscasts. Comments upon the direction of the wind would inform whether diplomatic relations were about to be broken with the United States, Great Britain, or Russia, or all of them. Thereafter, American listeners were posted to catch the signals.

Nomura placed Proposal B before Hull on November 20. The English text, as cabled some days before, had been intercepted and read. Hull knew that it was regarded in Tokyo as the last bargain; the hinge on the breech of the cannon.

There were five numbered points on the white piece of paper which Nomura gave to Hull. They have been printed in many other places, but I think the reader will want them before him as he follows the narrative:

    1. Both the Government of Japan and the United States undertake not to make any armed advancement into any of the regions in the South-eastern Asia and the Southern Pacific

area excepting the part of French Indo-China where the Japanese troops are stationed at present.

2. The Japanese Government undertakes to withdraw its troops now stationed in French Indo-China upon either the restoration of peace between Japan and China or the establishment of an equitable peace in the Pacific area.

In the meantime the Government of Japan declares that it is prepared to remove its troops now stationed in the southern part of French Indo-China to the northern part of the said territory upon the conclusion of the present arrangement which shall later be embodied in the final agreement.

3. The Government of Japan and the United States shall cooperate with a view to securing the acquisition of those goods and commodities which the two countries need in Netherlands East Indies.

4. The Government of Japan and the United States mutually undertake to restore their commercial relations to those prevailing prior to the freezing of the assets.

The Government of the United States shall supply Japan a required quantity of oil.

5. The Government of the United States undertakes to refrain from such measures and actions as will be prejudicial to the endeavors for the restoration of general peace between Japan and China.

Whoever insisted on the last paragraph—Tojo [Prime Minister] and the Army certainly did—insisted on war.

Hull glanced over the text to make sure it was the same as that which was known. It was. Then, on two points in particular he spoke out. Linking Japan's treatment of China to Hitler's actions, he defended our aid to China. Kurusu remarked that perhaps this point (No. 5) in the Japanese terms might be construed to mean that the United States would end its help only at the time when talks between Japan and China would have started. Hull also dwelt on the fact that this truce would leave Japan a full member of the Axis pact, and hence still a potential enemy of the United States and Great Britain. To this Kurusu had no answer.

Hull found no dissent, either within the State Department or at the White House, to his opinion that the proposal was "clearly unacceptable." His reasons for finding it so are summed up again in his "Memoirs":

> The commitments we should have to make were virtually a surrender. We on our part should have to supply Japan as much oil as she might require, suspend our freezing measures, and resume full commercial relations with Tokyo. We should have to discontinue aid to China and withdraw our moral and material support from the recognized Chinese Government of Chiang Kai-shek. We should have to help Japan obtain products of the Netherlands East Indies. We should have to cease augmenting our military forces in the western Pacific.
>
> Japan, on her part, would still be free to continue her military operations in China, to attack the Soviet Union, and to keep her troops in northern Indo-China until peace was effected with China. . . . Japan thus clung to her vantage point in Indo-China which threatened countries to the south and vital trade routes.
>
> The President and I could only conclude that agreeing to these proposals would mean condonement by the United States of Japan's past aggressions, assent to future courses of conquest by Japan, abandonment of the most essential principles of our foreign policy, betrayal of China and Russia, and acceptance of the role of silent partner aiding and abetting Japan in her effort to create a Japanese hegemony over the western Pacific and eastern Asia.

Inspection of such Japanese records as I have seen leaves room for doubt about some features of this judgment. It is not certain that the meaning which Hull attached to some of the points in Proposal B is the necessary meaning; or that his total estimate of the Japanese offer to begin to retreat was just. Perhaps so, probably so, but not surely so.

It would be a barren exercise, I think, now to re-examine, feature by feature, the face and soul of this last Japanese formula for peace. The result would be inconclusive; for even its authors were divided and mixed up in their intentions. And even a less suspicious reading would have, I think, led to the same rejection. For the situation had grown too immense and entangled for haggling. Japan had forced the creation of a defensive coalition more vast than the empire of the Pacific for which it plotted. This was not now to be quieted by a temporary halt along the fringe of the Japanese advance.

Acceptance of this Japanese proposal would have imperiled the trustful unity of the coalition. As the next few days were to show, China would have felt itself deserted, if not betrayed. Elsewhere the will to carry on the fight against Germany without pause or compromise might have been corrupted. The Japanese Army and Navy would have been left in place to take advantage of any future weakness.

Even—to carry conjecture further—if the American government had taken these risks and entered into this accord, there would have been war in the Pacific. For it seems to me almost certain that the truce would have broken down as soon as signed. Quarrels would have started over the military movements in which both sides were engaged. Japan would not have ceased its preparations for attack. Nor can it be thought that we or the British would have ended the movement of planes and ships and anti-aircraft and radar to the Philippines and Malaya. Each side would have thought the other to be taking crooked advantage of the truce.

If these disputes did not bring the truce to a quick end, arguments over oil would have done so. Very different notions existed in Tokyo and Washington as to what was expected under the phrase "a required quantity of oil." The Japanese government had told Nomura to let us know before signing how much it had in mind. It wanted four million tons a year from the United States, and one million tons a year from the Indies. The American government would not have agreed to supply anything like such quantities, which were enough to keep Japanese reserves intact.

In sum, the paper given by Nomura to Hull on November 20 would have marked only the start of new disputes, not the end of old ones.

War might be in the secret messages; it might be in the nerves, but the wish to avoid it was still alive. Hull began to compound a counteroffer to Proposal B which might defer the climax without giving Japan an advantage, or destroying the faith of our allies. The drafting squad ransacked the files for old memoranda, and drew upon a refreshingly new one from the Treasury.

The President sent across to the State Department his ideas of the terms on which a simple stay might be arranged. These were: some oil and rice for Japan at once, and more later; an introduction of the Japanese and Chinese governments, so that the two could talk the situation over in a friendly fashion without American participation. Japan, in return, was to promise not to send any more troops south or north and to agree not to invoke the Tripartite Pact, even if the United States got into the European war.

Hull was afraid both of being tricked and of being misunderstood. Therefore he resorted to a form of response that might have provided useful protection if a truce had been effected, but which surely would have prevented one. Along with the counterproposal for a *modus vivendi* Japan was to be asked to subscribe to a statement of principles to be observed by both countries thereafter.

Tentative drafts of these two papers were, by the 22nd, ready for submission to other governments. Hull called to his office the emissaries of Great Britain, Australia, the Netherlands, and China. He explained to them that the heads of the Army and Navy were beseeching him to postpone the crisis, if he could, to gain some more time. He showed the visitors copies of the drafts, from which they took notes. Casey spoke out incisively, saying that he felt that the wish of the military was enough to command. The others said little. But Hull had the sense that all except the Chinese Ambassador fell in with his thought. He asked whether under the accord Japan would be obligated not to extend its invasion into China. Hull answered that it would not. The diplomats left to report to their governments.

Later that day Hull talked with Nomura and Kurusu in an attempt to find out whether they held any further concessions in reserve. They had none. The news drawn from the caught cables and elsewhere did not encourage the opinion that it was any use to stretch our principles. Large Japanese forces were moving into their bases in Southern Indo-China, and Japanese transports were gathering at the point in the Japanese mandated islands nearest the Indies. A "Magic" cable sent from Tokyo on the 22nd (Tokyo time) informed Nomura that it was awfully hard for the Japanese government to consider a change in the deadline for the American reply, "for reasons beyond your ability to guess." But, the message continued, "if you can bring about the signing of the pertinent notes we will wait until November 29." "After that," the "Magic" cable read, "things are automatically going to happen."

Another message sent out on the same day by Admiral Yamamoto, the Commander in Chief of the Combined Fleet, to the Task Force in the Kuriles, was not intercepted. It began:

> The Task Force will move out from Hitokappu Wan on 26 November and proceed without being detected to Rendezvous set for December 3.
> X-day will be December 8.

Over the weekend the drafts of the two texts were retouched, and agreement with the Army and Navy confirmed. The military men strongly favored the effort to buy time. But since they esteemed it as a chance to make the Pacific outposts stronger, they wanted a truce which would not immobilize them. On this point they were satisfied.

Then on Monday, the 24th, the diplomats of the ABCD powers were consulted again. Hull made a vigorous exposition of the benefits to all of committing Japan to a peaceful course for three months. He sensed apathy in their comment. "They seemed to be very much gratified," he noted after the meeting was over, "[but] they seemed to be thinking of the advantages to be derived without any particular thought of what we should pay for them, if anything." The Dutch Ambassador reported that his government would support the truce. None of the others had as yet heard from home. Aggrieved at having to worry through this miserable decision with so little aid, Hull said to them: ". . . each of their Governments was more interested in the defense of that area of the world than this country, and at the same time they expected this country, in case of a Japanese outbreak, to be ready to move in a military way and take the lead in defending the entire area." In mind were the urgent current pleas of the British and Dutch military representatives in Singapore and Batavia for full agreement on combined military action if Japan moved south.

The intercepts, which Hull could not mention, made clear that time left for talk was all but gone. He merely said, on parting from the diplomats, that he did not know whether or not he would present the text discussed without knowing the views of their governments.

That evening the President, at Hull's initiative, sent a message to Churchill, outlining the terms of the offer in mind. In return primarily for a Japanese promise not to advance north or south, the American and other governments were to permit Japan to obtain a monthly quota of oil for civilian needs, and limited amounts of foodstuffs, drugs, cotton, ship bunkers and supplies. "I am not very hopeful," the message ended, "and we must be prepared for real trouble, possibly soon." This last sentence was added by the President himself to the draft which Hull had submitted.

At noon the next day (the 25th) Hull, Stimson, and Knox went to the White House where they were joined by Stark and Marshall. The talk seems to have been more concerned with what to do when and as Japan attacked than with the patchwork truce. The President, according to Stimson's notes, "brought up the event that we were likely to be attacked perhaps (as soon as) next Monday [December 1], for the Japanese are notorious for making an attack without warning, and the question was what we should do. The question was how we should maneuver them into the position of firing the first shot without allowing too much danger to ourselves." The Secretary's language was, I think, hurried and elliptic. The Japanese force was the attacking force. If left to choose the place and time for the first encounter, the defense might suffer. But if any of the defenders fired the first shot, they might be regarded as attackers. The problem of keeping the roles straight—without paying heavily for it—was far from easy.

After this meeting the members of the War Council returned to their offices. Stark and Marshall were disturbed by the rate at which the situation seemed to be heading to a showdown. They resumed work upon a joint memorandum to the President which was already well started.

Stimson found further news waiting for him. The Japanese were embarking a large force—from thirty to fifty ships—at Shanghai and the first elements of this expedition had been sighted proceeding south of Formosa along the Chinese coast. This news he telephoned to the President and Hull. Then he met again with Marshall and Stark. He was concerned lest the paper which Stark and Marshall were finishing should be construed by the President as a recommendation to reopen the talks with Japan on a basis of compromise. They assured him it was not to be so understood. Warnings to be sent to our commanders in the Pacific were also drafted.

Hull returned from the White House to a schedule of appointments. Halifax brought an unhelpful message from Eden. This stated that the British government, having complete confidence in Mr. Hull's handling of the negotiations, would support him if he felt it best to put forward a counterproposal. But he added that in his, Eden's, view, ". . . our demands should be pitched high and our price low." The Japanese government, the message went on, should be asked to withdraw all its armed force from Indo-China, and to promise to suspend further military advances in China. It also expressed doubt about the resumption of any oil shipments. Hull briefly reviewed with Halifax the advantages of a truce, but did not say what he would do.

Loudon, the Dutch Minister, came next. He again reported his government to be in favor of the truce proposal, but was of the opinion that the quantities of oil to be delivered should be limited, so that Japan's war potential would not be increased.

The Chinese Ambassador, Hu Shih, was waiting. He had anxious complaints from Chiang Kai-shek. In essence, the Generalissimo said that he had the impression that the American government had put China to one side and was inclined to appease Japan at its expense. He was afraid that if the economic blockade was relaxed, the morale of the Chinese troops would be sorely shaken, and the spirit of resistance of both people and Army might collapse. Chiang Kai-shek took pains to see that this message got to the President and friends in the cabinet quickly and undiluted. He sent an even stronger version to T. V. Soong, his brother-in-law (who was in Washington), for transmission to Knox and Stimson. Owen Lattimore, an American appointed by Chiang Kai-shek to be his political adviser, cabled Lauchlin Currie, one of the President's secretaries, asking him urgently to inform the President of the Generalissimo's very strong reaction.

A few months before, the Chinese government had shown itself similarly adverse and frightened. Alarmed by reports of a deal whereby, in return for Japanese promises in regard to the rest of the Pacific area, the United States would resume shipments of oil and scrap iron, it had protested. Hull on September 4 had sent assurances that the American government would not enter any arrangement that would allow aggression in China to continue. Further, he said that it would not alter or end the measures taken to impede Japan unless Japan altered the situations which had caused the United States to resort to them. The Chinese Foreign Minister had then half apologized for his anxieties. His way of doing so had been to tell a Confucian anecdote, of the mother at the spinning wheel, who, because of faith in her son, ignored the first two reports that he had committed a murder, but rose to investigate when a third neighbor brought the same story. The episode showed, whether realized or not, that the policy of the United States was almost as closely linked to the fate of China as to that of Britain. Both had been encouraged to spend themselves. How, then, could the United States, unless they freely concurred, treat with their enemy?

Now, in this crisis, Chinese trust faltered again. Chiang's messages seemed to both the President and Hull foolishly excited and unjust. Was not American fidelity amply proved? Hull explained to the Chinese Ambassador, Hu Shih, how all the opponents of Japan would gain by a truce; how China would be relieved by the retirement of Japanese troops from Indo-China, which he intended to ask; how even, perhaps, the war from which China was suffering so much could be brought to a good end. His exasperation found words before the call ended. The American government, he remarked, could, of course, cancel the proposal; but if it did so it was "not to be charged with failure to send our fleet into the area near Indochina and into Japanese waters, if by any chance Japan makes a military drive southward."

It was dark outside by the time Hu Shih left. Still Hull called together again the members of his staff who had shared with him the long and failing effort to convince or outwit Japan. Those present at this late afternoon session recall several interrupting telephone calls from outside. The identity of the talkers on the other end of the wire is no longer remembered; perhaps the President called, perhaps some reporter of further news of Japanese military movements. But they caused a further ebb in the belief that it was worth-while to proceed with the idea of a truce.

The group separated for a hurried half-eaten dinner, then met again at Hull's apartment in the Wardman Park. All agreed that the meager American offer would only be for the record; that Japan would not accept it or any tolerable variant of it. Time and again, as Hull knew, the Japanese envoys had been told that the proposal made to the United States was Japan's last word. The gesture, therefore, would not prevent or delay the Japanese southward invasion.

The very making of the offer seemed likely to have troublesome, if not ruinous, effects. It would be self-defeating to give a true and full explanation to the American people. A confused domestic debate was apt to follow and be in full flow when the war crisis came. More worrisome still was the prospect that, despite whatever was said, the other nations fighting the Axis would feel let down. There was no time to convince Chiang Kai-shek that China would not suffer and would not be deserted. The other members of the coalition were showing themselves lukewarm—not opposing the truce, but not welcoming it. Was it, as Hull averred, only a maneuver, or was it a wavering in the ranks?

Sometime during the night of the 25th, Churchill's answer to the President arrived. It left the American government free to do what it thought best, but seemed to fall in with the view that a truce with Japan was unfair to China. Doubt seemed to overrule enthusiasm. The text is given so that the reader may judge for himself:

> MOST SECRET FOR THE PRESIDENT FROM THE FORMER NAVAL PERSON. Your message about Japan received tonight. Also full accounts from Lord Halifax of discussions and your counter project to Japan on which Foreign Secretary has sent some comments. Of course, it is for you to handle this business and we certainly do not want an additional war. There is only one point that disquiets us. What about Chiang Kai-Shek? Is he not having a very thin diet? Our anxiety is about China. If they collapse our joint dangers would enormously encrease. We are sure that the regard of the United States for the Chinese cause will govern your action. We feel that the Japanese are most unsure of themselves.

Hull, in the course of the night, added up the sum of pros and cons. The reason for going ahead with the counterproposal had come to seem unreal. What we had to offer, it was all but certain, would not buy even time. The objections seemed many and hard to meet. He decided to discard it and let events take their course. The verdict was reached after tormenting uncertainty. But once reached, a calm sense followed that he had done all that a man could do.

One other happening of this day, November 25, might have been pertinent had our decision taken the other turn. Hull and Knox concurred in a recommendation of Admiral Land, Chairman of the Maritime Commission, that merchant vessels, under the American flag, be sent to Archangel and Britain, hitherto forbidden zones. They agreed that ships should be put on these routes gradually and when properly equipped. There was to be, at all events, no letup in the program of resistance to Germany. The mind is left to wonder what would have happened had the truce been signed, and this extension of our aid to Britain and Russia been made.

As Stubborn as Ever; the American Answer, November 26, 1941

Hull wrote out what he proposed to say to the President: "In view of the opposition of the Chinese Government and either the half-hearted support or the actual opposition of the British, the Netherlands and the Australian Governments, and in view of the wide publicity of the opposition and of the additional opposition that will naturally follow through utter lack of an understanding of the vast importance and value otherwise of the *modus vivendi,* without in any way departing from my views about the wisdom and the benefit of this step to all the countries opposed to the aggressor nations who are interested in the Pacific area, I desire very earnestly to recommend that at this time I call in the Japanese Ambassadors and hand to them a copy of the comprehensive basic proposal for a general peaceful settlement, and at the same time withhold the *modus vivendi* proposal."

Early on the 26th he read this to the President, who quickly agreed. Both knew, it may be surmised, that the Japanese would have ignored the discarded sketch of a truce. For what was offered, they would not have recalled the expeditions then heading south and west.

That afternoon at 5 o'clock Hull gave the Japanese Ambassadors his "comprehensive basic proposal." In this statement the American government had its full say. Described as

92   *The Road to Pearl Harbor*

"Strictly Confidential, Tentative and Without Commitment,"
it plotted out both present and future in the Far East. Only
a student of dead detail, an ironist besides, would now read
it through. Both memory and judgment will now, I think, be
sufficiently served by a summary of the three main features.
Japan and the United States were mutually to promise to
abide by the principles for which we had been standing right
along. They were to sponsor a non-aggression pact among all
countries concerned in the Far East which, in effect, would
have been re-validation of the Nine-Power Treaty. Japan was
to withdraw all military, naval, air, and police forces from
China and Indo-China.

The system of political and social order proposed was in
direct contrast to the dream that had driven Japan on. It
conceived of a community of orderly and equal states, who
would respect each other's independence and security, and
treat and trade with one another on identical terms. The
Japanese program conceived that Japan would be the stabi-
lizing center of life throughout East Asia. All other countries
of the region would be clustered about Japan. It would be
the roof of the temple; they the pillars. It would be the
organizer; they the followers. It would be the lawgiver; they
the grateful recipients. Here in this document there was a
denial of all that Japan had set out to do by stratagem or by
force.

But there seems to me no warrant for making it an ultimatum—either in the political or the military sense. Japan
was left with four choices: to assent to the American proposal
and reverse its policy; to abstain from any further armed advance north or south, but to continue the war in China as
best it could; to begin its retreat and see what return for
doing so might be had from China, the United States, and
Great Britain; or to carry through its bid for victory to the
end. It chose the last.

The American officials who knew of our answer had little
doubt that it would. Their thoughts switched further from
the tactics of negotiations to the tactics of war. On the next
day (the 27th) Hull told Stimson, "I have washed my hands

of it, and it [the situation] is now in the hands of you and
Knox, the Army and Navy."

Stimson had no regrets or misgivings. Knox and Stark came
that morning to his office. General Marshall was out of town
and General Gerow was again acting in his stead. There were
two crucial matters to be decided. What action should the
American government take in the face of threatened Japanese
assault? What further warnings should be sent to the commanders of our forces in the Far East?

The Army and Navy had for weeks past been trying to
extract a conclusive answer to the first question from the
President, the Commander in Chief. There was a war plan,
"Rainbow No. 5," which had been prepared for the con-
tingency that now was in sight. But there was no enacting
decision or agreement to put it into force. It had been shaped
in conference with the British and Dutch authorities, and was
based on the conception that if war came all would be in it
together. The British and Dutch governments had made a
score of attempts to obtain assurances that in the event of attack upon their territories (or Japanese entry into Thailand)
the United States would join in the defense. But the American government had just as persistently refused to give any
explicit promise to that effect.

Admiral Hart, Commander of the United States Asiatic
Fleet, to which it was expected the first call for action would
come, had been authorized to talk the situation out. The
British military commanders in the Far East (under Admiral
Phillips) were echoing Churchill's plea for firm assurances,
and again urging that the United States join in a warning to
Japan that a new transgression would mean war. The American naval men had said that they could not agree to this, but
that they would take the matter up with the President and
make a recommendation.

Stark and Marshall had been trying to frame an answer to
Hart. This was the prompting reason for the paper on which
they had been at work, and which they had held back pending
the outcome of the last diplomatic turn. Now the decision
could no longer be put off. It was November 27; and the

Japanese warships and troop transports were just around the bend, headed for no one knew where. Were the American ships and planes in the neighborhood to wait till they landed? Were they to wait even longer if territories under the American flag were left alone?

Stark and Marshall tendered their advice to the President in a memorandum sent to him that day (the 27th). The phrasing of one paragraph was a leftover from earlier drafts. "The most essential thing now, from the United States' viewpoint," it read, "is to gain time." Therefore, "precipitance of military action on our part should be avoided so long as consistent with national policy." Stimson received assurance that the authors did not mean by this statement to urge a reopening of the talks.

The line laid down was definite and conformed essentially to that which had been drawn in the conferences held in Singapore in the spring of the year.

It is recommended that:

prior to the completion of the Philippine reinforcement, military counteraction be considered only if Japan attacks or directly threatens United States, British, or Dutch territory as above outlined:

in case of a Japanese advance into Thailand, Japan be warned by the United States, the British, and the Dutch governments that advance beyond the lines indicated may lead to war;

prior to such warning no joint military opposition be undertaken; steps be taken at once to consummate agreements with the British and Dutch for the issuance of such warning.

Stimson and Knox agreed with these conclusions, and Stimson tried at once to get the President to rule upon them. But he would not, still keeping clear of any open promise to go to war, or joint warning which would be the equivalent. The problem of arranging for coordinated action was again passed back to the local commanders in the Asiatic region. The idea was that they should arrive at an "executory supplement" to "Rainbow No. 5." They were so engaged when the war started.

Whether or not the American forces would have gone into action right away if American territories had not been attacked remains a matter of conjecture. But it seems most probable that, at the point and hour where the danger flared high and clearly, the President would have followed the advice that his two senior military advisers gave on November 27. It may be guessed with confidence that he thought (1) that if the Philippines (or Guam, or Hawaii) were attacked the question would settle itself; (2) that if they were left alone the best tactic to be pursued was similar to that being followed in the Atlantic—a gradual movement of the American naval and air forces into combined action with the British, Dutch, and Australians. The Asiatic fleet would almost certainly have become engaged at once in the defense of the Malay Barrier.

On that same day (November 27), also, the war warnings that failed to protect were dispatched. Stimson proposed and the President approved the transmission to MacArthur and other field commanders of the "final alert," informing them of the situation and telling them to be on the "qui vive for any attack." These were sent off—the message to Admiral Kimmel at Pearl Harbor beginning, "This dispatch is to be considered a war warning."

The American people were vaguely aware that talks with Japan had come to a lingering end. But they were not clearly told that we might very soon be at war with Japan. Whatever else Japan might do, they did not expect it to attack territory under the American flag; and, short of that, they thought only of supporting operations, as in the Atlantic. Even those men who walked the corridors of the State, War, and Navy Buildings did not truly feel the great change that lay ahead.

Up to then we had been managers of the war, riders of the storm. Now we were soon to become part of it, of its flame and fire. We were going soon to land men on the bare coral ledges in the vast Pacific, on the African beaches, on the shores of Italy, and where the Atlantic rolled over the Normandy sands. The faces of the Japanese soldiers were going

to be closer to many Americans than the image of home.
That was, within a few days, to be decided in Tokyo.

The Last Arrangements and
Formalities for War

There, the resolution approved at the Imperial Conference
on November 5 dictated the future. It had followed a pattern
set by earlier use; a pattern cut to suit divided authority. Time
and again since 1931 the more aggressive elements in Japan, especially the Army, had set a mark. Having done so, they
allowed diplomacy a short time to reach this mark by persuasion, guile, or threat. Meanwhile the armed forces got
ready to act if diplomacy failed. The advances into China
and Indo-China had been arranged that way. Once again the
Army had agreed to give diplomacy a last chance. A brief
and bound chance.

The talkers had been allowed the days that were left in the
month of November. They had ticked away like a hidden
bomb. Scores of messages were exchanged between the Japanese government and its Embassy in Washington. But they
were all one in meaning. The first said the same thing as the
last: the American government will not choose peace on fair
terms; it will not agree to end aid to China and to provide
oil, unless we give up everything for which we have been
waging war.

On November 13 both the plans and the time schedule of
action in the event that no accord was reached with the United
States had been confirmed at another Liaison Conference in
the presence of the Emperor. Within the Foreign Office and
court circles there had been some scant expectation that we
would agree to Proposal B. Hearing from Nomura that Hull
had said that he must have more time to consult other governments, the Japanese cabinet had agreed to wait for the
American answer a few days longer—till the 29th. "After
that," the answer to Nomura said, "things are automatically

going to happen." Indeed they were; the task force assembling in the Kuriles was being told that on the morning of the 26th it was to proceed to the Hawaii area.

The long Ten-Point Memorandum on principles, which was our response to Proposal B, was received in Tokyo on the morning of the 27th. Along with it Nomura and Kurusu sent a convoy of troubled comment. They thought the answer hard and dumbfounding. But they found nothing in it compelling Japan to resort to war. They were afraid, as "Magic" let Washington know, that the United States and Britain might try to forestall Japan by occupying the Indies, thus bringing on war. Even this late, Nomura advised his government to keep on with the effort to reach a peaceful accord. He recalled a remark the President had made in an earlier talk—that there would be "no last words." But, he added, if his counsel was not taken, it would be best not to keep up a false front of friendliness, and to strike from behind it. Kurusu, also, tried to be calming. He attributed our statement in part to knowledge of the Japanese military movements and concentrations in the south.

Another Liaison Conference was called as soon as the American paper was read (November 27). This summarily dismissed our statement of principles as a humiliating ultimatum. It was resolved to proceed with the program adopted on November 5; that is, to go to war as soon as the striking forces were in position. Stratagem had failed. Force would be used. Japan would do or die.

As was natural, the men who made this decision pleaded later that it was compelled by the terms placed upon peace by the United States. Thus, the former Foreign Minister, Togo, one of the more conciliatory members of the government, argued that "Japan was now asked not only to abandon all the gains of her years of sacrifice, but to surrender her international position as a power in the Far East. That surrender, as he saw it, would have amounted to national suicide. The only way to face this challenge and defend ourselves was war."

This was not a valid attitude. The idea that compliance with the American terms would have meant "extinction" for Japan, or so deeply hurt it that it could not guard its just interests, is an absurdity. Japan was not asked to give up any land or resources except those which it held by force of arms. Its independence was not in peril. Its Army, Navy, and Air Force would have remained in being. Its chances to trade with the rest of the world would have been restored. Its struggle against the extension of Communism could have combined with that of China and the West. Extinction threatened the plan for expansion in Asia, but not Japan or the Japanese.

On the 28th, Tojo turned down Nomura's appeals. So did the Lord Privy Seal, Kido. They were not, as Nomura probably hoped, reported to the Emperor. Nomura and Kurusu were duly told: "With the report of the views of the Imperial Government that will be sent to you in two or three days, talks will be de facto ruptured. This is inevitable. However, I do not wish you to give the impression that the negotiations are broken off. . . . From now on do the best you can." This was read in Washington.

The coming day (the 29th, Tokyo time) was the day of the deadline—the day after which things were automatically going to happen. It was spent in continuous consultation. The Senior Statesmen met with the cabinet in the morning, with the Emperor at lunch, and with the cabinet again later in the afternoon. Several of them plainly spoke their doubts as to whether Japan should attempt to fight a great war.

Thus Konoye said: "To my great regret I am forced to conclude . . . that the continuance of diplomatic negotiations would be hopeless. Still is it necessary, however, to resort to war at once even though diplomatic negotiations have been broken off? Would it not be possible, I wonder, while carrying on things as they are to later find a way out of the deadlock by persevering to the utmost under difficulties?"

Another former Prime Minister, Yonai, uttered a prayer that "We may take care not to lose everything by trying to avoid becoming poor gradually."

To all such words of prudence, to wait or watch longer, Tojo had the same flat answer: To go on with broken economic relations would mean gradual weakening of Japan. The Senior Statesmen, thus having served their Emperor, went home to dinner and to bed. They were only a group of respected callers, whose time seemed past. Four years later some would be sought out again to manage the surrender.

That same day the government received a repetition of assurances that if Japan got into war with the United States and Great Britain, Germany would enter at once. Ribbentrop quoted Hitler as saying that there were fundamental differences in the very right to exist between Germany and Japan and the United States. To wipe out any doubt about the military prospect, he also informed the Japanese government that Hitler said he was now determined to crush Russia to an even greater extent than he had planned at first; that next spring German troops would cross the Urals and chase Stalin deep into Siberia. This was also intercepted and read in Washington.

A mite of worry still bothered the Emperor. His brother, Prince Takamatsu, had told him that as the Navy's hands were full it wished to avoid war. But the Navy Minister and Chief of the Naval General Staff, when called to the Palace, answered the Emperor's questions with confidence. Thereupon the Emperor acceded to Tojo's request that an Imperial Conference be held the next day to review for the last time the plan of war.

Without waiting for morning to come around the Japanese government began to complete its war pact with Germany and Italy. Oshima was instructed (on November 30) to inform Hitler and Ribbentrop that the talks with the United States were at an end. He was to tell them "that there is an extreme danger that war may suddenly break out between the Anglo-Saxon nations and Japan through some clash of arms and that the time of the start of this war may be quicker than anyone dreams." He was to explain further that Japan wanted to move south and to refrain for the time being from any direct move against Russia. The authors of this cable gave

Oshima the answer to any possible reproach that Hitler might make. He was to say, if need be, that during the whole period of the talk with the United States "the Japanese Government stuck adamantly to the Tripartite Alliance as the cornerstone of its national policy." It had hoped to find the solution within the scope of the alliance in order to restrain the United States from entering the war. But when in the later meetings it became clear that the United States demanded a divorce from the alliance, Japan could no longer continue the talks.

The Imperial Conference met at 2 o'clock in the afternoon of December 1. Tojo presided. It was now clear, he declared, that Japan's claims could not be obtained through diplomatic measures; and it was wholly out of the question, both from the viewpoint of national power and of military strategy, to allow the present situation to continue longer. The heads of the Army and Navy said they were ready and burning to serve the nation. The Emperor spoke not a single word. The decision for war was transmuted into "the way of the Emperor."

The drafting of the final statement to be given to the American government was begun. Tojo and Kido conferred about the text of the Imperial Rescript which was to be issued. On the next day (December 2) the Chief of Staff of the Army informed commanders in all South Sea areas that the war would start on December 8 (Tokyo time). An Imperial naval order sent the same notice to naval commanders. If, they were also told, an accord was reached before then, all the forces of the combined fleet would be ordered to reassemble and return to their bases. They were on their way, to be turned about only by a signal from Heaven.

The few remaining days of peace were spent in trying to keep the Americans and Britishers lulled, and in sealing the war pact with Germany and Italy. Nomura and Kurusu kept contact with Hull. Togo was suavely patient with Grew.

On the 3rd, the Japanese Ambassador in Rome informed

Mussolini that war with the United States and Britain in the immediate future was possible. Mussolini said he would declare war on the United States and Great Britain at once if Japan did. The Duce, according to Ciano, was pleased by the news and said: "Thus we arrive at the war between continents, which I have foreseen since September 1939." The British intercepted the report of the promise which was sent to Tokyo.

The Japanese government had trouble in getting from Hitler a final confirmation of the similar German promise. Ribbentrop gave as the reasons the storm around Berlin, and Hitler's faraway absence and absorption in the Russian battle-front. Perhaps these were the only reasons, perhaps not. There might well have been a tardy tremor of doubt as to whether Japan in the role of ally would count for as much as a belligerent United States. Ciano noted in his diary on December 4: ". . . the Berlin reaction to the Japanese step is extremely cautious. Maybe they will go ahead, because they can't do otherwise, but the idea of provoking American intervention is less and less liked by the Germans. Mussolini, on the other hand, is happy about it." On the 5th, Ribbentrop submitted to Mussolini a plan for triple action on Japan's entry into the war. The first article of the proposed treaty began: "Should a state of war arise between Japan and the United States, Germany and Italy for their part shall also consider themselves to be at war with the United States, and shall conduct this war with all the armed forces at their disposal."

Ciano complained that after delaying two days, Germany was now insisting on an answer at once. But it was given, at once. The British interceptors learned of all this also.

One thing remained to be settled, whether to strike without warning. The Army and Navy, particularly Admiral Nagano, the Chief of the Naval General Staff, wanted to avoid any risk of spoiling the surprise attack. The Foreign Minister, Togo, objected. He said it was improper not to give some advance formal notice and that Japan's good repute and honor would suffer. He had been the First Secretary of the Japanese

Embassy in Washington when the Briand-Kellogg Pact for the renunciation of war was signed. This was his last gesture towards a foregone ideal.

The Liaison Conference of November 30 had agreed to permit the Army and Navy to set the time of notice. The Navy suggested 12:30 p.m. on December 7 (Washington time). This, it said, would allow sufficient time before the attack to preserve Japan's good name. The Foreign Office was not told of the exact hour of the attack. Later, the Navy asked that the hour be put off till 1 p.m., and again the Foreign Office agreed. Had the notice been presented precisely at the arranged time, there would have been some twenty minutes before the planes arrived over Pearl Harbor. That long, at least, would have been needed to read to the revealing final sentence. This was the last and foolish stratagem.

But the Pearl Harbor attack was only a disabling action. The real invasions about to begin were in the south—in the Philippines, Malaya, the Indies, Borneo. The Japanese soldiers were sent there to conquer colonial lands, which for several centuries had been under the hands of the West. Their mission, their rulers avowed, was to bring peace and stability throughout Greater East Asia. They were, rather, time has since shown, the destroyers of peace and order there, as they had been in China. Before the Japanese invasion the peoples of the countries in the Pacific south of Japan had a secure and improving way of existence, though not as free or just a way as could be wished. The Japanese armies ruined this without bringing justice or freedom. In the Southwest Pacific —as in China—they widened the already open path for suffering and for revolution.

The Clasp of War Is Closed

During the last few days of somber waiting the President faced three entwined questions. First: should he promise the

British and Dutch that the United States would join them if
Japanese forces attacked their territories or crossed certain
bounds? Second: should he so warn Japan—openly or secretly?
Third: should he inform Congress about the fast-coming crisis
and the action he proposed to take?

The President, at one time or another, was on the point of
doing each or all of these things. After listening, to Hull
most especially, he did none of them. His mind could not
settle on any program that seemed to fit the many uncalipered
angles of the situation. Until the objects of the Japanese
military movement that was under way became clear, it was
hard to know what action was essential, and what Congress
and the people would approve. And in the event that Japan
struck at the Philippines, Guam, or Hawaii, he would not
have to argue with those who still believed that the United
States should take no part in foreign wars. It was best, he
concluded, to wait until the event itself dramatized the danger
and marked the response.

Japan, in other words, was left not only to strike the first
blow, but to decide, as well, whether and in what way the
issue of war or peace was brought before the United States.
This course lessened the risk of blunder and costly confusion
at the instant hour. But it caused the growth, as the American people learned more of what had taken place before the
Japanese attack, of a sense that they had been led in ignorance.

Behind the scenes there was hurried suspense—intent reading of the news of Japanese ship movements, grim talk as to
whether and how American forces should be engaged, anxious
uncertainty over when and what to tell the country and Congress.

The Japanese envoys continued to drive down each day
from the Embassy on Massachusetts Avenue to the State Department. They still bowed as they entered Hull's office. But
no chance of change any longer attached to their visits. They
had been told, it was known, to keep on talking in order to
make military surprise the more complete. Hull listened only

for clues to the Japanese program of action, and to keep the record straight.

On the 28th the War Council, meeting with the President, agreed (in accord with the Stark-Marshall memo) that if the Japanese attacked British or Dutch territories, or if they rounded the southern point of Indo-China and landed in the Gulf of Siam, and the British fought, the United States would have to fight. It favored the issuance of a warning to that effect. When the group dispersed it was understood that the President would send a private message to the Emperor. This was to be at once a friendly expression of the wish for peace and a warning. He was also to "deliver a special message to Congress reporting on the danger and reporting what we would have to do if the danger happened."

The State Department was put to work at once on these two messages, using material and ideas sent by Stimson and Knox. There was no time to be lost, for Congress was going to meet on Monday (December 1) and unless held together would adjourn almost at once. The President left for Warm Springs, remarking to reporters that the Japanese situation might bring him back any time. Stimson rushed such drafts as he had written down to him by plane on the 29th. Then he and Knox again worked over with Hornbeck the message for the Emperor. "This was in the shape of a virtual ultimatum to Japan that we cannot permit her to take any further steps of aggression against any of the countries of the Southwest Pacific, including China."

During these same days (November 27–December 1) the British government again tried its utmost to get a definition of our intentions. On the 30th Halifax asked Hull what the American government would do if the British resisted a Japanese attempt to establish a base on the Kra Isthmus. Hull answered that he would submit the question to the President, who would be back in Washington the next morning. Later that day a message came from Churchill, urging a declarative warning.

"It seems to me," this read, "that one important method remains unused in averting war between Japan and our two

countries, namely a plain declaration, secret or public as may
be thought best, that any further act of aggression by Japan
will lead immediately to the gravest consequences."

About this and other messages to the same effect the scepti-
cal mind can still play. Ever since learning of Hull's decision
to discard the truce counter-offer, the British, Australian, and
Dutch Ambassadors in every visit to the State Department
expressed regret and stressed a desire for more time to prepare. It is hard to believe that Churchill thought a warning
could now halt Japan; that the Japanese government had not
already taken American entry in the war into full account.

Churchill commented later about this message, "I did not
know that the die had already been cast by Japan or how far
the President's resolves had gone." Besides, at a hazard, his
pen may have been touched by a wish to bring the President
to the point of final decision; to have him say, through the
warning, whether or not the United States would fight at
once even if its lands were not attacked. This was an answer
to which the British felt themselves entitled.

In any case, the President, on Hull's advice, postponed the
warning message to the Emperor until the attack had all but
begun. Of the reasons which caused him to do so, I have
found no convincing record or account.

Hull had also been poring over drafts of the message to
Congress. This, too, he concluded, had better be reserved
"until the last stage of our relations, relating to actual hos-
tility, has been reached." He so advised the President. For
this counsel, Hull, then and later, gave two reasons. A full
account of the situation, he thought, would give material to
Japanese advocates of war with which to rouse their people
against us. Further it would cause excitement in Congress
where isolationist feeling was still strong, stir division within
the United States. This might be taken as a sign of weakness
and bring on the war crisis sooner than otherwise.

Who is to know whether that is how, and how far, his mind
and the President's along with his, traveled? There is reality,
sad reality, in the fact that a revelation of the whole situation
probably would have produced a serious, even though brief,

division in the country. Old fights would have been fought again. Old and bitter charges would have been heard again. Even old slurs against the foreign countries with which now, more closely than ever, the United States would have to stand. But there is little reality in the thought that this quarrel might have hastened the war crisis or made a difference in Japanese morale. The attack was known to be actually in motion—though the points of attack were not spotted.

Whatever the inner core of thought and purpose, the message to Congress was also deferred. The President went down the road a little longer by himself. He told Hull (December 1) to query Nomura again about the meaning of the reported large troop movements into Indo-China. He asked for a copy for his own private files on the intercept of the cable sent on November 30 by the Japanese Foreign Minister, Togo, to the Japanese Ambassador in Berlin, Oshima. One passage, at least, of this message for Hitler and Ribbentrop, will return to the reader's mind: "that there is an extreme danger that war may suddenly break out between the Anglo-Saxon nations and Japan through some clash of arms and that the time of the start of this war may be quicker than anyone dreams."

The next three days (December 1–4) thus passed without any new American initiative. On the 4th Congress adjourned for a long weekend.

The signs that the end was close became as plain as though they were written on a blackboard for children. "Magic" produced more telltale cables. One from Tokyo (the 5th, Tokyo time) ordered most of the members of the Japanese Embassy staff to leave Washington by plane within the next couple of days. Another from Nomura (the 5th, Washington time) informed Tokyo, "We have completed destruction of codes . . ."

The President now decided (on the 6th) that the time had come for the last-minute note to the Emperor. It said nothing that had not been said before. Washington knew that it was being addressed to a throne that rested on weak silence. Whether or not it was truly expected that an answer, a significant answer, would be received before some first clash, somewhere in the Pacific, is not to be known from the records in hand. Probably a wan hope, nothing more. How could there have been more?

From the Far East and London reports came that two large fleets of Japanese cruisers, destroyers, and transports were moving around the southern point of Indo-China. Cambodia Point is about 250 miles from Kota Bharu (where the Japanese landed first in Malaya) and about 500 miles from Singapore.

The Dutch and British were still asking to be told what we would do if the expeditions at sea landed in the Indies, Malaya, or Thailand. To the Dutch, Admiral Stark, after consulting the President, had given advice (on the 4th) that Japan might be warned that if its ships entered certain waters close to the Indies, it would be considered an act of war. But he had given no promise that the American government would, for its part, so regard it.

The British government was similarly holding back from any warning or anticipatory measures. Thus on December 6 the President was informed, via Harriman and Hopkins, that it was Churchill's belief that "it would be the policy of the British to postpone any action—even though this delay might involve some military sacrifice—until the President has taken such action as, under the circumstances, he considers best."

On that same evening (the 6th, Washington time) the Navy and Army Departments received the report of the arrangements worked out among Admiral Hart, Commander of the Asiatic Fleet, General MacArthur and Admiral Phillips. MacArthur cabled Marshall: "Complete coordination and cooperation most satisfactorily accomplished." Hart cabled Stark: "Am sending Glassford to command TF [Task Force] 5. Recommend you empower me to put all or part of the command under British strategic direction or even direct command . . ." Hart was so sure of approval, and so sure the battle was about to start that he began to carry the arrangement into effect without waiting for the answer. On the evening of the

6th (Manila time), as recorded by Morison, he told Admiral Phillips: "I have just ordered my destroyers at Balikpapan [Borneo] to proceed to Batavia on the pretext of rest and leave. Actually they will join your force."

In the War Department, too, some lights burned late on this night of the 6th. Ships with important military supplies for the Philippines were on the ocean; and a flight of big bombers had just left the West Coast for Hawaii, en route to the Philippines.

After dinner the awaited message to Nomura was taken out of the air. The assistant to the Naval Aide hurried to put before the President the first thirteen (of fourteen) sections of this final answer from Japan. The President read them, and to Hopkins, pacing back and forth, said, in effect, "This means war." War from the east. He would still wait, and not because of secret knowledge begin it. The roles of disturber and of resister must not be confused in the last minute.

In private houses and on the streets of Washington, the morning of the 7th seemed like any other quiet Sunday morning. Even the readers of "Magic" did not greatly change their routine or manner.

The last of the fourteenth part of the note which Japan was about to present had been caught and deciphered. It was in the President's hands soon after breakfast. Japan was saying that all talk was at an end, and bitterly placing the blame upon us. The Japanese intent seemed clear; even before seeing this last section of its answer the President had concluded Japan was about to take some action that would mean war. But would it make some further declaration? And when?

In one way or another we would soon learn, the President must have thought. For a little later the carrier of the "Magic" messages brought another. This informed that the Japanese government had ordered its envoys to present its answer to Hull at one o'clock that day—little more than two hours off. The President waited to let events instruct. He may well, though it is not of record, have spent part of that time in study of the text of a joint warning to Japan—submitted by Churchill.

In the Pentagon building Marshall and his staff fumbled with and over a last minute alert to the commanders at the outposts—the Philippines and Hawaii. In the Navy building Stark and his staff discussed Hart's reports of the arrangements he had made with Phillips.

At half-past ten Stimson and Knox went to Hull's office. Soon after, his secretary entered to say that the Japanese Embassy was on the telephone asking for an engagement for Nomura and Kurusu at one o'clock. With the flimsies of the last two "Magic" messages in mind, but out of sight, Hull agreed to the hour. It would be early dawn over the Pacific islands. The three cabinet officers stayed together till past noon, wondering where the action would start and going over plans for what should be said or done. "We three," Stimson recorded in his diary, "all thought we must fight if the British fought." They were ready so to argue before Congress and the nation with all the authority of their office.

At twelve-thirty the President received the Chinese Ambassador, Hu Shih, who had shuttled back from New York on learning that he was sought. With an air of leisure and gusto Roosevelt read aloud the text of his note to the Mikado. Now and again he paused to explain why he used such and such a phrase. When Mrs. Roosevelt came in to remind that time was getting on (and a big family luncheon assembling), he motioned to the Ambassador to resume his seat, and went on to the last word.

The President then told his thoughts of the moment. In Hu Shih's present memory these remain very much alive in words believed to be close to the original. "This is," Hu Shih recalls his saying at the end of the reading, "my last effort for peace." And then, "I am afraid it may fail." The President went on to say that if he got no reply to his message by the evening of the 8th, the American government would publish its text. But he added that he had just learned that "those fellows" (his term for Nomura and Kurusu) had asked for an urgent appointment with Hull. The Japanese government, he thought, was probably hurrying its answer to our last note (of November 26). In this hurry, the President went on to state he expected "foul play"; he had a feeling that within forty-eight hours something "nasty" might happen in Thailand, Malaya, the Dutch Indies, and "possibly" the Philippines.

Hu Shih took his leave at 1:10.

Undetected, a Japanese task force was coming upon Hawaii. Over the flagship *Akagi* flew the flag which had been displayed on the battleship *Mikasa* when, in 1905, the Japanese fleet moved into battle against the Russians in Tsushima Straits. The planes were leaving the decks of the carriers. Their errand, each crew had been told, was to destroy the power of the United States to cheat Japan out of its deserved place on the earth.

In the Japanese Embassy a great scurry was going on. The code clerks had selected trivial messages to decipher before the fourteenth part. A diplomatic secretary was doing over pages his awkward fingers had wrongly typed. There were a few last-minute revisions from Tokyo to be made. Nomura and Kurusu could have snatched what was ready and kept their one o'clock engagement with Hull. But they put it off till the typed message was in fair shape. The Ambassadors arrived at the State Department at two. They were shown into Hull's room at twenty minutes past two. This was about two and a half hours after the landing at Kota Bharu (British Malaya) had begun; an hour after the first bomb fell on Pearl Harbor. American battleships were settling in the sand.

The envoys sat awkwardly in the deep black leather chairs. Nomura gave over the accusing paper. Hull made a show of looking at it. Both refrain and phrases were familiar; Japan had sought only to bring stability to East Asia and peace to the world; the United States had failed to grasp its true intentions. With quickened voice, Hull called it false and distorted in every line. The envoys made no answer. Now enemies, they opened the door for themselves. The elevator was waiting, empty, to take them to the street. As they walked

across the sidewalk to their car, the light but gleaming structure of the White House stood before them. The President
was talking on the telephone to Hull. The clasp of war was
closed.

For Further Reading

A fine, brief summary of events leading to war in both the Atlantic and Pacific is Robert A. Divine, *The Reluctant Belligerent; American Entry Into World War II* (1965). Of equal merit
is the survey of events and literature by John E. Wiltz, *From
Isolation to War, 1931–1941* (1968). A more detailed, able
analysis is Selig Adler, *The Uncertain Giant: American Foreign Policy Between the Wars* (1965). Two other readable
surveys are Allan Nevins, *The New Deal and World Affairs,
1933–1945* (1950); and Jean-Baptiste Duroselle, *From Wilson
to Roosevelt: Foreign Policy of the United States, 1913–1945*
(1963). On an even broader scope for Japanese-American relations, see the brief but superb Edwin O. Reischauer, *The
United States and Japan* (1957). Although some of the more
recent historiographic trends are not covered, Wayne S. Cole,
"American Entry into World War II," *Mississippi Valley Historical Review* 43 (March 1957), pp. 595–617, is still a valuable interpretative survey of the literature.

For the "Court" historians' view, in addition to the Feis
volume, see the two-volume work by William L. Langer and
S. Everett Gleason, *The Challenge to Isolation, 1937–1940*
(1952) and *The Undeclared War, 1940–1941* (1953); Robert
E. Sherwood, *Roosevelt and Hopkins* (1948); Donald F. Drum-
mond, *The Passing of American Neutrality, 1937–1941* (1955);
Basil Rauch, *Roosevelt: From Munich to Pearl Harbor* (1950);
and most recently, T. R. Fehrenbach, *FDR's Undeclared War,
1939 to 1941* (1967).

The best of the revisionists' early statements are Charles
A. Beard, *President Roosevelt and the Coming of the War,
1941* (1948); and Charles C. Tansill, *Back Door to War:*

Roosevelt Foreign Policy, 1933–1941 (1952). Other revisionist works are William Henry Chamberlin, *America's Second Crusade* (1950); Harry Elmer Barnes, ed., *Perpetual War for Perpetual Peace* (1953); and Frederic R. Sanborn, *Design for War: A Study of Secret Power Politics, 1937–1941* (1951). A more recent scholarly study, Paul W. Schroeder's *The Axis Alliance and Japanese-American Relations, 1941* (1958) concludes that Hull's diplomacy barred peaceful remedies to Japanese-American disputes. For an overall assessment of the implications of the Open Door policy, see William Appleman Williams, *The Tragedy of American Diplomacy* (1962); and more explicitly, Lloyd Gardner, *Economic Aspects of New Deal Diplomacy* (1964).

Memoirs, diaries, and biographies assist the reader in piecing together the varied perceptions of the world crisis from 1937 to 1941. For Cordell Hull, see his own two-volume *Memoirs* (1948); Julius Pratt, *Cordell Hull, 1933–44,* vols. 12 and 13 of *American Secretaries of State and Their Diplomacy* (1964); and Norman A. Graebner, ed., *An Uncertain Tradition: American Secretaries of State in the Twentieth Century* (1961). For the U.S. ambassador to Japan Joseph C. Grew's critical views of his superiors, see Walter Johnson, ed., *Turbulent Era: A Diplomatic Record of Forty Years, 1904–1945* (2 vols., 1952); Joseph C. Grew, *Ten Years in Japan* (1944); and Waldo H. Heinrichs, *American Ambassador: Joseph C. Grew and the Development of the United States Diplomatic Tradition* (1966).

There are some excellent monographs that concentrate on Japanese-American relations, like Schroeder's (cited above), and on the formation of Japanese policy: David C. Lu, *From the Marco Polo Bridge to Pearl Harbor: Japan's Entry into World War II* (1961); Robert J. C. Butow, *Tojo and the Coming of the War* (1962); Francis Jones, *Japan's New Order in East Asia, Its Rise and Fall, 1937–45* (1954); James Crowley, *Japan's Quest for Autonomy* (1966); and, for a slightly earlier period, Dorothy Borg, *The United States and the Far Eastern Crisis of 1933–1938* (1964).

On the hotly disputed controversy over President Roosevelt

and the Pearl Harbor attack, see the revisionists George Morgenstern, *Pearl Harbor: The Story of the Secret War* (1947); Rear Admiral Robert A. Theobald, *The Final Secret of Pearl Harbor: The Washington Contribution to the Japanese Attack* (1954); and critical, but less extreme, A. A. Hoehling, *The Week Before Pearl Harbor* (1963). To the President's defense has rushed Walter Millis, *This Is Pearl! The United States and Japan—1941* (1947). More balanced and perhaps definitive are two scholarly works: Ladislas Farago, *The Broken Seal: "Operation Magic" and the Secret Road to Pearl Harbor* (1967); and Roberta Wohlstetter, *Pearl Harbor: Warning and Decision* (1962).

The United States Overplays Its Hand

William Appleman Williams

*F*rom 1941 to the present the
United States has been locked in combat. A brief Indian summer in late 1945 and early 1946 merely un-
derscores the seemingly interminable conflict, a struggle that sometimes is marked by armed force, sometimes
by extensive economic sanctions, alliance-making, and
propagandizing. Stout hearts are needed to contemplate
the past: a global hot war, 1941–1945, during which
American technological prowess helped defeat three
major nations and, in the process, destroy millions of
people, civilian and military alike; and a global cold
war, 1946–present, pock-marked by skirmishes in Korea
and Southeast Asia.

Prolonged strife breeds elaborate self-justification. Almost without exception, regardless of party affiliation,
American leaders since 1945 have subscribed to and
helped maintain a world-view that pictures the Soviet
Union and the United States as mortal enemies. What
leaders have proposed, scholars and commentators until
recently have generally endorsed. Perhaps responding to

Source: William Appleman Williams, *The Tragedy of American
   Diplomacy* (New York: World Publishing Co., 1962, Delta
   Books Edition), pp. 244–276. Copyright © 1959, 1962 by
   William Appleman Williams. Reprinted by permission of
   The World Publishing Company.

some organic societal need, the American people have attributed this cold war to initial hostile acts by the Soviet Union.

A simplified version of what may be called the "cold warrior" interpretation of post-1945 world affairs, rests on a historical perception that runs somewhat as follows: Following the Bolshevik Revolution in 1917, the Soviet Union embarked on a threefold program. First, it sought to consolidate the internal revolution in Russia, a process that took years of repressive social control. Second, it attempted to strengthen itself so that it could continue the centuries-old Russian aim of achieving defensible frontiers and warm-water outlets. Third, the Soviet Union ceaselessly perfected its techniques as a launching pad for the world-wide Communist goal of hastening the inevitable downfall of capitalism. This trio of aims, the cold warriors have contended, has posed a real threat to the free world, especially to its leader, the United States.

The Soviet Union's joining with the Allies during World War II to defeat Hitler (and later Tojo) did not alter the basic Russian thrust. Even as an Ally, Russia proved intransigent. Moscow would not permit, for example, the stationing of her Western allies' airplanes in Soviet-controlled territory to facilitate the bombing of Germany. The wartime conferences, particularly the Crimean, drove home to all who were alert the Russian preoccupation with its basic aims. Consequently the Soviet Union, although a signer of the 1941 Atlantic Charter and numerous subsequent international agreements including the United Nations' Charter, did not intend at any point to uphold the pacific principles upon which those agreements rested. Events after Yalta proved the case: the Soviets ruthlessly suppressed democratic elements in East European countries beginning with Poland in 1945, followed by Czechoslovakia in 1948, Hungary and East Germany in 1956, and Czechoslovakia again in 1968. Russian refusal to honor the Yalta and Potsdam agreements concerning unification and pacification of Germany, as well as its erection of the Berlin Wall, exposed again its hostile attitude. In the Far East and even in Latin America, the Russians played a disruptive role: from the successful Chinese Communist revolution in 1948, to the Korean crisis, to the continuous Communist attempts to subvert the entire Southeast Asian subcontinent, and to Fidel Castro's rise in Cuba. Finally, Russian refusal to act responsibly as a guarantor of international peace and order—manifested by its spurning of the Baruch atomic proposals of 1946, of the Marshall plan's offer of cooperation in 1947, and of the Eisenhower Open Skies idea of 1956—gave added emphasis to the cold warrior's argument. The Soviet Union, in brief, was implacably and unalterably engaged in a program of forceful and covert conquest of the world; it understood and could be "contained" by economic or military force alone. On the obverse side, the United States was the initiator of peace proposals and programs that materially aided the poorer nations; its rare and temperate use of force came as a reaction to earlier Soviet probes.

This interpretation of recent history has found recruits from conservatives and liberals alike. In fact, the consensus that emerged in the post-1948 period has been quite remarkable. Right and Left have converged. Variations and different emphases of course exist. The more conservative position tends to stress the Soviet ideological consistency and world domination aspiration; the liberal seems more impressed with the limited but nonetheless serious Russian desire to protect its extended frontiers. Both, to repeat, see the Soviet Union as an expanding power with designs that threaten American national interests.

The consensus has not gone unchallenged. During the 1945–1948 period individual leaders—particularly liberals—provided alternative interpretations of Soviet behavior. Henry A. Wallace, FDR's former Vice President (1941–1945) and his and Truman's Secretary of Commerce (1945–1946), was an outspoken advocate of a "soft" approach to Russia. He believed that Russian intransigence was but the natural suspicion of a nation that had long been in a beleaguered international position. Wallace, thinking that he was continuing Roosevelt's policy, formed a rallying point for a more sympathetic and conciliatory attitude.

Wallace's approach, however, suffered a series of setbacks. His own defeat in the 1948 election, associated as it was with American Communist support of his Progressive Party ticket, removed him as a legitimate spokesman. The disclosures of Communist infiltration of the U.S. government with the Chambers-Hiss case and the Julius and Ethel Rosenberg trials also undermined the soft approach to the Soviet Union. Lastly, the sometimes frantic attempt of the non-Communist Left during the McCarthy period to dissociate themselves from the taint of Communism reduced domestic support for the Wallace position.

The "hard" consensus thus held sway, not to be seriously challenged until well into the post-Stalin period (1953–present). The replacement of the old Bolsheviks with a more genial appearing power structure in the Soviet Union, coupled with an increasingly truculent and anti-American Chinese Communist ruling group, opened the way for reappraisal of the cold war by some American observers. Soviet expansion began to look less ominous than a future confrontation with the Chinese.

The blurring of the former hard outlines of Soviet-American relations, however, did not mean the end of the cold war consensus. Presidents Eisenhower, Kennedy, Johnson, and Nixon in succession saw a continued menace to America from Communist expansion in the Far East. Although Eisenhower refused to intervene in Indo-China to save the French from defeat at Dienbienphu in 1954, he and his successors stepped in to shore up the various pro-American regimes in South Vietnam.

The spectacular escalation of the Southeast Asian war more than any other factor has brought in its train increasingly sharp challenges to the cold war synthesis. The pioneer in this assault on the official interpretation is William Appleman Williams. The outline of what later historians and analysts have begun to detail can be seen clearly in the following selection from Williams' important and provocative survey of American foreign relations since the Spanish-American War. Criticized for his lack of "documentation," Williams nonetheless provides an overarching framework for a critique of American foreign policy. It is tempting to liken Williams to Charles Austin Beard, the noted revisionist of an earlier day. Both have offered novel and unflattering interpretations of the motives of policymakers during a critical period of American history; both have attempted to restore the economic or materialistic motive to what they believe have been unnecessarily idealistic interpretations. If the analogy between the two holds, then one can confidently predict that Williams' contribution will be sorely contended for years to come.

A New Vision of Omnipotence and a Misreading of History Prompt the United States to Overplay Its Hand

*F*ollowing upon President Roosevelt's clear expression of a desire to retain "complete freedom of action," the United States Government under President Truman initiated and sustained a vigorous drive to undercut the Stalin-Churchill agreement of October 1944, concerning eastern Europe, and to replace it with the Open Door Policy. Churchill supported that determined effort to subvert the understanding which he himself had originally and voluntarily written out and pushed across the table to Stalin. Truman and Churchill undertook that course, moreover, in the full knowledge and open acknowledgment that Stalin had honored his part of the bargain in Greece.

This insistence upon applying the Open Door Policy to eastern Europe (and, of course, to Asia) was decided upon before anyone knew for sure that the atom bomb would work. Along with the feeling among American policy-makers that Russia's war-caused weakness would enable them to secure major concessions from Moscow, that consideration must be kept constantly in mind when following the sequence of events after the defeat of Germany. The success of the bomb strength-

ened an existing attitude and a traditional strategy—it did
not call forth a new approach.

Stimson's diary entry covering a conversation with Truman
on June 6, 1945, indicates that American leaders were conscious of the relationship between the bomb and their general
strategy at an early date. Truman "said that he had been
thinking of that," Stimson noted, "and mentioned the same
things that I was thinking of, namely the settlement of the
Polish, Rumanian, Yugoslavian, and Manchurian problems."
By the end of the month, in preparation for the Potsdam
Conference, the American position concerning the countries
of eastern Europe had become clear and firm. The United
States planned "to insist on the reorganization of the present
governments or the holding of free general elections." The
broad objective was phrased in the classic terms of the Open
Door Policy: "To permit American nationals to enter, move
about freely and carry on commercial and government operations unmolested in the countries in question."

The goal was "access, on equal terms, to such trade, raw
materials and industry" as existed and developed. In the meantime, such access was sought "to modify existing arrangements." As part of that general effort, American officials
planned to demand unrestricted movement for American
newspapermen so that "the spotlight [can be] trained on these
areas." And finally, the United States emphasized the specific
objective of internationalizing the commercial waterways of
the Danube River system with a Western majority on the
board of control.

Similar stress was laid on guaranteeing the Open Door
Policy in Asia. American leaders seem to have entertained a
particularly vivid hope that the defeat of Japan would turn
the clock back to 1903–1904; a maneuver that would enable
the United States to step back on the mainland of Asia at the
moment of its greatest success in Manchuria with the expectation that this time it would not be frustrated as before. The
Russians posed the only danger to this idyllic picture. On the
eve of the first general session at Potsdam, for example, Stimson seems to have set himself the role of special tutor to

Truman and Byrnes on the importance of the Open Door Policy in the Far East. Even though the lessons had apparently been going on for some time, Stimson saw Truman again on July 14, 1945. "[I] went over [it] with him carefully," Stimson wrote in his diary, "again and again warning him to be absolutely sure that the Russians did not block off our trade."

Still concerned, Stimson wrote the President a special letter on July 16. Concentrating on "our clear and growing interests in the Orient," the Secretary all but hammered the words through the page in the course of his pounding on the crucial importance of the Open Door Policy. Ideally, of course, Russia should not have anything to say about handling Japan or the general problems of the Far East. At most, and only if it became absolutely necessary in the face of Soviet complaints, some kind of "token occupation" would be arranged.

Stimson next had a briefing session with Byrnes on July 17. The subject had not changed. Neither had the dedication of the tutor. "I impressed on him," Stimson recorded, "the importance of the Open Door Policy." A series of special reports made the same point. Harriman, for example, prepared one which placed—even in that context—a noticeable emphasis on "the development of commerce and trade of the United States." Perhaps his service as an artillery officer in World War I had inured him to such bombardments, for Truman seemed never to blink at the hammering on the same point. Obviously pleased, Stimson reported on July 18, 1945, that the President "was confident of sustaining the Open Door Policy."

Stalin arrived in Potsdam with a noticeably different set of priorities. He was still concerned about Russia's frontiers in Europe, about preventing Germany from trying it all over in another 25 years, and about a major economic transfusion for the Soviet Union's battered economy. Apparently shrewd enough to realize that he had but little chance to obtain a large loan from the United States, and in any event unable to plan on that basis in the summer of 1945, Stalin laid immediate and heavy emphasis on being treated as an equal and upon obtaining massive reparations from Germany and its former allies.

THOMAS Y. CROWELL COMPANY

THOMAS Y. CROWELL COMPANY

Name
College
May we quote you? ☐ Yes ☐ No

Please accept with our compliments this examination copy of:

THE STRUCTURE OF AMERICAN HISTORY, Volume VI:
Recent America: 1933 to the Present

edited by Davis R. B. Ross, Alden T. Vaughan and John B. Duff

We look forward to learning your opinion of this text and something of your plans for its use in your classes. A reply card is attached for your convenience.

Student price $2.75

for your comments on:

THE STRUCTURE OF AMERICAN HISTORY
Volume VI:
Recent America: 1933 to the Present

THOMAS Y. CROWELL COMPANY

COLLEGE DEPARTMENT

116

"This Council," Stalin remarked in explaining the Soviet view of the conference at its first general session, "will deal with reparations and will give an indication of the day when the Peace Conference should meet." The primary political issue, he continued, was that of dealing with Germany and its former allies. That was "high policy. The purpose of such a policy was to separate these countries from Germany as a great force." Recurring often to the "many difficulties and sacrifices" brought upon Russia by those Axis partners, Stalin argued that the proper strategy was "to detach them once and for all from Germany." As for reparations, Russia would if necessary "compel" such deliveries.

The American response on reparations was crucial to the outcome of the Potsdam Conference, and also, very probably, to the whole course of subsequent events. "Reparations," Byrnes told Molotov on July 20, "do not seem to the United States to be an immediate problem." He then added that "the United States does not intend to make advances to any country in order that reparations may be paid by them." "We do not intend, as we did after the last war, to provide the money for the payment of reparations." The full significance of those remarks by Byrnes cannot be grasped without understanding both the background of each of them, and the interrelationship between them. It seems wise, therefore, to discuss them separately before putting them together.

First of all, and as revealed in Byrnes' remark about loans, American policy-makers had misread the history of their experience with reparations after World War I. They concluded that American loans to Germany had simply ended up as reparations to England and France, who themselves had not repaid their debts to the United States. In the American view, therefore, the United States had been twice played the fool. The vigorous assertion by Byrnes reflected a determination not to fall into the same trap still another time.

That reaction was based on a seriously distorted interpretation of the World War I experience. It neglected, on the one hand, the creative role of American loans and the harmful effects of having actually collected money from England and

France. On the other hand, and regardless of the estimate made of those and similar factors, the World War I situation blinded American leaders to the vastly different one that existed at the end of World War II. It was not so much that they had learned no lesson from history but rather that they had become almost obsessed with the wrong lesson.

The real point was that the capital for reconstruction at the end of World War II had to come from some place. Alternative sources were available. Either it could come from the United States under more relevant conditions and terms than had been arranged at the end of World War I, or it could come in the form of reparations taken by Russia—reparations which could be stopped only by recourse to another war. American policy-makers had used history to block their view of the present.

In order to avoid the second alternative, American leaders would obviously have had to negotiate a loan to Russia in conjunction with their discussion and settlement of other issues. But that approach was never even initiated, let alone put into sustained operation. The contradiction involved can be explained, however, by reference to the atom bomb. *Byrnes knew, when he told Molotov on July 20 that reparations were not "an immediate problem," that the atom bomb was a success.* The first news reached Potsdam on July 18. And as Stimson noted in his diary, Truman and other American leaders were "highly delighted" and "very greatly reinforced." It seems very likely, therefore, that the information on the bomb (even though the first dispatches were not complete accounts) served to convince the United States that it could hold the line on reparations and bargain from a position of formidable power.

But this reaction actually served, in a deeply ironic way, to close both the intellectual and the psychological jaws of the trap that American policy-makers had set for themselves. For in fact it left the United States with no moderate, flexible policy. It hardened both the feeling that the Russians would have to come to terms and the reading of history to the point that no loans should be granted if they would end up as reparations. That attitude left the United States with no choice but to acquiesce or use the bomb if the Russians refused to give way and accept American conditions for economic aid.

The extent to which this analysis explains American policy can be seen by the response to further news about the bomb test. Truman had already indicated, in a private conference with Churchill, that he was very favorably inclined toward the old Roosevelt idea of an Anglo-American entente. He was also aware of the understanding between Churchill and Roosevelt of September 18, 1944, concerning the bomb: "The suggestion that the world should be informed . . . with a view to an international agreement regarding its control and use," the two had agreed, "is not accepted."

Churchill seems to have insinuated in his masterful way that the secret might be kept from Stalin. This was by no means a novel idea. It had, after all, been kept from him up to that point. And Stimson records that he and others were very "doubtful" about sharing the news of the test bomb. However it evolved, and Truman appears to have refused to consider saying nothing to the Russians, the final compromise was to tell Stalin in a brief, casual way that the United States had developed a new weapon. Much has been made of the fact that Stalin already knew about the bomb through espionage. That is of course true, but he probably learned more of direct importance in observing how the news of the successful test firing affected the attitude and manner of Truman and Byrnes at the next session of the Potsdam Conference.

Stimson reports that Truman was "immensely pleased" and "tremendously pepped up by it." The President "said it gave him an entirely new feeling of confidence." This change is apparent even in reading the third-person stenographic account of the meeting with Stalin on July 21, 1945. One of the first questions to arise concerned the governments in eastern Europe, and this is the official account.

PRESIDENT TRUMAN: The American Government was unable to recognize the governments of the other satellite countries [besides Italy]. When these countries were established on a proper basis, the United States would recognize them and not before.

The President stated that the meeting would proceed and that this question would be passed over.

After he returned to England, Churchill told the House of Commons that "we possessed powers which were irresistible." His comments to Stimson at the time, in Potsdam, are perhaps even more revealing. "He [Truman] stood up to the Russians in a most emphatic and decisive manner, telling them as to certain demands that they absolutely could not have and that the United States was entirely against them. . . . He told the Russians just where they got off and generally bossed the whole meeting."

Truman bossed the meeting but he did not change American policy on reparations. That oversight served to subvert the power of the bomb. An astute American observer warned on the next day, July 22, that the Russian position on reparations should not be discounted. It was backed by "intense popular feeling and fresh experience." But the old block against loans, when combined with the new vision of omnipotence, led the United States into a dead end. In order to avoid financing Russian reparations through loans to Germany, Italy, or other former Axis partners, and with the myopic confidence induced by the news of the bomb, Byrnes proposed to Molotov on July 23 that "each country tak[e] reparations from its own zone."

Now the fascinating thing is that the Russians fought that proposal for one whole week—from July 23 to July 31—before Stalin finally agreed to it. Even then, he remarked very sharply that it was "the opposite of liberal."

Those two sentences have been set apart, and even further emphasized, for two reasons. First: the Byrnes offer to Molotov of July 23 clearly meant that the Russians would have a free hand in their zone of Germany and throughout eastern Europe. The freedom to control economics implied—demanded—political control. Assistant Secretary of State Clayton understood this point and commented on it with great perception in a memorandum of August 16, 1945, after the offer had been accepted by the Soviets. Although he was formally denying the point he was raising, the tone of his remarks needs no comment. "There appears to be," he noted ruefully, "an unfortunate tendency to interpret the reparations operating agreement as an indication of complete abandonment of four power treatment of Germany. This is not stated in the texts and should not be accepted as a necessary conclusion. . . ." But whether accepted or not, that was the meaning of the final arrangement.

To argue that the Russians did not understand the implications of the Byrnes offer of July 23 even though Clayton did is to argue that they were fools. To argue that they did understand it and still acted as they did is to argue that they played Byrnes and Truman and Stimson along for one entire week as a matter of private amusement. Those positions can be held and defended as viable explanations of Russian behavior. But the evidence indicates that the Russians very deeply wanted a firm commitment on reparations in the form of heavy industrial equipment from the restored production of the Ruhr Valley more than they wanted anything else. Such reparations would not only provide crucial help at home, but the agreement providing for them would be based on an Allied control of German industry that would in turn limit Germany's ability to start another war. Clayton himself, certainly as conservative and hard-headed an operator as the United States had produced, concluded in a memorandum of July 27, 1945, that this was the correct analysis. Molotov's behavior between July 23 and July 31 further supports that interpretation.

Molotov connected the issues of reparations and German war potential very simply: "The question of reparations was even more urgent because unless this was settled there could be no progress on economic matters" involving the future strength of German industry. Hence the Soviets wanted "clear replies to the questions." Byrnes gave them one by suddenly remarking that the United States now considered the Yalta figure of 10 billions for Russia to be "impractical." Molotov then shot back that the Soviets were "entitled to a clear answer" on what figure the United States did find acceptable. Failing to obtain one, Molotov then raised—very directly and

without any frills—the central implication of the proposal
that Byrnes had offered on July 23.

> MR. MOLOTOV: My understanding, Secretary Byrnes, is that
> you have in mind the proposal that each country should take
> reparations from its own zone. If we fail to reach an agree-
> ment the result will be the same. . . .
> THE SECRETARY [BYRNES]: Yes. . . .
> MR. MOLOTOV: said would not the Secretary's suggestion mean
> that each country would have a free hand in their own zone and
> would act entirely independently of the others?
> THE SECRETARY [BYRNES]: said that was true in substance. . . .

In spite of those candid and revealing remarks by Byrnes,
the Soviet Union nevertheless continued its efforts to reach
an agreement involving all of Germany. Molotov was still
"anxious" about the issue on June 29 and 30. He wanted "a
fixed sum or quantity agreed upon," including materials from
the Ruhr, because the Soviets feared "they would be left with
very little equipment as reparations in spite of the fact that the
Germans had destroyed Soviet industries. They needed agricultural machinery and [goods] to rehabilitate their railroads."
They also wanted to settle what Stalin had on the first day
of the conference referred to as the issue of "high policy"—
preventing Germany from attacking Russia in another 25
years.

Finally, in the face of continued American refusal to discuss
the issues in that related way, Stalin accepted the Byrnes
proposal of July 23, 1945. He then extended it in a way that
clearly foreshadowed the division of Europe. The specific issue
involved the assignment of German assets in other European
countries, but the discussion immediately picked up overtones
of a far broader nature.

> PREMIER STALIN: . . . with regard to shares and foreign in-
> vestments, perhaps the demarcation lines between the Soviet
> and Western zones of occupation should be taken as the divid-
> ing lines and everything west of that line would go to the
> Allies and everything east of that line to the Russians.

THE PRESIDENT [TRUMAN] inquired if he meant a line running from the Baltic to the Adriatic.

PREMIER STALIN replied in the affirmative. . . .

[BRITISH FOREIGN SECRETARY] BEVIN said he agreed and asked if Greece would belong to Britain. . . .

PREMIER STALIN suggested that the Allies take Yugoslavia and Austria would be divided into zones. . . .

MR. BYRNES said he thought it was important to have a meeting of minds. Mr. Bevin's question was whether the Russians' claim was limited to the zone occupied by the Russian Army. To that he understood Mr. Stalin to say 'yes.' If that were so he was prepared to agree.

PREMIER STALIN replied in the affirmative. . . .

THE PRESIDENT [TRUMAN] said that he agreed with the Soviet proposal.

The American decision to give the Russians a free hand on reparations throughout eastern Europe can in the end be explained only in one of three ways. The first would be to assert that the United States knowingly handed eastern Europe over to the Soviet Union. This is absurd on the face of it. It is also belied by Truman's actions during the conference, and by his blunt public remarks after the meeting was over. The eastern European countries, he announced on August 9, 1945, were "not to be spheres of influence of any one power." The Open Door Policy was thereby reaffirmed. A second explanation would be based on the idea that the United States made the reparations deal without understanding its political implications. But that interpretation is undercut by the analyses prepared by Clayton and other American officials who did see those possibilities.

The third explanation is supported by direct and indirect evidence. It is, simply, that the United States—confident in its vast economic and military superiority over Russia—made the reparations agreement to avoid any indirect financing of Soviet recovery. American leaders were certain that the bomb, and Russia's great recovery needs, provided them with the leverage to re-establish the Open Door, and pro-Western governments, in eastern Europe.

This vision of omnipotence was apparent in Truman's remarks of August 11, 1945. "We must constitute ourselves," he explained, "trustees of this new force to prevent its misuse." As for the possibility that the Soviets would construct their own bomb, Byrnes recalled that "no one seemed too alarmed at the prospect." But perhaps the best evidence of the American attitude came in connection with the use of the bomb against Japan. Byrnes later remarked that American leaders had eastern Europe as well as Asia in mind when they reached the decision to use the weapon as soon as possible.

That recollection is borne out by the evidence of the time. The decision to bomb Japan as quickly as possible was made during the Potsdam Conference, and at the very time of the toughest discussions about eastern Europe. In a very candid meeting on July 23, 1945, Truman, General George C. Marshall, Stimson and others generally agreed that the Russians were no longer needed in the war against Japan. They also talked very directly of using the bomb before the Russians could enter that conflict. Actually, however, that was not a new approach. Stimson had recommended as early as July 2, 1945, that the bomb should be dropped at a time when "the Russian attack, if actual, must not have progressed too far." And once it had proved out in the test, Truman was "intensely pleased" with the chance of using it before the Russians even entered the war.

This sense of urgency about using the bomb makes it possible to advance beyond the question of whether the United States dropped the bomb to end the war against Japan, or whether it did so in order to check the Russians. The evidence provided by the government archives and private American leaders converges on one explanation: The United States dropped the bomb to end the war against Japan *and thereby stop the Russians in Asia, and to give them sober pause in eastern Europe.*

Once it was known to work, the atomic offensive against Japan could have been delayed as much as a month or six weeks—if all that had been at stake was the saving of American lives which might be lost in the invasion of Kyushu that was projected for the fall. By that time, for example, the United States would have had a small arsenal of the weapons, so that it would have made little difference if the first drop during a demonstration had misfired, or otherwise failed. As for the saving of lives, they would still have been spared by using the weapon in September. But the bomb had to be used quickly, and if necessary repeatedly, if the war was to be ended before the Russians honored their promise to attack within three months after Germany was defeated.

Secretary of State Byrnes has offered this very explanation of the dropping of the bomb—and with equal directness. Indeed, he has done so twice. He was asked in 1960, on the fifteenth anniversary of the bomb, whether there was "any urgency to end the war in the Pacific before the Russians became too deeply involved?" "There certainly was on my part," Byrnes replied. "We wanted to get through with the Japanese phase of the war before the Russians came in." Even earlier, in 1958, Byrnes revealed how the United States encouraged Chiang Kai-shek to drag out his negotiations with Stalin over their arrangements in Manchuria. Referring to an American dispatch to Chiang of July 23, 1945, Byrnes explained the meaning and importance of a particular sentence. "The second sentence was to encourage the Chinese to continue negotiations after the adjournment of the Potsdam Conference. . . . If Stalin and Chiang were still negotiating, it might delay Soviet entrance and the Japanese might surrender. The President was in accord with that view."

American leaders were becoming so enthusiastic and confident over the power of the bomb that Secretary of War Stimson undertook a very courageous and searching review of the existing attitude. Even before Roosevelt died, Stimson was somewhat disturbed over the way various members of the government were reacting to the progress reports on the weapon. True enough, he felt that the bomb should be used against Japan, and kept from the Russians until safeguards had been established; but he also fretted that the attitude of the majority of American leaders would lead neither to peace nor prosperity. During the next five months, Stimson grew progressively more convinced that the American attitude and policy concerning the bomb was leading into another armament race, and perhaps even to a horrible war with Russia. On the eve of the Potsdam Conference, for example, he cautioned Truman that war would become inevitable if the United States took the position that all differences with the Soviet Union were irreconcilable. The Secretary's increasing concern was very probably caused by the interaction of four factors: the strong line taken by Truman and Byrnes at Potsdam; the awful destruction caused by the bombs at Hiroshima and Nagasaki; the clear evidence that Byrnes and the President had been encouraged by the bomb to maintain and even increase their pressure on Russia at the upcoming foreign ministers' conference scheduled for September in London; and his own searching thought and reflection on the problem, which was certainly provoked in part by his own great responsibility in recommending the use of the weapon.

The evidence suggests very strongly that Stimson devoted most of his intellectual and moral energy to the problem of the bomb from the end of the Potsdam Conference through the time when he received reports on the havoc caused in Japan. The result was a performance very similar, though of course more courageous and dramatic, to the one resulting from his experience in the late 1920's with armed intervention in Latin America. In that instance he concluded he had been wrong and set about to bring the Marines home from Nicaragua and to change the basic policy.

Stimson decided in the late summer of 1945 that the United States "was on the wrong path" in handling Russia in connection with the bomb. Having made that judgment, he undertook a brave, serious effort to persuade Truman and Byrnes to change their policy. He saw Byrnes on September 4, 1945, only to discover that the Secretary of State "was very much against any attempt to co-operate with Russia." Stimson noted that Byrnes was "full of his problems with the coming meeting of the foreign ministers and he looks to having the presence of the bomb in his pocket, so to speak, as a great weapon."

Byrnes left for London on September 5, unmoved by Stimson's arguments. Deeply concerned, and aware that his long government service was coming to an end, Stimson took his case directly to the President. His formal letter and memorandum to Truman dated September 11, 1945, made two crucial points. The first involved his conclusion, based on a careful evaluation and analysis of all the evidence he could obtain, that American efforts to force the pace, or determine the nature, of internal relaxation or liberalization in Russia by applying pressure "would be so resented that it would make the objective we have in view less probable." It followed from that estimate that the most vital issue of American foreign affairs concerned the way that the United States dealt with Russia in connection with the bomb. Stimson outlined the consequences of the then existing attitude and policy of Truman and Byrnes with a degree of accuracy that seems almost eerie in view of subsequent developments. "Unless the Soviets are voluntarily invited into the [nuclear] partnership upon a basis of co-operation and trust, we are going to maintain the Anglo-Saxon bloc over against the Soviet in the possession of this weapon. Such a condition will almost certainly stimulate feverish activity on the part of the Soviet toward the development of this bomb in what will in effect be a secret armament race of a rather desperate character. There is evidence to indicate that such activity may have already commenced."

He continued in a passage so important that he italicized it when making the document public in 1948. *"Those relations may be perhaps irretrievably embittered by the way in which we approach the solution of the bomb with Russia. For if we fail to approach them now and merely continue to negotiate with them, having this weapon rather ostentatiously on our hip, their suspicions and their distrust of our purposes and motives will increase."*

In conclusion, Stimson stressed the need for a direct approach *"to* Russia." *"I emphasize perhaps beyond all other considerations,"* he wrote, *"the importance of taking this action with Russia as . . . peculiarly the proposal of the United States. Action of any international group of nations, including many small nations who have not demonstrated*

*their potential power or responsibility in this war would not,
in my opinion, be taken seriously by the Soviets."*

Stimson's powerful argument may have caused Truman to
pause, and perhaps momentarily to reconsider the militant
anti-Soviet policy he had laid down on April 23, 1945. If so,
the second thoughts were quickly set aside. Byrnes arrived in
London determined to apply the strategy of the Open Door
Policy in every area of the world. On the question of Axis
colonies, for example, the American proposal was to place
them under a trusteeship guaranteeing the open-door principle. And as far as Japan and the Asia settlement were concerned, the United States took its control so much for granted
that Byrnes was truly and literally "surprised" when the Russians asked for some share in making the decisions.

The clash in London was most fully revealed in connection
with the two issues that had dogged American-Soviet relations
ever since 1944. The first involved the continued efforts of the
United States to abrogate the Churchill-Stalin bargain of
October 1944, which had underwritten Soviet predominance
in eastern Europe. The second was defined by the refusal of
the United States to commit itself on the reparations issue,
which for their part the Russians stressed above all else. On
both questions, furthermore, Byrnes had in Labor Foreign
Secretary Ernest Bevin an ally whose militance measured up
to the standard set by Churchill.

As it happened in London, moreover, the United States
used its power to attempt to displace an existing agreement.
As Byrnes later explained to the Congress, the American objective was "the maintenance of the open door in the Balkans." Specifically, Byrnes was "disturbed" by, and sought to
limit or stop completely, the Soviet moves to establish close
economic partnerships with eastern European nations. In the
positive sense, he sustained Truman's drive launched during
the Potsdam meeting to internationalize the entire Danubian
waterway system.

That move of Truman and Byrnes in 1945 was in many
respects similar and comparable to Secretary of State Knox's
attempt in 1909 to internationalize the Manchurian railway

system. The analogy is illuminating. The American objective was the same in both cases: as the London *Times* described the postwar maneuver, to establish the conditions under which there would be "free entry into the Danube Valley and Eastern Europe for the goods and capital of the Western countries." And just as it had been assumed in Manchuria, so it was also assumed in eastern Europe in 1945 that such free access for American economic power would in turn help to create and sustain political predominance. The American demand for free elections in eastern Europe was considered by American policy-makers as much a means to such economic and political ends as a philosophic or moral end in and of itself.

But as Knox had failed in 1909, so did Byrnes fail in 1945. As they had done in 1909, the Russians in 1945 evaluated the American proposal for exactly what it was. And as in the earlier episode, so also in the later one—the Russians resisted. One exchange between Byrnes and Molotov summarized not only the impasse at London in 1945, but much of the diplomacy of the succeeding 15 years. The Secretary of State tried to persuade Molotov that the United States, despite its demands for the Open Door and its refusal to come to terms on reparations, was not trying to weaken or close out Soviet influence in eastern Europe. "I must tell you," Molotov replied, "I have my doubts as to this."

The Diplomacy of the Vicious Circle

The *New York Times* correspondent Herbert L. Matthews wrote from London on September 25, 1945, what probably remains the best short analysis of what happened between the spring and the early fall of that fateful year. "France, Britain, and the United States, in seeking to absorb eastern Europe into a unified continental system, are aiming to weaken the Eastern bloc, and at the same time they are being forced with varying degrees of reluctance into the formation of that very Western bloc that Russia dreads.

"It is a vicious circle. . . ."

Soviet Russia's initial response to the American outlook and action was ambivalent. On the one hand, and by necessity, it launched a major program of reconstruction based on labor and capital extracted from a war-weary and weakened populace, supplemented where possible by reparations from Germany and eastern Europe. On the other hand, and as feared by former Secretary of State Hull as early as April 1945, it sought to "establish outposts, bases, and warm-water harbors in many areas and add buffer territory and otherwise prepare her own outward defenses just as fully as if the United Nations were not in existence." Yet in every case but one, that involving eastern Europe, Russia retreated from these efforts in the face of America's vigorous and militant opposition.

Thus Russia withdrew from Iran, leaving the Western powers in a predominant strategic and economic position. Thus it also retreated from its efforts to modify Western supremacy at the entrance (and exit) of the Black Sea. And thus it acquiesced, though under vigorous protest, when on May 3, 1946, the United States abruptly and unilaterally announced that it was terminating reparations to Russia from the Western zones of occupied Germany. These reparations, never large, had been arranged as part of interzone economic rehabilitation after the Potsdam Conference.

This decision, apparently taken on his own responsibility by General Lucius Clay, the Military Governor of the American zone, very probably had a crucial effect on the deteriorating relations between the United States and the Soviet Union. It can of course be debated whether any single action can or should be called decisive when the general situation already exhibited such momentum toward sustained and embittered antagonism. On the other hand, Soviet officials stationed in Germany who later came to the West testified that it was "one of the pivotal events." And it provoked the first all-out postwar propaganda attack by the Russians upon American policy. Those considerations make it useful to examine the episode more fully.

It is essential first of all to realize the issue was economic.

Given that, the importance and the impact of the action can best be understood by placing it in its general and specific context. At the beginning of the year, on January 5, 1946, Truman had declared that World War III was inevitable unless Russia was "faced with an iron fist and strong language." By the end of January, Byrnes had discontinued "the practice of having private meetings with the Russians," even though "they were always eager to do so." Then, on March 5, Truman applauded from the platform as Churchill delivered his extremely violent and unrestrained anti-Soviet "Iron Curtain" speech at Fulton, Missouri.

Stalin promptly and bluntly called Churchill's performance "a dangerous act." He went on to speak of it as "something in the nature of an ultimatum: 'Accept our rule voluntarily and then all will be well; otherwise war is inevitable'." A bit later, on April 4, 1946, Stalin told the American Ambassador to Russia that in his opinion the United States had "definitely aligned itself with Great Britain against the U.S.S.R."

Clay's action on reparations was intimately bound up with American conditions for a loan to Russia. American representatives persistently tied such aid to the question of the Open Door Policy in eastern Europe. Secretary of Commerce Wallace warned Truman on March 14, 1946, that such an approach was increasing the tension. He suggested that it would be more fruitful "to talk with them in an understanding way" about "their dire economic needs and of their disturbed sense of security." Contrary to the impression created by all the vicious attacks on Wallace, he was not proposing anything that could be called appeasement. He wanted a calm and less adamant approach to economic discussions as a means of persuading the Russians to modify "many of their assumptions and conclusions which stand in the way of peaceful world cooperation." Wallace wanted neither to demand nor to surrender, but only to bargain in a mature fashion. But quite in keeping with his support for Churchill, Truman reports that he "ignored this letter of Wallace's." Note that the President does not say merely that he considered but finally rejected Wallace's analysis and proposal. He "ignored" it. In that difference lies considerable insight into the state of the cold war as of March 1946.

By cutting off reparations so soon thereafter from the western, industrial zones of Germany, Clay in effect put real and positive, as well as verbal and negative, pressure on the Russians. The Soviets no doubt interpreted Clay's actions as proof of America's double standard of judgment. For at the very outset of the four-power occupation of Germany, long before the Russians took any such steps, the French had refused to be bound by any joint Allied decisions. They handled their zone as they pleased. To the Russians, at any rate, the conclusion was obvious. Not only could they not negotiate a loan, as the French had been able to do, but they were being punished in a very vital area for the kind of behavior that, when taken by the French, was tolerated by the United States.

Clay's action was also important as background for a subsequent and very significant move by the United States. His termination of reparations came less than six weeks before the United States offered its long-heralded plan to control and ultimately share the secrets of atomic energy. The point here is not only that Clay's clamp-down on reparations squeezed a very tender Russian nerve, and thereby increased the general tension; but that it was an economic nerve that was very quickly pinched again and even harder by the American proposal on nuclear energy.

The American approach to the atom appeared first as the so-called Acheson-Lilienthal Report of March 1946. During the next three months it was transformed, under the general direction of Bernard Baruch, from a general analysis and report into a proposal involving sanctions against violators. Then, on June 14, it was presented to the United Nations. The final policy proposal is usually considered to be proof positive of American statesmanship and generosity, and its rejection by the Russians as the final evidence of their intransigence. While that matched set of conclusions can be, and has been, advanced with great power and persuasion, it nevertheless seems worthwhile to review the essential elements of the episode.

The strongest part of the generally accepted favorable interpretation concerns the point that the United States offered the proposal even though it enjoyed a monopoly of nuclear power. It is usually implied, furthermore, that America did this without any prompting or pressure. Let there be no misunderstanding on two points. It was a positive move, and there is no reason to question either the sincerity or the good intentions of American leaders. In a similar way, it can be argued that it is unrealistic and even unfair to criticize the United States on the grounds that it should have done more—or should have done differently what it did. This may be, even probably is, true in the sense of being highly improbable.

But it *is* fair to point out at the very beginning of any evaluation of the American plan that such criticism is *not* unrealistic or unfair in the sense of being made outside the context and obligations of direct governmental responsibility. For Stimson made exactly such criticism in September 1945, while he was Secretary of War.

Stimson's memorandum to Truman offers or suggests three crucial insights into the general nature of the American attitude and policy. The first stems from his blunt warning that the United States would not secure its objectives if it merely continued to negotiate with Russia *"having this weapon rather ostentatiously on our hip,"* or if it did so in a way that involved *"many small nations who have not demonstrated their potential power or responsibility."* The American proposal on atomic energy ignored and violated both those danger signals. Secondly, the rapid development of a tough American policy in the summer and fall of 1945 that prompted Stimson's memorandum also provoked serious concern and fears on the part of the British. Prime Minister Clement Attlee told Truman that the question uppermost in his mind was a fundamental one: "Am I to plan for a peaceful or a warlike world?" Attlee's subsequent visit to Washington in November 1946 was clearly undertaken to influence Truman to take the former course in connection with atomic energy, and did unquestionably have some effect. This British pressure has to be credited in any assessment of American action. Finally, Stimson's memorandum bears directly, and in two ways, on the whole question of American disarmament at the end of the war. The official and widely accepted view is that the United States disarmed almost completely. This conclusion seems to have stemmed from three things: the extremist rhetoric and rather frantic behavior of Secretary of Defense James V. Forrestal who replaced Stimson (and similar assertions by assorted newspaper columnists and other pundits); the annual scare campaigns conducted by the Army, Navy, and Air Force in connection with their budget requests; and various formal and pseudohistorical accounts of the immediate postwar period prepared by the State Department, other government agencies, and associated intellectuals as part of cold-war propaganda.

But the striking thing is that neither Stimson nor Truman thought that the United States stood disarmed and defenseless before the Russian bear. Neither did Churchill. The Stimson letter to Truman of September 1945 is based on the assumption that the possession of the bomb and the capacity to deliver it gave the United States a clear military advantage: it meant having "this weapon rather ostentatiously on our hip." Churchill stated the same thing very simply in March 1946: the bomb kept the Russians under control. And Truman, on July 10, 1946, in a letter to Baruch about the American control plan, phrased it with perfect candor. "We should not under any circumstances throw away our gun until we are sure the rest of the world can't arm against us."

The fact is that the United States had not disarmed just because it had demobilized the mass army created to fight World War II. Nor did its leaders think it had disarmed. Men like Forrestal merely wanted more conventional weapons to exploit the basic advantage of nuclear supremacy. Granted their assumptions, it was an intelligent proposal, but it had nothing to do with a desperate need to provide a disarmed United States with the means of its survival. Indeed, Forrestal himself admitted during his own campaign—as in his diary entry for June 10, 1946—that "the Russians would not move this summer—in fact at any time."

Truman's remark about "our gun" brings into clear focus the first of three essential points concerning the Acheson-Lilienthal-Baruch plan for the atom. The American proposal not only failed to set any time for giving up the nuclear weapons monopoly held by the United States, but it never committed the United States to do so in any firm manner. "The plan," explained the joint committee, "does not require that the United States shall discontinue such manufacture [of the bomb] either upon the proposal of the plan or upon the inauguration of the international agency. At some stage in the development that is required." But the United States never specified the conditions of that stage. Let the motivations of the United States be accepted as stated by its protagonists and defenders, that demand for an immediate *quid* from Russia without a clear commitment to supply the *quo* by America remains a gaping weakness in the plan.

This suggests very strongly that J. Robert Oppenheimer was being accurate and candid in his recounting of the proceedings of the Acheson-Lilienthal committee, of which he had been a member. He makes the second principal point about the American proposal: it was conceived in the spirit of Truman's remarks in August and October 1945. "The prevalent view," he explained, "saw in the problems of atomic energy . . . an opportunity to cause a decisive change in the whole trend of Soviet policy." "There appears to be little doubt that we yearn for the notion of a trusteeship more or less as it was formulated by President Truman in his Navy Day Address of late 1945." At that time, on October 27, the President had invoked the "righteousness and justice" of American foreign policy, and had assured the public that he would refuse to participate in "any compromises with evil."

Finally, the American plan demanded even more of the Russians than that they trust the United States with a nuclear weapons monopoly for an indefinite period. It asked in the meantime that the international authority established to administer the program should be granted extensive control over the nuclear economic affairs, and by indirection all economic affairs, of the Soviet Union. This is clearly one of the points that Oppenheimer had in mind when he spoke of the committee's idea of changing Soviet policy.

This proposed international authority was to be one, according to Baruch, "to which should be entrusted all phases of the development and use of atomic energy, starting with raw materials and including: 1. Managerial control or ownership of all atomic energy activities potentially dangerous to world security. 2. Power to control, inspect and license all other atomic activities."

Baruch seems to have understood from the beginning what this meant as far as winning approval from the Russians. For this phase of the plan amounted to applying the traditional Open Door Policy to atomic energy, and backing it up with sanctions. If this seems at first glance to be an exaggerated or mistaken analysis, it appears that way only because of the matter of timing involved. Fundamentally, the plan proposed the same kind of internationalization of the atom that Secretary Knox advocated for the Manchurian railways in 1909, and that Truman demanded for the Danubian waterways in 1945.

The Baruch plan held out the prospect of an open door for the development and use of atomic energy. The only difference was that in this case the United States was going to retain the job of doorman for an indefinite period. It was as if the United States had enjoyed monopoly control of the Manchurian railroad system in 1909, and had proposed to admit other nations to participate in the venture on American terms and according to an American timetable. At some unspecified time, the United States would remove all restrictions on share purchasing—assuming that it would retain 51 per cent of the voting stock. In the meantime, the new but still American-controlled board of directors was to have the power to prevent the construction of competing lines either across Siberia or in China proper.

That analogy should also help in understanding why the Russians refused to agree to the Baruch plan. Baruch himself explained it on June 16, 1946, as well as—if not better than—

the Soviet spokesmen did in their own speeches. Russia, he commented, "has no intention of permitting a situation whereby the national economy of the Soviet Union or particular branches of that economy would be placed under foreign control." That was fair and accurate enough, but then neither did the United States have any such intention. The result was precisely what Stimson had predicted: "A secret armament race of a rather desperate character."

Secretary of Commerce Wallace had become, by September 1946, so disturbed by the tone and tempo of this race that he spoke out even more forcefully than Stimson had done exactly a year earlier. He bluntly told Truman and the American public that it was time to stop using a double standard in dealing with the Soviet Union. "We should be prepared to judge [Russia's] requirements against the background of what we ourselves and the British have insisted upon as essential to our respective security. We should be prepared, even at the expense of risking epithets of appeasement, to agree to reasonable Russian guarantees of security." He also reiterated his suggestion of March 1946 to make "a new approach along economic and trade lines."

Truman did not agree with Wallace. Neither did Secretary Byrnes, then engaged in being firm with the Russians during negotiations in Paris. Neither did Truman's other advisors, or the top men in the Department of State. And neither did the Congress. Wallace was dismissed from the Cabinet on September 20, 1946. The Russians no doubt interpreted the firing of Wallace for what it was—a resounding reassertion of the tough policy. And as if to make sure they got the point, Byrnes, on October 16, 1946, canceled an existing Export-Import Bank loan to Czechoslovakia.

Most commentators make a great deal of Andrei A. Zhdanov's rise to power in setting and enforcing the Soviet interpretations of intellectual and political questions. He did win this authority, and he advocated a very tough and even vulgar anti-Americanism derived from his argument that the world was divided into two hostile camps. But Zhdanov did not reach his position as commissar of the party line until the same period that Wallace was fired for challenging Truman. Figuratively speaking, Wallace and Zhdanov passed each other going in opposite directions aboard their elevators in the respective power systems during the last week in September 1946. And as the Varga debates of May 1947 indicated, Zhdanov cannot really be said to have fully consolidated his position for at least six months.

In this, as in so many other aspects of the cold war, the timing of apparently disparate, incidental, and unrelated events is crucial to an understanding of what was going on inside and between the two countries. In a similar way, it is a grave error to evaluate or interpret the diplomatic moves of 1945 and 1946 in an economic vacuum. This is true in three respects. First, a good many of them were specifically economic in character. Second, all of them were intimately bound up with Russia's concern to obtain either a loan from the United States or extensive reparations from Germany and its former allies in eastern Europe. And finally, the determination to apply the Open Door Policy to eastern Europe, which led directly to the policies of "total diplomacy" and "negotiation from strength" later made famous by Secretary of State Acheson, evolved concurrently with a deep concern over economic affairs in the United States.

This fear had never really disappeared after the Recession of 1937–38. It was even present, though in its most subdued forms, during the concentrated drive in 1942–43 to win the war by out-producing the Axis. It regained all its former vigor, and power over the thinking of American leaders, beginning with the congressional hearings of 1943 on postwar planning and economic policy. By March 1946, the *New York Times* reported that "in all groups there is the gnawing fear that after several years of high prosperity, the United States may run into something even graver than the depression of the Thirties." The Employment Act of 1946, designed to relieve such anxiety, did not seem to reassure very many people.

Perhaps an explanation was the growing feeling that the welfare state approach of the New and Fair deals had not changed the essential characteristics, or power structure, of

America's corporate political economy. By the end of 1946, in any event, even government spokesmen warned that the United States might "produce itself into a bust" if it did not obtain more foreign markets and overseas investment opportunities. Complementing that fear was the increasing concern over America's "staggering" consumption and waste of raw materials. Open-door expansion, it appeared, was the answer to all problems—the Russians, markets, and raw materials.

That traditional outlook was given further support by two events early in 1947. First, the President's Council of Economic Advisors expressed concern about the probability of a serious economic slump. Second, western Europe failed to recover from the war and take its place in the American scheme of things. Hence the problem was to coerce the Russians, help western Europe, and thereby establish the reality of an open-door system throughout the world. These two themes converged during the spring of 1947 in George F. Kennan's famous policy of containment and Dean Acheson's proposal for solving the "hard task of building a successfully functioning system" at home by reinvigorating America's expansion. These and other American leaders shared John Foster Dulles' view of February 1947, that "peace lies not in compromising but in invigorating our historic policies."

Among the many ironies of Kennan's policy of containment, perhaps the greatest is the fact that he had so internalized the assumptions and principles of the Open Door Policy that he thought he was proposing a radically different program. This indeed is the final act in the transformation of a utopia into an ideology. As Kennan himself later acknowledged, containment and liberation are "the two sides of the same coin"; and it was Kennan—not Dulles—who first stressed the traditional open-door faith in America's overwhelming economic power to force the Soviet Union along a path preferred by the United States. Even in 1957, when he felt "at liberty" to admit that containment had not prevented Russian economic development, Kennan reasserted the traditional objectives of the Open Door Policy in Europe.

Kennan's condemnation of earlier exponents of the Open

Door Policy who moralized about foreign policy (and other nations) provided another striking paradox. For, as a fellow foreign-service officer noted, Kennan was "constantly making moral judgments about the behavior of states." Thus, for example, he judged the Soviet system "wrong, deeply wrong," and ruled by a "conspiracy within a conspiracy." His blanket denial that the Soviets had ever considered that they could work with the United States was another such moral judgment, as well as being an error of fact.

Kennan's later remark that one of his objectives in 1947 was to counter the tendency of Americans "to take a despairing and dramatic view of Soviet relations" indicates still another facet of the ideological nature of the thought of American leaders. For he described the Soviets as moving "inexorably along the prescribed path, like a persistent toy automobile wound up and headed in a given direction, stopping only when it meets with some unanswerable force." Hence it was absolutely necessary, he warned, to "confront the Russians with unalterable counterforce at every point where they show signs of encroaching" and to block the Soviet Union with "superior force" and with "unassailable barriers in its path." This language was not only dramatic and despairing, but it had a very great deal to do with the "overmilitarization of our thinking about the Cold War," about which Kennan complained ten years later.

The policy of containment was supplemented in 1947 by the Truman Administration's stress on the necessity of economic expansion. Aware of the warning made by government economists that "without a new aid program there would be a sharp drop in American exports," the President explained and stressed that problem very candidly *before* he enunciated the Truman Doctrine. In two speeches prior to that dramatic performance, the President asserted the need to "act and act decisively" to sustain the Open Door Policy. "The pattern of international trade which is most conducive to freedom of enterprise," he pointed out, "is one in which major decisions are made not by governments but by private buyers and sellers." On the assumption that America was "the giant of the economic world," Truman announced that "the choice is ours" to sustain and expand private enterprise.

Hence it is misleading to overemphasize the differences between the Truman Doctrine and the Marshall Plan. They were the two sides of the same coin of America's traditional program of open-door expansion. As the direct descendant of Winston Churchill's militantly anti-Russia "Iron Curtain" speech of March 1946, the Truman Doctrine blamed the Soviet Union for the troubles of the world and announced the determination of the United States to halt the spread of revolutionary radicalism. It was the ideological manifesto of American strategy, described by the head of *Time*'s Washington bureau as a program to promote "trouble on the other side of the Iron Curtain." As Acheson revealed to the Congress, the American Government entered upon "no consultation and no inquiry" about the possibility of achieving the stated objectives either through negotiations with the Russians or within the framework of the United Nations. The approach proceeded from the assumption, openly avowed by Harriman in 1945, and by Truman in 1946, that the cold war was inevitable.

Considered in isolation, however, the Truman Doctrine provides a one-sided impression of American policy. Some of its crusading fervor seems clearly to have been the result of a conviction, most candidly expressed by Senator Vandenberg, that it would be necessary to "scare hell out of the American people." On the other hand, it contained no references to the economic difficulties that worried American leaders. It concentrated instead on the political dangers of communism.

For his part, however, Secretary of State George C. Marshall did not initially emphasize the Russian danger. In his speech at Harvard on June 5, 1947, he offered the aid program as an expression of America's warm humanitarianism. There can be no question but that it did represent America's generous urge to help the peoples of western Europe, and that it did play a vital role in the recovery of that region. Approached solely as a humanitarian gesture, however, the Marshall Plan raises several troubling questions. China and Latin America were excluded, for example, though their needs were certainly great from a humanitarian (or even a policy) point of view. Perhaps Marshall's own testimony before the Congress provides a broader understanding of the program.

Prior to Marshall's famous address at Harvard, moreover, the Congress and the Department of State had been preoccupied with the danger of another depression. Undersecretary of State for Economic Affairs Clayton redefined *the* problem as that of disposing of America's "great surplus." "The capitalistic system, whether internally or internationally," he explained in May 1947, "can only work by the continual creation of disequilibrium in comparative costs of production." Clayton was saying implicitly what Acheson had argued explicitly in 1944: the profitability of America's corporate system depended upon overseas economic expansion. Given this consensus among American leaders, it is not too surprising that Marshall took a similar approach before the Congress: "The paramount question before us, I think, can be stated in business terms." The consequences of failing to carry through on the plan, he explained, would be to confront America, "if not [with] a trade barrier, certainly with a great detriment to our ordinary business, or commerce and trade."

Marshall and other advocates of the program also spoke openly of the parallel between their policy and America's earlier westward expansion across the continent. Marshall presented the program in those traditional terms as the way to avoid the loss of democracy at home. Assuming that it offered the only solution to America's economic difficulties, the Secretary argued that the nation faced an either-or situation. Unless the plan was adopted, he asserted, "the cumulative loss of foreign markets and sources of supply would unquestionably have a depressing influence on our domestic economy and would drive us to increased measures of government control." By thus defining America's expansion as the key to prosperity, Marshall defined foreign policy as the key to domestic problems and to the survival of democracy at home. The intellectual continuity of his thought with the frontier thesis and the policies of John Hay, Woodrow Wilson, Herbert Hoover, and Franklin D. Roosevelt was apparent.

Other Americans were even more explicit. Secretary of the Interior Julius A. Krug defended the plan as "essential to our own continued productivity and prosperity." Another enthusiastic supporter remarked that "it is as if we were building a TVA every Tuesday." Even in the most restrained temper of judgment, this might well be the biggest "as if" in American history; for whereas TVA qualified as one of what Alvin Hansen has described as "frontiers in our own back-yard," the Marshall Plan was a concerted program to sustain and expand a frontier overseas.

The testimony of liberal and conservative leaders indicated that they viewed the frontier thesis as the answer to the theories and prophecies of Karl Marx. Chester Bowles, for example, warned specifically that it "was wholly possible that within the next ten years Karl Marx's judgment will have proved correct." Concretely, he thought the United States was "heading toward some sort of recession which can be eased by quick approval of the Marshall Plan." Nelson Rockefeller explained that "with the closing of our own frontier, there is hope that other frontiers still exist in the world." Spruille Braden also saw the program as a way to "repeat what had been done in the development of our own great west."

One of Truman's Cabinet members preferred to think of the whole operation as a "logical extension of the good-neighbor policy, that the Fair Deal for all cannot flourish in isolation." Another Cabinet official saw it as the "restoration of Europe as a paying market for United States goods." And such widely different men as William Henry Chamberlin and Marquis Childs pointed directly to the analysis and program advocated by Brooks Adams in 1900 as a wise guide for 1947. Writing in *The Wall Street Journal,* Chamberlin thought it was "high time to face the problem created by what Brooks Adams called 'America's vast and growing surplus.'" Childs republished Adams's recommendations for the deployment of "America's economic supremacy" in behalf of the open door, and pointedly remarked that Adams "would have . . . to alter scarcely anything to relate his views to the world of today." Perhaps Childs, along with others, was struck by Adams's praise for Britain's traditional policy of "containing" the Russians.

From the very beginning, for that matter, many American leaders stressed the desirability and possibility of making the countries of eastern Europe "independent of Soviet control" and the importance of the "struggle for the preservation of Western civilization." Even a casual reading of the *Congressional Record* makes it clear that John Foster Dulles was a latter-day missionary for the doctrine of liberation. Coupled with this thought was a general acceptance of the idea of ending Soviet rule in Russia. Hardly any American leader failed to contribute his insights to the "cheerful discussion of how America ought, and ought not, to try to remake Russia." Some thought it might be necessary, and certainly magnanimous, to allow the Russians to retain some features of socialism. Others proposed a Heavenly City of the American Century. All agreed on the morality and the practicality of the objective.

This emphasis on open-door expansion and the assumption of the inevitable downfall of the Soviet Union again indicated that American leaders were not motivated solely by fear of Russian military attack. When asked point blank, *even after the Russians had tested their first nuclear bombs and the Chinese communists had defeated Chiang Kai-shek,* whether or not "our position on foreign policy with respect to communism is not relative to Churchill's in 1940," Secretary Acheson replied in the negative. "I do not mean to infer at all that there is that desperate a situation. I said I was not discouraged and was not taking a pessimistic view at all." "The problem which confronts us," he explained, "can be stated very simply: To maintain the volume of American exports which the free world needs and which it is our national interest to supply as a necessary part of building a successfully functioning political and economic system, the free world must obtain the dollars to pay for these exports."

For their part, the Russians clearly interpreted the Marshall Plan as the over-all economic equivalent of Baruch's pro-

posal on atomic energy. It was to them an American strategy
for setting and maintaining conditions on economic development in eastern Europe and the Soviet Union. That estimate
prompted them first to refuse to participate, and then to em-
bark upon a series of actions which most Americans mistak-
enly think had already occurred. They initiated a program
of general political repression in Rumania. They sharply cur-
tailed freedom of the press in Bulgaria, Rumania, and eastern Germany. They shot the Peasant Party leader Patlov in
Bulgaria. And within the year the Communist Party in
Czechoslovakia seized a monopoly of political power.

These events typified the nature of the cold war as it continued on into the 1950's. In the United States, President
Truman repeatedly blamed all the troubles of the world on
the Soviet Union, and American leaders in and out of government "bombarded the American people with a 'hate the
enemy' campaign rarely seen in our history; never, certainly,
in peace time." This American propaganda barrage prompted
analyses by two government figures that received little publicity. A congressional committee headed by Representative
Forrest A. Harness concluded its long study of the problem
with this estimate in 1947: "Government propaganda distorts
facts with such authority that the person becomes prejudiced
or biased in the direction which the Government propagan-
dists wish to lead national thinking." Exactly ten years later,
General Douglas MacArthur offered an even more biting
commentary on the same pattern of distortion. "Our government has kept us in a perpetual state of fear—kept us in a
continuous stampede of patriotic fervor—with the cry of a
grave national emergency. . . . Yet, in retrospect, these dis-
asters seem never to have happened, seem never to have been
quite real."

Perhaps it was true that the community of American policy-
makers "fell in love with its Cold War plan." That was the
considered conclusion of James P. Warburg, an eminent conservative student of foreign affairs. It was more likely, however, that the ideology of the Open Door Policy had come to
be so firmly believed by American leaders that they never

questioned either the freedom or the necessity of their program for America and the world.

Certainly the attitude of American leaders toward the underdeveloped societies of the world suggested that explanation. Kennan, for example, took an extreme position on
China, discounting almost completely its immediate significance or its potential importance. Others defined the poorer
areas in the traditional open-door manner, seeing them as
markets for exports and as sources of raw materials. Even
when they spoke of the need to help such regions—or provided such assistance—they did so from the point of view of
developing them as part of America's corporate system. It was
quite normal, given that conception of the world, for American leaders to consider such regions as dependent variables
of the situation in western Europe. The problems and difficulties in the underdeveloped areas could be handled through
their existing ties to European empire countries. Time after
time, therefore, the United States endeavored to support the
crumbling ruins of eighteenth- and nineteenth-century co-
lonialism against the impact of nationalistic and radical on-
slaughts.

No American leader personified all aspects of the ideology
of the Open Door Policy more dramatically than Secretary of
State John Foster Dulles. In the 1920's, he supported the
Hughes-Hoover policy of expansion based on a "community
of ideals, interests, and purposes" with Germany and Japan,
and specifically pushed American penetration of underdeveloped areas in line with his emphasis on the necessity of
markets for surplus goods and capital. He followed the same
policy throughout the 1930's. Arguing that it was necessary to
accept changes in the world, and asserting the Christian way
of compromise, he labored diligently as late as 1939 to work
out a broad understanding with Nazi Germany and a mili-
tarized Japan.

Dulles continued to advocate and practice this approach
after 1945. Understandably, he worked very well as an advisor
and assistant to Secretary Acheson during the early years of
the cold war. His definition of compromise did not include a

fundamental rapprochement and accommodation with the
Soviet Union, or the acceptance of fundamental changes in
the underdeveloped regions. On the threshold of his lifelong
ambition to be Secretary of State, Dulles provided in 1952 the
definitive statement of the Open Door Policy. Synthesizing the
moral imperialism of his missionary background with the
necessity of economic expansion of his banking experience,
Dulles announced that he would liberate the Russians and the
Chinese from "atheistic international communism" and usher
in the American Century.

Perhaps Dulles himself provided the most accurate picture
of the final failure of the Open Door Policy. Against the background of constant and record-breaking travels all over the
world, Dulles undertook yet another mission to Latin America.
He was greeted by his official host with the pleasant and
gracious remark that it was "good to have you here, Mr.
Secretary." "You shouldn't feel that way," Dulles replied, "for
I go only where there is trouble." And trouble indeed there
was for the policy of the open door.

A bit later, when it appeared that negotiations with Russia
could no longer be avoided, Dulles inadvertently laid bare the
basic flaw of the open-door conception of the world. He worried about such a meeting with the Soviet Union, he explained, because it might tempt Americans to turn their attention and energies away from the cold war. But only a view
of the world which defined freedom and necessity in terms of
expansion could lead to that response. For a growing number of Americans were beginning to join millions of others
throughout the world in a reassertion of the elementary fact
that man was born to achieve and exercise his self-knowledge
in more fruitful endeavors than a cold war which persistently
threatened to erupt in nuclear horror. Dulles apparently failed
to realize that he felt anxiety for the wrong reasons and was
pursuing a policy that had now become a denial of the spirit
of man.

Though not as extreme as Dulles in their reactions, most
other American leaders were slow to grasp the real meaning
of the revolutions throughout the world—their ability to de-

stroy a cherished American illusion in Asia, to manage the transfer of power in Russia, to initiate and carry through a major conference of underdeveloped societies without American leadership, and even to defy the United States to use its nuclear weapons in retaliation. But only such an understanding and acceptance of the revolutions, followed by the development of a program based upon their reality, would enable the United States to play its warranted role in the new society arising on the foundations of the old.

For Further Reading

The output of books and articles on American foreign relations for the post-1941 period is phenomenal; only the more outstanding can be mentioned here. Any one of the following three able, balanced accounts of wartime diplomacy are good points at which to begin: Robert A. Divine, *Second Chance: The Triumph of Internationalism in America During World War II* (1967); Divine, *Roosevelt and World War II* (1969); and Gaddis Smith, *American Diplomacy During the Second World War* (1965). John W. Spanier, *American Foreign Policy Since World War II* (3rd rev. ed., 1968) is the most competent survey of the postwar period.

There are outstanding, illuminating memoirs and biographies already published, some of high literary merit. The relevant portions of George F. Kennan's *Memoirs, 1925–1950* (1967) are vital for the views of the chief architect of the containment policy. Dean Acheson, *Present at the Creation* (1969) is the best defense of the cold warrior view with plenty of persuasive factual data to back it up. James MacGregor Burns focuses on the President's wartime policy in his excellent biography of F.D.R., *Roosevelt: The Soldier of Freedom* (1970). Other memoirs and biographies of important wartime and postwar policymakers are: Elting E. Morison, *Turmoil and Tradition: A Study of the Life and Times of Henry L. Stimson* (1960); Henry L. Stimson and McGeorge Bundy, *On Active Service in Peace and War* (1948); Robert E. Sherwood,

Roosevelt and Hopkins (1948); Cordell Hull, *Memoirs of Cordell Hull* (2 vols., 1948); Walter Millis, ed., *The Forrestal Diaries* (1951); James F. Byrnes, *Speaking Frankly* (1947) and *All in One Lifetime* (1958); Edward R. Stettinius, *Roosevelt and the Russians*, ed. by Walter Johnson (1949); John R. Deane, *The Strange Alliance: The Story of Our Efforts at Wartime Cooperation with Russia* (1947). The memoirs of both Harry S Truman and Dwight David Eisenhower, cited in the bibliographic note following the next selection, should also be consulted.

The cold war is the subject of a number of fine summaries. For an able survey, in addition to Spanier's, see Paul Y. Hammond, *The Cold War Years: American Foreign Policy Since 1945* (1969). For excellent, detailed discussions of the formative period of Soviet-American relations see George F. Kennan, *Russia and the West Under Lenin and Stalin* (1960); William H. McNeill, *America, Britain and Russia* (1953); and the volumes by Herbert Feis: on World War II and early postwar U.S. policy toward China, *China Tangle* (1953); on Allied war relations, *Churchill-Roosevelt-Stalin* (1957); on the Potsdam conference, *Between War and Peace* (1960); on the fall of Japan, *The Atomic Bomb and the End of World War II* (rev. ed., 1966); and on the Soviet-American struggle in the Far East, *Contest Over Japan* (1967). John Lukacs, *A New History of the Cold War* (3rd ed., 1966); and David Rees, *The Age of Containment: The Cold War, 1945–1965* (1967), accept the cold warrior view. Louis J. Halle, *The Cold War as History* (1967); and William L. Neumann, *After Victory: Churchill, Roosevelt, Stalin and the Making of Peace* (1967) are excellent recent accounts. The revisionist approach, following Williams' lead, but expanding on it, may be explored in Gabriel Kolko, *The Politics of War: The World and United States Foreign Policy, 1943–1945* (1968); Gar Alperovitz, *Atomic Diplomacy* (1965); Walter LaFeber, *America, Russia and the Cold War, 1945–1966* (1968); Ronald Steel, *Pax Americana* (1967); N. D. Houghton, ed., *Struggle Against History* (1968); and Denna F. Fleming, *The Cold War and Its Origins, 1917–60* (2 vols., 1961).

The Eisenhower Equilibrium

Eric F. Goldman

*A*s thoughtful Americans peered forward in 1945 they could hardly help remembering the experiences of the 1920's. That postwar decade had been marked by an apparent headlong flight from America's role within the international nation-state system. Prewar social and moral standards had been abandoned. Americans seemed to embrace the domination by business of both the economy and political life. Indeed, the mood of the "Flapper Age" had been attributed to disillusionment born of frustrated ideals; after all, the repudiation of the League of Nations severed the last threads of Wilsonian idealism.

Some trends in American society during the closing days of World War II portended withdrawal from world responsibility once again. With the defeat of Germany in May 1945, a clamor arose to bring the troops home; after the Japanese collapse three months later, the clamor turned into a roar. In January 1946, American GIs—stationed throughout the globe in India, Japan, the Philippines, Guam, Germany, France, Great Britain, and even in the United States—staged a series of spontaneous "amiable mutinies." "Lincoln Freed the Slaves, Who Will Free Us?" "Japs Go Home, How About Us?" and "Service Yes, But Serfdom Never" became the slogans of troops weary of war and bored with occupation duty.

Source: Eric F. Goldman, *The Crucial Decade and After* (New York: Alfred A. Knopf, Inc., 1956), pp. 261–294. Copyright © 1956 by Eric F. Goldman. Reprinted by permission of Alfred A. Knopf, Inc.

The American people supported their soldiers' and sailors' sentiments. Harry S Truman and his military advisers had no choice but to order a speedup in discharge policy; they presided reluctantly over the "disintegration" of the armed forces, seeing the number shrink from 12 million in 1945, to 3 million in 1946, and to a nadir of 1.4 million in 1948. The people had spoken emphatically: The United States may indeed have international responsibilities, but those needs would have to be met by means short of armed force.

The dismantling of the military machine during 1945–1948 rested in part on the public's high expectation that the newly proved atomic bomb would make standing armies a thing of the past. Although most military authorities disagreed (General George S. Patton observed in August 1945 that "If we put our trust in the atomic bomb we are selling our birthright." He continued prophetically, "The enemy, too, will have it. . . ."), this mood seemed very much like an earlier faith in the League of Nations. Instead of an institution, a bomb in benevolent and wise hands would ensure peace.

Yet another parallel to the 1920's emerged in 1945–1946. President Truman, attempting to resuscitate the New Deal's social and economic programs in housing and public health, ran into a stone wall of "back to normalcy" sentiment. The formidable wartime economic control structure that he wished to continue in order to forestall inflation came crashing down after the 1946 Congressional elections proved that the people wished to disengage rapidly.

Anti-Communist sentiment, never entirely submerged in American life, surfaced again in the period 1945–1948 as it had in 1919–1920. Directly related to the hardening of United States-Russian relations, concern about Communist subversion began to take on the proportions of a crusade. Politicians pursued career opportunities by appealing to public fears of a worldwide aggressive Communist expansion. Richard M. Nixon's early career is not unusual for the period. His political success in California was largely due to his ability to portray both his Congressional opponent in 1946, Jerry Voorhis, and his

Senatorial antagonist in 1950, Helen Gahagan Douglas, as being "soft" on Communism. Once in Washington, the future President earned a reputation as a vigilant defender of the American citadel, particularly for his role in exposing the relationship between Whittaker Chambers, a former Communist, and Alger Hiss, a one-time high official in the State Department. In 1948, the notorious Hiss case and the contemporaneous disclosures by the government that Julius and Ethel Rosenberg had allegedly "given the secret" of the atomic bomb to the Russians, combined to "prove" the existence of a vast subversive conspiracy.

Upon these underpinnings there rested another political career, that of Joseph R. McCarthy. Although the precise configuration of McCarthy's national political constituency is debated, few deny that for a brief period the Wisconsin Senator had enormous influence. Elected officials and civil servants trembled at the prospect of being named by McCarthy or his aides as a Communist sympathizer. But, as Eric Goldman recounts in the selection that follows, McCarthy's demise came quickly. Analysts have attempted to explain the McCarthy phenomenon in a variety of ways, ranging from the straightforward attribution of support by people who perceived Communism as a real threat to America, to the more subtle explanation that certain groups (such as Catholics, German-Americans, and rural dwellers) used Communism as a scapegoat for their larger, more diffuse dissatisfaction over tendencies in modern American life.

Despite the many similarities between the 1920's and the 1950's, the differences seem more significant. Although the army and navy were dismantled, the United States did organize and join the United Nations, it did organize and join the North Atlantic Treaty Organization, and it did use force in conjunction with the UN in the Korean "police action" to uphold its concepts of world order and peace. Equally as important, in domestic affairs the first Republican administration in twenty years decided not to undo the achievements of the New Deal. As Professor Goldman so ably discusses in

the following excerpt, Eisenhower accepted the imperatives of the "Half Century of Revolution"—the end of
the Harding-Coolidge brand of laissez-faire, the coming
to grips with industrial modernity.

One last admittedly superficial similarity between the
1920's and the 1945–1955 period should be noted. Both
have been chronicled by superb storytellers: Frederick
Lewis Allen for the 1920's, and Eric Goldman for the
later period. Goldman, like Allen before him, saw his
work as "history in the most direct sense of the word."
"It is a narrative, . . . an effort to place events in the
long perspective," Goldman wrote; he assumed "that the
history of man is the story of men."

*A*t first the war scares kept right on coming. The Korean
truce was hardly signed when the civil war in Indochina, which
had been dragging on since 1946, erupted into a major Communist assault on Dien Bien Phu. A number of high Administration figures, including Vice-President Nixon and Secretary
of State Dulles, let it be known that the United States might
well send troops. Dien Bien Phu fell, an armistice was signed
(giving the Communists 60,000 square miles containing a
population of 14,000,000), and Indochina quieted. Six months
more and the Chinese Communists seized Yikiang, north of
Formosa, and talked loudly of invading Quemoy, Matsu, and
Formosa itself. President Eisenhower asked Congress for broad
authority to use American armed forces in the area and, with
the country expecting a Chinese thrust any day, the Senate
passed the resolution by the sweeping majority of 85 to 3.

Over everything, more than ever, hung the knowledge that
another major war could be a war of oblivion. On March 1,
1954 American scientists set off the first explosion of an H-
bomb and the scientists themselves were surprised at the range
of its ability to injure. Radioactive ash fell on a Japanese fishing boat eighty miles away and twenty-three fishermen were
hospitalized for burns. A chill went through the United States.
Scores of cities reported that automobile windshields were
suddenly pock-marked as if by some exhalation from the H-

bomb. The scientific explanation was normal erosion—plus mass jitters.

Yet during all the fears of 1954 and 1955 a quite different feeling was growing in the United States. Cautiously, incredulously, Americans were asking: Was not the danger of World War III definitely receding? For one thing, whatever the threats to peace, armies were no longer fighting each other. With the signing of the Indochinese truce on July 20, 1954, no shooting war existed anywhere on the globe for the first time since the Japanese invaded Manchuria twenty-three years before. The failure of the Chinese Communists to carry out their threats continued the fact of actual peace. For another thing, strange and hopeful events were happening in the Soviet Union. The post-Stalin Russian leaders were not only continuing their conciliatory language. On occasion they were acting in a way which strongly suggested that the bear could change his habits.

Early in 1955 Premier Georgi Malenkov resigned with the explanation of "insufficient experience . . . I see clearly my guilt" and went right on staying alive while the premiership was taken over by Nikolai Bulganin and Nikita Khrushchev emerged as the power in the Communist Party organization. On the international scene, the Soviet government did things which had the authentic ring of a desire to soften the East-West clash. In June 1955 Americans really rubbed their eyes. Russian fliers shot down a United States plane over the Bering Strait and the Soviet government quickly expressed its regrets and offered to pay half the cost of the plane.

Probably most important of all, the feeling was growing in America that science had made large-scale war so terrifying that no nation would start one. 1954–5 was the period when it became clear that both the United States and the Soviet Union had an effective H-bomb and that both were far along in the development of intercontinental missiles. President Eisenhower expressed the spreading American attitude when he said: "We have arrived at the point . . . [where] there is just no real alternative to peace."

In the new climate of expectations of peace the United States naturally relaxed and sought to go back to its customary ways. But just what was normal for 1954–5? To what extent could one apply the pre-F.D.R. conception of America as a nation determining by itself its role in the world, zestfully individualistic, cherishing Home and Mother, delighting in a free economy and all the values that went with it?

Certainly the tug toward the traditional was powerful in American thinking. Every area of living showed the trend. Most of the college girls were telling the pollsters they wanted babies, not careers. The vogue among men was to stay home at night and do-it-yourself (insurance statisticians said more than 600,000 men a year were cutting their fingers with saws, setting themselves afire with spray paints, or shocking themselves with electrical tools). The intellectuals were showing greater and greater interest in a "new conservatism." And Dwight Eisenhower, who more than any President since William McKinley liked to deliver little homilies on Home and Mother, held on to his enormous popularity—in part, observers agreed, because of his emphasis on traditional values.

Yet if the trend was unmistakable, it was no plainer than certain counter facts. One of the assumptions of old-style America had been the acceptance of a society in which great differences in economic and social standing existed. The United States of 1954–5 was not only a product of the Half-Century of Revolution in domestic affairs; the revolution was not only continuing; the pressures for still more economic and social gains were strong and sustained. By 1955 the inflation had definitely slackened. The Republicans said their policies had brought about the change; the Democrats declared it came from long-term programs and the end of the Korean War. Whatever the cause, the result was a girding of all lower- and middle-income groups to see to it that the altered situation brought no wage cuts or other obstacles in the way of a continually rising standard of living.

Citizens of lower social status kept pressing hard for opportunities to improve their standing in the community. Those

of less esteemed nationality and religious backgrounds had
never been so persistent. Negro leaders battled untiringly. On
May 17, 1954 they won the critically important Supreme Court
decision declaring that no child could be barred from a public
school simply because of his color. Without a pause, the National Association for the Advancement of Colored People
threw tremendous energies into efforts to get the decision
speedily enforced and to remove Jim Crow from further parts
of American life.

Partly because of the techniques that had been used to
bring the social upsweep, partly for a dozen other reasons,
millions of Americans now found themselves in a position
where the genuine attitudes of individualism were not so much
wrong as irrelevant. The average industrial worker belonged
to a union and the average farmer was deeply involved in at
least one occupational organization. The typical clerical
worker was employed by a corporation or a business with
more than two hundred employees, and the typical executive
was not the owner but an employed manager of the business.
A web of relationships bound most Americans in with state
and federal governments. The very manner of living was having its effects. The unquestionable trend was toward a home in
a suburb—the mushrooming miles of middle-class and worker's suburbs—where the prime virtue was adjustment to what
the neighbors thought and did. Under the circumstances the
urge was not so much for individualism as it was for getting
oneself into the most profitable and comfortable relationship
with some larger group or organization.

Particular developments in the United States were making
large numbers fearsome of facing society by themselves and
deeply concerned with keeping and extending special governmental and nongovernmental protections. In the existing
state of the American economy and of the world market,
farming was simply not profitable without a subsidy. The
decades-old urbanization of the nation had brought a huge
segment of the population to the complexities and the ano-
nymity of city living. The relative number of women had been
steadily mounting and many of them were in a vulnerable eco-

nomic position; in 1954 a female headed about one in ten households. The population was growing older, bringing all the fears and uncertainties of age. In 1900, one person in seven was forty-five to sixty-four; by the early 1950's the ratio had changed to one in five and one in every twelve persons was sixty-five or over. The white, Protestant, "Anglo-Saxon" had long felt especially secure in the United States. But now year after year a smaller percentage of Americans were white, Protestant, and born of parentage which traced back to "Anglo-Saxon" lands.

Whether in a special category or not, the American of 1954–5 was likely to be a man who could not forget the crash of 1929. No matter the rampant boom, no matter the fact that during all the years since the beginning of World War II most families had been prospering; the edginess about a possible depression continued. Any dip in the economy, any flutter of the stock market brought wide concern. The very quieting of the international scene had many Americans asking: Wouldn't a peaceful situation and the cutting down of defense expenditures bring the crash? "Depression psychosis," the economist John Galbraith called it. Whether it was psychosis or good sense, the apprehensions about depression brought an added element into the national response to any governmental talk or action that smacked of the 1920's.

As for Home and Mother, attitudes were inevitably adjusting somewhat to the facts. In a thousand ways, little and big, the general reactions of the American had been growing less sentimental. Family living itself had been undergoing important changes. There was not only the possibility that mother was the head of the household; there was the decidedly better chance that she was out working (women were making up about 21,000,000 out of a total working force of roughly 64,000,000). Scores of other developments in the home, decidedly unsettling of the old ways in themselves, were dwarfed by the television revolution. By 1954–5 it had gone so far that for many Americans home was close to meaning the place where the TV set was located.

In 1954 the Water Commissioner of Toledo, puzzled why

water consumption rose so startlingly during certain three-minute periods, checked and rechecked his charts, theorized and retheorized, finally hit on the answer: Toledo was flushing the toilets during the commercials. That same year the "TV dinner" was born—the turkey, sweet potatoes, and peas pre-cooked in a compartmented tray—and the family did not have to talk to each other even during supper. The offerings of TV were hardly dominated by lavender and lace. The plunging necklines had plunged to a point where only an abyss could provoke comment. More people were murdered on TV in 1954, one dour commentator estimated, than the United States lost in Korea. And Lucille Ball of *I Love Lucy,* redefining the decorous, proceeded to give a week-by-week viewing of most of her pregnancy period, including Desi Arnaz's sympathetic morning sickness.

If the American scene itself was sharply untraditional, the feelings of world peace which were settling over the nation were still more unconventional. They lacked the fundamental of the usual American conception because they did not permit the country to forget about the world. The Soviet leaders might be cooing, but Communism in and outside Russia was obviously as much of a reality as ever and constantly threatening to increase in strength. In fact, the apparent Soviet swing away from attempts to advance Bolshevism by wars was merely being replaced by an intensified drive to extend Communism by internal subversion and by political, diplomatic, and economic techniques. If this was peace, it was plainly no 1865 or 1919 or even 1945 but a peace that constantly had to be worked at.

A strong urge toward the traditional amid situations that were inescapably new—here was the general pattern of the America that was relaxing in 1954–5. Such a nation could find its normality only along some wavering, in-between path.

Ever since the beginning of the 1952 campaign, Dwight Eisenhower had frequently used the term "middle-of-the-road" in describing his approach to public affairs. His Administration up to the winter of 1953–4, with its restrained Executive leadership, its toleration of extreme right-wing Republicans, its tendency toward the past in domestic and foreign policies, had certainly moved down the right side of the middle. But even in the most conservative days of 1953–4, other elements were present in Eisenhower's thinking.

All the while that he was emphasizing that the Executive should respect Congress and pointing to Roosevelt and Truman as men who had tried to lead too much, the President liked to repeat some remarks made by his old friend, General George Patton. One day Patton was discussing leadership and his eye fell on a plate of spaghetti. Leadership was like trying to get a piece of spaghetti across a table, Patton said. Push it and you would only break it. But get a bit in front of the piece of spaghetti, pull it gently, and you would get it across the table intact. Dwight Eisenhower, however much he was a leader who wanted to keep the Republican Party intact, nevertheless was quite conscious of the importance of getting out ahead a bit and pulling gently.

The President's attitude toward specific domestic and foreign problems also had its varying aspects. He was, as he frequently remarked, "basically conservative." But it was just as true to say that he was—and more so than any President in recent American history—generally non-ideological. Eisenhower tended to look for an *ad hoc* solution to a given situation and was willing to listen sympathetically to quite contrasting points of view. If he was inclined to believe that a successful businessman had thereby proved his sagacity, he deeply admired his younger brother Milton ("Milt inherited all the brains in the family"), whose mind had been shaped by years of high New Deal and Fair Deal positions.

Any policy in any field had to stand the test of the President's persistent tendency to react less along the lines of doctrine than according to the human aspects of the problem. The journalist Stewart Alsop has recalled an incident of the 1952 campaign. At first Eisenhower was strongly inclined to make a major issue of what seemed to him the excessively pro-labor attitude of Truman in dealing with a serious steel strike. Before committing himself, he asked to be briefed on the facts and some of his labor advisers explained the demands of the union in terms of what the benefits meant to the men's families in a period of rising prices. Eisenhower's reaction was, "Why maybe they ought to have had more than that," and the steel strike never became an important campaign issue.

Around the President were a group of men who were also "basically conservative," most of them more so than Eisenhower, but they had their own flexibility. All of the principal aides had spent their mature careers learning to operate within a New Deal-Fair Deal society. A number of them had served in specific functions for a Democratic Administration. This was particularly true of Eisenhower's chief adviser on foreign affairs, Secretary of State Dulles, who had worked with the State Department during most of the post-World War II period and who played a part in bringing about the highly untraditional decision to intervene in Korea. The two most influential advisers in domestic and defense matters, Secretary of the Treasury George Humphrey and Secretary of Defense Charles Wilson, were decidedly not businessmen of the 1920's type. They were part of the new, more adaptable managerial class.

In 1948 Wilson, wearied by the struggles between General Motors and the United Automobile Workers, had invented the famous "escalator clause" (tying wages to the cost of living) which labor liked so much and which was important in preserving industrial peace in the following years. In 1947 Humphrey demonstrated a similar flexibility. Facing a coal strike, he and Benjamin Fairless of United States Steel met with John L. Lewis for private talks and brought about a settlement largely on Lewis's terms. Many industrialists and a large section of Congress were indignant but Humphrey defended the move on pragmatic grounds, including the statement that Lewis's demands were largely reasonable. Discussing these episodes, the astute journalist Robert Coughlan has commented that "Wilson and Humphrey . . . have about as much resemblance to the Republican Big Businessman of the Coolidge-Hoover era as the Indian elephant has to the hairy mammoth—the general outline is the same, but there are vital differences in detail. . . . These two performances were neither 'conservative' nor 'liberal.' They were, however, practical."

Practical men, headed by an essentially non-ideological President, trying to govern a nation with conflicting urges— after the winter of 1953–4 the Administration moved increasingly from the severe conservatism of its early phase. The shift was evident in many ways, but it was clearest of all in the fact that Eisenhower was departing somewhat from his pre-F.D.R. conception of the Presidency.

He talked less and less about offending no one in Congress, left fewer major decisions to subordinates, spoke out more frequently on public issues. He was giving the appearance at press conferences that he no longer merely tolerated them but intended to use them to press forward his purposes. Only occasionally did he still remark that he just didn't know about the matter under discussion. No one quite said it but a dozen newsmen now came close to applying to this President Bert Andrews's remark about Harry Truman after the election of 1946: Dwight Eisenhower is becoming President of the United States.

The most immediate problem facing an Executive who was genuinely trying to lead was the rampant right-wing of the Republican Party, particularly one Joseph McCarthy. A relaxing America was stirring against the extremities of the Senator from Wisconsin. As Secretary of the Army Stevens apparently yielded to McCarthy on February 24, 1954, feelings were at white heat throughout the country. Within the next ten days Adlai Stevenson bluntly called the Republican Party "half McCarthy and half Eisenhower." The Republican Senator from Vermont, Ralph Flanders, took the floor of the Senate with anger and scorn. "He dons his warpaint," the elderly Vermonter said. "He goes into his war dance. He emits his warwhoops. He goes forth to battle and proudly returns with the scalp of a pink Army dentist. We may assume that this represents the depth and seriousness of Communist penetration at this time." That night Edward R. Murrow used his CBS documentary TV show, "See It Now," for a film-clip program which was potently anti-McCarthy. CBS stations reported a flood of applauding calls (15–1 against the Senator in San Francisco and New York, 2–1 against him in Chicago).

From the day of the Memorandum of Agreement the Administration moved against McCarthy, sometimes indirectly but steadily. Secretary Stevens countered the Memorandum with a strong statement and the President made plain that he backed his Secretary "one hundred percent." On March 11, 1954 the Army attacked with the charge that Senator McCarthy, Roy Cohn, and Francis Carr, the Subcommitee staff director, had sought, separately and collectively, by improper means, to obtain preferential treatment in the Army for G. David Schine, the Subcommittee consultant who was now a private in the Army. McCarthy and "associates" promptly replied with forty-six charges against the Army, of which the key one was that Secretary Stevens and John Adams, the department counselor, had tried to stop the Subcommittee's exposure of alleged Communists at Fort Monmouth and that they used Private Schine as a "hostage" to this end. Four more days and the Subcommittee voted to investigate the Army-McCarthy clash, with TV cameras in the room and with McCarthy temporarily replaced by the next ranking Republican, Senator Karl Mundt of South Dakota. Once again a TV spectacle would transfix the country and once again television would have a major part in shaping opinion on a critical national issue.

Shortly after 10 a.m. on April 22, 1954 the red lights in the cameras went on amid the florid Corinthian columns and the brocaded curtains of the large Senate Caucus Room. Senator Mundt tapped his big pipe, leaned forward, and delivered a little speech about how everything was going to be done with "dignity, fairness, and thoroughness." The ranking Democrat, John McClellan, said a few words to the same effect.

"Thank you very much, Senator McClellan," Chairman Mundt declared. "Our counsel, Mr. Jenkins, will now call the first witness." Ray Jenkins opened his mouth but the words came from down along the table. "A point of order, Mr. Chairman," McCarthy was saying. "May I raise a point of order?"

For thirty-six days and more than 2,000,000 words of testimony the hearings went on. A thousand impressions were driven into the public mind—Senator Mundt, roly-poly and pliable and so torn between his McCarthyite sympathies and the fact that he was supposed to be an impartial chairman that someone thought to call him the "tormented mushroom"; the Subcommittee's special counsel, Ray Jenkins, the homicide lawyer from Tellico Plains, Tennessee, chin stuck forward, intoning away with his questions; Senator John McClellan of Arkansas, the real terror of the Subcommittee, cadaverous and saturnine and pursuing everyone with a rasping logic; Robert Stevens, earnest and decent but having to pour out his, the Secretary of War's, pathetic attempts to mollify the friends of buck private G. David Schine; Roy Cohn, leaning over to make a point to McCarthy with a mouth that seemed perpetually pouting, obviously tremendously attached to Schine, obviously tremendously attached to Roy Cohn; Cohn and Schine, endlessly Cohn and Schine. But with each passing day one impression was having an increasingly potent effect on the millions at their TV sets. It was Joseph McCarthy, full-life, acting precisely like Joseph McCarthy.

"Point of order, point of order, Mr. Chairman," the Senator would interrupt in his scowling, sneering way until the children of the United States were imitating him on the streets. He repaid loyalty, like that of bumbling Senator Henry Dworshak of Idaho, by riding contemptuously over what the supporter was trying to say. He seized the floor from opponents by physical force, repeating in his strong, singsong voice until the opponent wearily gave way. McCarthy flung smears and constantly accused others of smearing; his aides tried to use a cropped photograph and he cried deceit at the Army; he sidetracked, blatantly sidetracked, and demanded the end of "diversionary tactics." Day after day he was still Joe McCarthy of the boyhood fights, ceaselessly, recklessly swinging for the knockout.

The more reckless McCarthy became, the more strongly the Administration opposed him. In mid-May the President threw the Constitution of the United States at him. McCarthy became involved in demands that were flagrant violations of the rights of the Executive and from the White House came a blunt statement of those rights, which "cannot be usurped by any individual who may seek to set himself above the laws of our land." No one, not even the President of the United States, not even a President of his own party, was immune to the Senator's standard weapon, the charge of softness toward Communism. McCarthy's answer to Eisenhower was to talk once again of "the evidence of treason that has been growing over the past twenty—" Then he paused and added darkly: "twenty-one years."

The hearings ground on. The changing national mood, the Presidential opposition, and the appearance McCarthy was making on TV were costing the Senator heavily in public support. But he was still not a ruined man. The evidence was certainly not giving either side a clear-cut victory in the issues immediately at stake. Had the McCarthy group sought preferential treatment for Schine? Clearly they had. Had the Army tried to stop McCarthy's investigation at Fort Monmouth? Equally clearly it had—though it was emphasizing that it was anxious to get "that type" of hearing ended because it demoralized the Army. Other charges and countercharges were tangled in a maze of conflicting testimony. Throughout the country a good many pro-McCarthy or anti-anti-McCarthy people were wavering but they were only wavering. The Senator could have emerged from the hearings partially intact if he had now made some moves to present himself as a reasonable, responsible person. But Joseph McCarthy was not interested in being partially intact. He went on looking for the haymaker and the right man was present to see to it that when the Senator swung his wildest, he swung himself flat on his face.

The chief Army counsel, Joseph Welch, was a senior partner of the eminent Boston law firm of Hale and Dorr and he had a well-deserved reputation as an infinitely shrewd trial lawyer. But friends emphasized more Welch's innate sense of human decency and his gift of ironic laughter. They associated him with his spacious colonial home in Walpole, where he puttered around studying his thermometers (there were twelve in the house), spending a day fishing or an evening in a game of carom or cribbage, delighting more than anything else in kindly, bantering talk about the cosmos. Mrs. Welch had a favorite story about the whimsicality of the man. She liked to tell how she had urged him to take up gardening, which he loathed, and he countered that he would garden if she would drink beer, which she detested. So on weekends the two would alternately garden in the broiling sun and stop for a beer in the shade, both grinning through their periods of suffering.

At the hearings Welch sat questioning away, his long, drooping face quizzical, his questions softly spoken and deftly insidious, dropping a damaging little jest and looking utterly surprised when people laughed. The sessions were only eight days old when the Army counsel drew blood. Welch was driving hard at a photograph which the McCarthy forces had produced, cropped to show only Stevens and Schine together although the original photograph contained two other men. The Army counsel brought out that the original had hung on Schine's wall and he questioned James Juliana, a Subcommittee employee who had arranged the cropping, as to why he had not brought the whole picture.

JULIANA: "I wasn't asked for it. . . ."
WELCH: ". . . You were asked for something different from the thing that hung on Schine's wall?"
JULIANA: "I never knew what hung on Schine's wall. . . ."
WELCH: "Did you think this came from a pixie? Where did you think this picture that I hold in my hand came from?"
JULIANA: "I had no idea."

There was a stir of voices and McCarthy interrupted. "Will counsel for my benefit define—I think he might be an expert on that—what a pixie is?"

Welch's face was beatific. "Yes. I should say, Mr. Senator, that a pixie is a close relative of a fairy. Shall I proceed, sir? Have I enlightened you?"

The spectators roared. Roy Cohn's pouting lips hardened into angry lines. The Senator glowered.

In the world of Joseph McCarthy nothing was more alien than the deft, and the Senator's feelings about Welch steadily mounted. He denied the Army counsel, or was wary of giving him, what he considered the ordinary camaraderie. McCarthy would walk up to friends and opponents alike, hand extended and the other hand grasping an arm, but he moved a wide circle around Joseph Welch. He first-named almost everybody —Secretary Stevens was "Bob" and the obviously hostile Senator Stuart Symington was "Stu." Welch was "Mr. Welch" or "the counsel."

Eight days before the hearings ended, on June 9, the Army counsel led Roy Cohn through a mocking, destructive cross-examination and McCarthy sat fuming. Now Welch was pressing Cohn as to why, if subversion was so serious at Fort Monmouth, he had not come crying alarm to Secretary Stevens. When Welch went ahead along this line, McCarthy began to grin broadly.

The Army counsel got in another dig at Cohn: "May I add my small voice, sir, and say whenever you know about a subversive or a Communist or a spy, please hurry. Will you remember these words?"

McCarthy broke in, bashed his way to attention. "In view of Mr. Welch's request that the information be given once we know of anyone who might be performing any work for the Communist Party, I think we should tell him that he has in his law firm a young man named Fisher whom he recommended, incidentally, to do work on this committee, who has been for a number of years a member of an organization which was named, oh, years and years ago, as the legal bulwark of the Communist Party. . . ."

The Senator was grinning ever more broadly, pausing now and then to lick his lips and savor his words. Roy Cohn sat in the witness chair, his legs dangling apart, the blood drained from his face, and once his lips seemed to be forming the words "Stop, stop." McCarthy went on: "Knowing that, Mr. Welch, I just felt that I had a duty to respond to your urgent request. . . . I have hesitated bringing that up, but I have been rather bored with your phony requests to Mr. Cohn here that he personally get every Communist out of government before sundown. . . .

"I am not asking you at this time to explain why you tried to foist him on this committee. Whether you knew he was a member of that Communist organization or not, I don't know. I assume you did not, Mr. Welch, because I get the impression that, while you are quite an actor, you play for a laugh, I don't think you have any conception of the danger of the Communist Party. I don't think you yourself would ever knowingly aid the Communist cause. I think you are unknowingly aiding it when you try to burlesque this hearing in which we are trying to bring out the facts, however."

Welch was staring at McCarthy with the look of a man who was watching the unbelievable. The puck was gone; his face was white with anger. "Senator McCarthy," Welch began, "I did not know—"

McCarthy turned away contemptuously and talked to Juliana. Twice the Army counsel demanded his attention and the Senator talked to Juliana in a still louder voice, telling him to get a newspaper clipping about Fisher so that it could be put in the record.

Welch plunged ahead. "You won't need anything in the record when I have finished telling you this.

"Until this moment, Senator, I think I never really gauged your cruelty or your recklessness. Fred Fisher is a young man who went to the Harvard Law School and came into my firm and is starting what looks to be a brilliant career with us.

"When I decided to work for this committee I asked Jim St. Clair . . . to be my first assistant. I said to Jim, 'Pick somebody in the firm who works under you that you would like.' He chose Fred Fisher and they came down on an afternoon plane. That night, when we had taken a little stab at trying to see what the case was about, Fred Fisher and Jim St. Clair and I went to dinner together. I then said to these two young men, 'Boys, I don't know anything about you except that I have always liked you, but if there is anything funny in the life of either one of you that would hurt anybody in this case you speak up quick.'

"Fred Fisher said, 'Mr. Welch, when I was in law school and for a period of months after, I belonged to the Lawyers Guild.' . . . I said, 'Fred, I just don't think I am going to ask you to work on the case. If I do, one of these days that will come out and go over national television and it will just hurt like the dickens.'

"So Senator, I asked him to go back to Boston.

"Little did I dream you could be so reckless and so cruel as to do an injury to that lad. It is true that he is still with Hale & Dorr. It is true that he will continue to be with Hale & Dorr. It is, I regret to say, equally true that I fear he shall always bear a scar needlessly inflicted by you. If it were in my power to forgive you for your reckless cruelty, I would do so. I like to think I am a gentle man, but your forgiveness will have to come from someone other than me."

The Senate Caucus Room was hushed. McCarthy fumbled with some papers, began saying that Welch had no right to speak of cruelty because he had "been baiting Mr. Cohn here for hours."

Welch cut off McCarthy. "Senator, may we not drop this? We know he belonged to the Lawyers Guild, and Mr. Cohn nods his head at me." Cohn was quite plainly nodding.

WELCH: "I did you, I think, no personal injury, Mr. Cohn."
COHN: "No, sir."
WELCH: "I meant to do you no personal injury, and if I did, I beg your pardon."

Cohn nodded again. The Army counsel turned back to McCarthy and his emotion was so great that on the TV screens his eyes seemed to be filling with tears. "Let us not assassinate this lad further, Senator. You have done enough. Have you no sense of decency, sir, at long last? Have you left no sense of decency?"

McCarthy tried to ask the Army counsel a question about Fisher. Welch cut him off again. He had recovered his composure now and his voice was cold with scorn. "Mr. McCarthy, I will not discuss this with you further. You have sat within

6 feet of me, and could have asked me about Fred Fisher. You have brought it out. If there is a God in heaven, it will do neither you nor your cause any good. I will not discuss it further. I will not ask Mr. Cohn any more questions. You, Mr. Chairman, may, if you will, call the next witness."

For a long few seconds the hush in the room continued. One of the few rules Chairman Mundt had tried hard to enforce was the one against demonstrations and six policemen were present to assist him. But suddenly the room shook with applause. For the first time in the memory of Washington observers, press photographers laid aside their cameras to join in the ovation for Welch. Chairman Mundt made no effort to interfere and instead soon called for a five-minute recess.

Joseph McCarthy sat slouched in his chair, breathing heavily. Spectators and reporters avoided him. Finally he found someone to talk to. He spread out his hands in a gesture of puzzlement and asked: "What did I do wrong?"

Joseph McCarthy would never know. And that June day, 1954, millions at their TV sets learned once and for all that Joseph McCarthy would never know.

The children stopped saying "Point of order, point of order." The housewives went back to *I Love Lucy*. A different subject was filling conversations. Agricultural prices were dropping, the textile and auto industries were laying off workers, general unemployment was mounting (by mid-1954 the government figures put it over 2,000,000). Everywhere in the United States there was talk of depression.

November 1954 was not far away and GOP political leaders shuddered at the thought of a Republican Administration having to face the polls during a decline in the economy. They were keenly aware that the success in 1952 had been much more an Eisenhower than a Republican victory and they did not ignore the association in so many people's minds between Republicanism and the depression of 1929. The elections of 1954 came, the Democrats did take both houses of Congress, and the point went on having its effects in high GOP circles. It was a continuing prod to an Administration which was not indisposed for other reasons to move from the conservatism of its early period.

The domestic policies that emerged in 1954 and 1955 represented no sharp break. The Administration kept its businessman tone. Just before the elections of 1954, Secretary of Defense Wilson was at it again with his observation, in discussing unemployment, that "I've always liked bird dogs better than kennel-fed dogs myself—you know one who'll get out and hunt for food rather than sit on his fanny and yell." As late as May 1956 another high Administration official, a deputy assistant to the President, Howard Pyle, was apologizing for his "off-hand comment" that the "right to suffer [by unemployment] is one of the joys of a free economy." Particularly in its policies toward government finance, power, and public resources the Administration continued the lines of its first period to such an extent that the New Dealish had tart words. Which was the more serious corruption? they demanded to know. Mink coats and deep-freezers or disposals of the national forests and utility contracts which could mean millions for a few corporations? And Administration figures were still capable of providing caricatures of the conservative leeriness of welfare expenditures by the federal government. When the Salk polio vaccine was announced on April 12, 1955, the problem arose as to how poor families were to get the protection without having to go through the humiliation of declaring that they could not pay for it. A bill was presented in Congress to have the federal government provide free vaccine for all children. Mrs. Oveta Culp Hobby, Secretary of Health, Education and Welfare, was horrified. The bill was "socialized medicine"—by "the back door."

Yet the shift, however restrained, was on. In late 1954 a White House adviser remarked: "The President's changed, George Humphrey's changed—we've all changed since we came here." Eisenhower was seeing more and more of Dr. Arthur Burns, a Columbia economist and now chairman of the Council of Economic Advisers, who believed that "it is no longer a matter of serious controversy whether the Government should play a positive role in helping to maintain a high

level of economic activity. What we debate nowadays is not the
need for controlling business cycles, but rather the nature of
governmental action, its timing and its extent." Humphrey,
who had taken Taftite steps to raise interest rates, was encouraging measures that would bring them down. "The first
moves," he explained in his pragmatic way, "were to stop price
rises and inventory inflation. Then, finding we had credit a
little tight, we turned around and loosened it."

In April 1954 Secretary of Agriculture Benson cut the price
support of butter from 90 to 75 per cent of parity. The dairy
industry was furious but Benson, probably the most dogged
free-enterprise man in the Cabinet, indicated he would stand
firm. The Secretary of Agriculture was soon summoned to the
White House. "Ezra," the President said, "I think maybe we
went a mite too far this time." Eisenhower pulled a pad of
paper toward him and drew a base and a summit line. He
pointed to the bottom line. "This is where we are." Then he
tapped the upper line. "And this is where we eventually want
to arrive. But we'll have to go more slowly with our changes—
like this." The pencil zig-zagged up the length of the sheet.
"This is the way we'll have to go—first this way, then that. But
we'll always be headed here"—*here* meaning an agriculture
more responsive to the play of market forces.

The threatened depression did not come but the Administration shift continued. The trend is summarized by a comparison
of the President's 1953, 1954, and 1955 State-of-the-Union messages. The 1953 document had an unmistakable Taftite tone.
By 1955 the nature of the address had changed to one which the
New York Times correctly characterized as a call "for limited
extension of measures along the lines of the New Deal." The
new direction was plain in the highway, school, slum-clearance,
medical insurance, and widened social security bills sent to
Congress. They were decidedly un-New Dealish in the amounts
of money called for, some of the methods proposed, and the
extent to which the Administration pressed for their passage.
But they were also decidedly non-Taftian in their assumption
that the federal government had to assume responsibility for
broad social needs. So far as amount of expenditure was con-

cerned, the programs would raise federal spending in these categories to an annual level four billion dollars higher than it had been under Truman.

Throughout the shift of his Administration, Eisenhower was feeling his way toward some general statement of the domestic aims of his Presidency. He no longer emphasized "conservatism" alone. He tried "dynamic conservatism," "progressive, dynamic conservatism," "progressive moderation," "moderate progressivism," "positive and progressive." But more and more he adopted a formula along the lines of the one he expressed in December 1954. The Administration, Eisenhower remarked then, "must be liberal when it was talking about the relationship between the Government and the individual, conservative when talking about the national economy and the individual's pocketbook."

Adlai Stevenson met a Chicago press conference and said: "I have never been sure what progressive moderation means, or was it conservative progressivism? [Laughter] I have forgotten, and I am not sure what dynamic moderation or moderate dynamism means. I am not even sure what it means when one says that he is a conservative in fiscal affairs and a liberal in human affairs. I assume what it means is that you will strongly recommend the building of a great many schools to accommodate the needs of our children, but not provide the money. [Laughter]" Unquestionably there was something ludicrously muddled about the Administration's efforts to describe itself in its new direction, but the very confusion bespoke the essence of where it was going. Conservative in economic matters and liberal in human affairs—the social gains of the New Deal and the Fair Deal were to be preserved, some extensions would be advocated but for the most part not vigorously pressed, and the whole was to be set within a severe budget consciousness.

The most striking fact about the Eisenhower domestic policies, in their earlier or later phase, was the same characteristic that had marked the programs of the Truman years—action on the home front was usually much less significant than action abroad.

In the all-important foreign field, the Administration was paralleling its domestic shift. It held to the main lines of the New Look defense policy. But it went along with an increasing number of amendments to it. It was noticeable, too, that the Administration was defending the policy less and less in terms of budget-balancing and more by that totally non-ideological argument—the world situation and the development of new weapons dictated a shift in the American defense. As time went on, the question arose just how new the New Look was. How much was it a reversion to Taftism and how much simply another instance of the immemorial American habit—practiced after every war and decidedly practiced by the Truman Administration—of slashing defense expenditures when the guns were quiet?

Still more change from the early Eisenhower days was evident in the attitude toward economic aid and technical assistance. The talk within the Administration of ending all such expenditures died down. The smallness of the appropriations asked for by the President continued to distress deeply men of a Point Four persuasion. Chester Bowles, Ambassador to India during the Truman Administration, cried out: "Let it not be said by future historians that in the second decade after World War II freedom throughout the world died of a balanced budget." But a degree of economic aid continued, with the Administration fighting off right-wing attempts to cut severely the amount or add hamstringing restrictions. Meanwhile Eisenhower was putting into effect something of an atomic age Point Four—his plan for the United States to join in spreading the peaceful uses of atomic energy by giving knowledge and by selling atomic reactors at half price.

The change in the Administration's policy toward the world was most marked in the most important aspect, the matter of general attitude. The basic question was the same as it had been throughout the post-World War II period: To what extent was the United States going to break with its deeply felt tradition of the quick, final solution, brought about largely by the United States alone? The specific debate was now less over the word "containment" than the word "coexistence," with all its implications of a long, slow process of adjustment during which the continued power of Communism would be assumed and the world would stay thoroughly entangled.

Any favorable mention of coexistence brought from Mc-Carthy-type sentiment cries of treason. To many Americans of less extreme views, the idea was dangerous nonsense. In particular Senator William Knowland, the Republican leader in the Senate, was arguing forcibly that coexistence was a "Trojan horse" that would lull America into a sense of false security, to be followed by disaster. The United States, Knowland solemnly warned, must take "every possible step"—often the Senator sounded as if this included war—to throw back Communism or in time it would find itself overwhelmed. "The civilizations that flourished and died in the past had opportunities for a limited period of time to change the course of history. Sooner or later, however, they passed 'the point of no return,' and the decisions were no longer theirs to make."

1954–5 saw Secretary Dulles move appreciably toward the coexistence position. His speeches became a good deal less impatient and bellicose. He dropped any emphasis on liberation and instead gave most of his enormous energies to building the Southeast Asia Treaty Organization—a NATO-type defense organization which certainly assumed a long, hard pull. Of still greater importance, President Eisenhower, who had never entirely shared his Secretary's belligerence, was more and more determining the general outlines and the tone of the country's foreign policy.

With each passing month the President increased his emphasis on the importance of the slow processes of conciliation and adjustment in world affairs. In July 1954 UN headquarters were filled with talk that Red China was about to be admitted. Senator Knowland, speaking for a considerable body of opinion in the United States, was bitter. America, he declared, should make plain that it would leave the UN the day Red China entered. As for himself, if the UN made the move he would resign his Republican leadership in the Senate to lead an agitation to take the United States out of the world organization. What did President Eisenhower think? reporters wanted to know. He did not believe that Red China would be admitted, Eisenhower replied. But if the UN should make this mistake, the attitude of the American government would have to be decided on the basis of how it could best advance the cause of peace. But what about Knowland's insistence on American withdrawal? the newsmen pressed. The President said he had not yet reached any such decision. No, he hadn't.

In November 1954 Red China announced that it had sentenced as spies thirteen Americans, eleven of them fliers who had fought in the Korean War. It was not only obvious that the charges against the fliers were fraudulent; Red China had clearly violated the Korean armistice agreement by not repatriating the airmen. A good many Americans besides William Knowland were furious, and the Senator demanded that the Chinese should be handed an ultimatum: Release the fliers or the United States would impose a naval blockade.

Eisenhower made plain to his press conference that he believed a blockade meant war and he was against imposing one. The President went further. He delivered a little fifteen-minute speech which he permitted the reporters to quote directly. A President, Eisenhower said, "experiences exactly the same resentment, the same anger, the same kind of sense of frustration almost, when things like this occur, as other Americans, and his impulse is to lash out. . . . In many ways the easy course for a President, for the Administration, is to adopt a truculent, publicly bold, almost insulting attitude." But the easy course had one terrible flaw—it led toward war. The sensible path was the hard way and "the hard way is to have the courage to be patient, tirelessly to seek out every single avenue open to us in the hope finally of leading the other side to a little better understanding of the honesty of our intentions. . . ."

The courage to be patient, the slow, hard way, using every possible avenue—a climax of coexistence was near and Eisenhower did not stand in its way. During all the bitternesses over foreign affairs in the post war, one image in particular had inflamed the critics of the Roosevelt-Truman policies. It was their picture of the President of the United States sitting in

Big Four conferences, joking and tossing off Martinis with the Soviet leaders, signing secret agreements that sold more millions down the river to Communism. As the summer of 1955 came on, the pressure for a Big Four conference steadily mounted. The Russians were calling for one; a good deal of world opinion agreed; in the Democratic-controlled Congress, Senator Walter George of Georgia, chairman of the powerful Senate Foreign Relations Committee, was pressing hard. President Eisenhower moved warily. He attempted to make certain that the time and the conditions were propitious for American purposes and he announced firmly that there would be no secret agreements—probably no agreements at all but merely exploratory talks. Then, on July 18, 1955, he joined the leaders of Britain, France, and the Soviet Union at a Big Four conference in Geneva.

The Russians tried hard to tell the world that they were men of peace. Party chief Nikita Khrushchev grinned endlessly for the photographers and said: "Things are different now." Premier Nikolai Bulganin went around in an open car beaming at everybody and waving his gray fedora. Foreign Minister Vyacheslav Molotov, he of the eternal *nyets* in the UN, got to talking of the photograph of him on a recent American visit wearing a ten-gallon hat. He'd like people to think of him, the Foreign Minister said to reporters, "as something more than a man who says no." The hat didn't fit, Molotov added, "but it's more important to have good publicity than to have a hat that fits."

If the Russians were friendly, Dwight Eisenhower was coexistence incarnate. He opened the conference with a moving appeal for "a new spirit. . . . No doubt there are among our nations philosophical convictions which are in many respects irreconcilable. Nothing that we can say or do here will change that fact. However, it is not always necessary that people should think alike and believe alike before they can work together." The President overlooked no amenity. Eisenhower, Bulganin later recalled delightedly, "opened the Martini road." When the President learned that the daughter of his World War II colleague, Soviet Marshal Georgi Zhukov, was about to be

married, he promptly sent to Moscow gifts of a desk pen in-
scribed "From the President of the United States" and a port-
able American radio. And then as the conference neared its
end, with many observers declaring that it was really getting
nowhere, the President rose from his seat, began reading his
formal paper prepared by the State Department, put it aside.
He took off his glasses, laid them on the table, continued ex-
temporaneously.

"Gentlemen," he said, "I have been searching my heart and
mind for something that I could say here that could convince
everyone of the great sincerity of the United States in approaching this problem of disarmament." Eisenhower turned and
directly faced the Russians. "I should address myself for a
moment principally to the delegates from the Soviet Union,
because our two great countries admittedly possess new and
terrible weapons in quantities which do give rise in other
parts of the world, or reciprocally, to the fears and dangers of
surprise attack."

The translations of the President's words were not yet coming through but his face alone, cocked to the side in earnest-
ness and gravity, told that he was speaking important words.
The usual bustle of the conference room quieted. "I propose,
therefore," Eisenhower went on, "that we take a practical step,
that we begin an arrangement very quickly, as between ourselves—immediately. These steps would include: to give each
other a complete blueprint of our military establishment. . . .
Next, to provide within our countries facilities for aerial pho-
tography to the other country." Firmly Eisenhower added:
"What I propose, I assure you, would be but a beginning."

The Russians were sitting bolt upright. In the United States
experts broke into puzzled discussion. How practical was the
plan? Why should the Soviet exchange something it had,
knowledge of the American military establishment, for something the United States might well not have and very much
wanted—information about the Russian facilities? What was
the essence of the Eisenhower foreign policy anyhow, with its
wariness toward the world on the one hand and on the other
hand its invitation to fly Soviet planes over America? The

President found no phrase to express his program in international affairs, at least nothing as simple as his conservative-liberal description of his domestic policies. Perhaps it was because the emerging program for abroad, with its restraints on defense money, its hesitancies about large-scale economic aid, and its acceptance of coexistence, was—even more confusingly than the domestic policy—a blend of conservatism and of New Dealism. Perhaps it was because the Eisenhower foreign policy, in a very real sense, was Robert Taft in many of its tactics and Dean Acheson in its larger strategy.

When the President's plane, the *Columbine III,* neared the Washington airport, a summer shower was spattering the Capital. Vice-President Richard Nixon issued an instruction to the officials going out to the airport. No umbrellas, the Vice-President said, because people might be reminded of Prime Minister Neville Chamberlain coming back with his umbrella from the Munich appeasement of Hitler. Nixon need hardly have been concerned. By the summer of 1955 Eisenhower's in-between concept of the President's role, his conservative-liberal domestic policies, his mixed attitudes in foreign affairs, his warm but unaggressive personality, were sweeping him to a political potency unapproached since the heyday of Franklin Roosevelt.

The right wing of the Republican Party lay at his feet, powerless if not shattered. Senator Knowland was issuing no more calls for ultimatums and he was making it very plain that he was for Eisenhower first and last. To the farthest right there were only occasional yawps breaking the still of the cemetery. Senator McCarthy was now duly censured by the Senate of the United States and by a vote of 67 to 22. Flailing away at the descending oblivion, he summoned a press conference and "apologized" for having supported Eisenhower in 1952. The President smiled and the nation yawned.

Harry Truman was stirring restlessly. Where were the give-em-hell assaults? Why were there so few calls for "real" liberalism? The head of the Democratic Party, Adlai Stevenson, would soon answer: "We must take care lest we confuse moderation with mediocrity, lest we settle for half answers to hard problems. . . . [But] I agree that it is time for catching our breath; I agree that moderation is the spirit of the times."

Moderation, middle-of-the-road—the phrases were filling the country until Charles Comiskey, vice-president of the Chicago White Sox, could say with a straight face: "Henceforth, we'll do our trading in moderation, we'll be middle-of-the-roaders." In every part of America, in every part of American living, people were working out the clashes created by a decade of turbulent change with a thousand conscious and unconscious compromises. If women were saying they wanted babies, not careers, they were also making sure that the phone number of a baby sitter was at hand. If the intellectuals were discussing a "new conservatism," the new conservatism, for the most part, was heavily streaked with the old liberalism. The trend was emphasized by the reports from the oncoming generation. The pollsters polled, the magazines questioned away, and in Los Angeles a UCLA coed summarized the findings in a few words. What, in general, did she want out of living? "Why, a good sensible life." The coed added quickly: "But, you know, of course not too darned sensible."

Somehow, amid all the bitter disagreements of the post-World War II period, the United States had felt its way to a genuinely national mood. It was not the kind of arrival that could be announced in ringing tones. It contained, in fact, a determination not to be too sure where you were or where you ought to go. It was nothing more or less than the decision on the part of a people who were so in-between in so many of their attitudes to go on cautiously, hopefully maintaining equilibrium. In the murky way of history, another era in the life of the United States was closing. The ten years from the end of World War II in the summer of 1945 to the Geneva Summit Conference in the summer of 1955 were over—and over not only in a chronological sense.

Some astute observers have found little good in the decade, only a muddled descent of American civilization. The "Dismal Decade," the "Years of Neuroses," the "Age of the Vacuum Tube," they have called the period. They see in it the culmination of deeply disturbing trends in the national life, and picture the end-product as a country dominated by a banal mass culture, a worship of the material, the gaudy, the violent, and the mediocre.

Certainly such portrayals cannot be airily waved aside. After all, the America of 1955 was a country where Altman's in New York City had quite a run on mink-handled openers for beer cans and a women's shop in Beverly Hills, California, sent out charge plates made of fourteen-carat gold; where the disc jockeys took off "O, Happy Day" only to put on "If a Hottentot taught a tot to talk ere the tot could totter"; where the stock-market craze reached the point that millions of shares of blatantly wildcat uranium ventures were snapped up; where a major crime was committed every fifteen seconds; where approximately one hundred million dollars a year—or just about four times the expenditures on public libraries—were paid out for comic books; where the most popular of all its citizens, Dwight Eisenhower, defined an intellectual as "a man who takes more words than is necessary to say more than he knows."

Yet there is another way of viewing the decade, a way with a quite different emphasis. The ten years from 1945 to 1955 were a decade of high importance in American history, a Crucial Decade. When World War II ended, the Half-Century of Revolution in domestic affairs had reached a critical state. It had gone far enough to influence profoundly American living and to pile up a strong and bitter opposition. During the years immediately after V-J Day, the problem of international affairs reached a similar critical juncture. The emergence of the world-wide Communist threat brought changes in American foreign policy fully as revolutionary as the trends which had been developing on the domestic scene, and these jolting breaks with tradition also provoked potent resistance. Intermingling with the mounting storm, taking strength from it and giving strength to it, was the surge of McCarthyism which, in essence, amounted to an exasperated urge to club everything back into a simpler, more comfortable pattern. At the height of the drive for the traditional, during the tensions of the goadingly untraditional Korean War, two fateful questions were emerging. Would the United States continue, through extensions of the welfare state and of welfare capitalism and a variety of other techniques, the Half-Century of Revolution in domestic affairs? Would it continue moving along the new international path marked by the attitudes clustering around the concepts of containment and coexistence? What is crucial about the Crucial Decade is that during the years from 1945 to 1955 the American people faced these questions and they answered them.

Whatever the swings from Democrats to Republicans, McCarthyism to moderation, intellectualish New Dealers to practical-minded businessmen, there was a basic continuity in the era. Gradually, with many a contrary movement and sidewise venture, a greater and greater percentage of the population decided that the Half-Century of Revolution in domestic affairs was here to stay and that it should be forwarded. Still more gradually, and with much more bridling, an increasing percentage came to the conclusion that the traditional idea of a quick, total solution to international problems, executed largely by the United States alone, simply would not do. The coming of a general attitude of equilibrium in the summer of 1955 was accompanied by the arrival of a broad consensus in the thinking of Americans about the basic public issues of the day. Most of them had come to agree on continuing social change at home, if not so much, so swiftly, and on a shift in their attitude toward the world, if not so sharply, so expensively.

The continuity of the period also expressed itself in political terms. In a very real sense, the Truman and the early Eisenhower years blended into one development. It was the Truman Administration that began codifying New Dealism in domestic affairs—slowing down its pace, pushing its attitude only in areas of outstanding need. (It is easy to overlook the fact that as early as 1949 Truman was describing his domestic policy as the "middle-course" and defining the phrase in a way that Eisenhower would not have found too hard to accept.) Meanwhile the Truman years were also bringing the departures in foreign policy. The Eisenhower Administration, whatever its modifications, continued the codification in domestic affairs and accepted and extended the breakaways in the foreign field. Moreover, it was bringing the Republican Party, a large part of which had been talking for twenty years as if it would do everything drastically differently, into line with the long-running policies and thus changing them from partisan to national programs. The consensus on fundamental public issues that was reached in the summer of 1955 was so genuine a consensus because it developed slowly and survived the test of savage political warfare.

From the perspective of future years the arrival at this consensus may well be considered one of the most important facts in all the American story. Over the centuries more than one powerful nation has, out of meanness and shortsightedness, tried to walk against a great tide of human aspirations and been swallowed ignominiously. The two problems Americans faced during the years 1945–55 were actually parts of one such tide—a world-wide struggle of poor people or men of lower status to achieve more income and more of a sense of human dignity. Inside the United States the surge took the form of the demands for the Half-Century of Revolution. Around the world it appeared as the stirrings of underdeveloped colonial lands under Communist, partially Communist, or non-Communist impetus. On occasion during the exasperating, frightening years after World War II, the American people came close to saying that they had enough of aspirations, foreign or domestic. But they never quite said it and in time they managed to say something quite different.

As the Crucial Decade closed in the summer of 1955, the American people could face the onrushing years and the onrushing crises with one solid fact to buttress them. Whatever their addiction to chrome, comic books, and comic-book politics, whatever their yearning for the prepackaged, one-minute solution to everything, they had not, however sorely tempted, committed the supreme foolishness of trying to defy history.

For Further Reading

Although Goldman's account remains the best survey of postwar America, a briefer interpretative essay by Herbert Agar, *The Price of Power* (1957) is a deft summary. Extensive factual treatments of the period may be found in twentieth-century textbooks, the best of which is Arthur S. Link and William B. Catton, *American Epoch* (3rd ed., 1967). Of exceptional interest is Samuel Lubell, *The Future of American Politics* (3rd rev. ed., 1965), especially with regard to his ethnic analyses of postwar politics. Works on American foreign relations are mentioned in the bibliographic note following the preceding selection of this volume.

For a sense of the home front during World War II, see Jack Goodman, ed., *While You Were Gone* (1946). Scholars have only recently begun to explore domestic wartime and early postwar politics in detail. Two early works, Roland Young, *Congressional Politics in the Second World War* (1956) and Joel Seidman, *American Labor from Defense to Reconversion* (1953) are good treatments of their topics. For a detailed examination of policymaking for World War II veterans during 1940–1946, see Davis R. B. Ross, *Preparing for Ulysses* (1969). Richard Polenberg has edited a useful collection of documents for the war period, *America at War* (1968).

The Truman years are covered more or less adequately by Cabell Phillips, *The Truman Presidency* (1966); Jonathan Daniels, *The Man of Independence* (1950); and Alfred Steinberg, *The Man from Missouri* (1962). Barton J. Bernstein's "America in War and Peace: The Test of Liberalism," in Bernstein, ed., *Towards a New Past* (1967), pp. 289–321, is a sharp critique by an able revisionist or New Left historian. Bernstein has edited two useful collections concerning the Truman period; the first, co-edited by Allen J. Matusow, contains documents, *The Truman Administration* (1966); and the second, essays, *The Politics and Policies of the Truman Administration* (1969). For the more advanced student, the Truman

Administration's reconversion, labor, housing, and agricultural programs are covered respectively in Stephen Kemp Bailey, *Congress Makes a Law* (1950); R. Alton Lee, *Truman and Taft-Hartley* (1966); Richard C. Davies, *Housing Reform During the Truman Administration* (1966) ; and Allen J. Matusow, *Farm Politics and Policies of the Truman Years* (1967). The President's memoirs are indispensable for an understanding of the period: *Years of Decision* (1955) and *Years of Trial and Hope* (1956).

The Eisenhower years are the subject of two fine journalistic accounts, Richard Rovere, *Affairs of State* (1956), and Samuel Lubell, *The Revolt of the Moderates* (1956). Three biographies of Eisenhower, the first two flattering, the third critical, are Robert J. Donovan, *Eisenhower: The Inside Story* (1956), Merle J. Pusey, *Eisenhower, the President* (1956), and Marquis Childs, *Eisenhower: Captive Hero* (1958). A good collection of essays and book excerpts is Dean Albertson, ed., *Eisenhower as President* (1963). The President's own memoirs, *The White House Years: Mandate for Change, 1953–1956* (1963), and *The White House Years: Waging Peace* (1965) form the core of the firsthand accounts. Members of the administration have added their voices, favorably in the cases of his executive secretary, Sherman Adams, *Firsthand Report* (1961); his Secretary of Agriculture, Ezra Taft Benson, *Cross Fire* (1962); his Vice-President, Richard M. Nixon, *Six Crises* (1962); and his Atomic Energy Commissioner, Lewis Strauss, *Men and Decisions* (1962); and critically in the case of his former speechwriter, Emmet John Hughes, *Ordeal of Power* (1963).

The McCarthy controversy has occasioned a spate of books and articles. Pioneering works on the underlying reasons for McCarthy's appeal are Richard Hofstadter, *The Paranoid Style in American Politics and Other Essays* (1965) and Daniel Bell, ed., *The New American Right* (1955). Although difficult, the first two chapters of Michael Paul Rogin's *The Intellectuals and McCarthy* (1967) contain penetrating summaries and analyses of the literature on McCarthy. The most readable indictment of McCarthy is Richard Rovere, *Senator Joe McCarthy* (1959); the ablest defense, William F. Buckley, Jr. and L.

Brent Bozell, *McCarthy and His Enemies* (1954). A dispassionate attempt to assess the extent of Communist infiltration is
Earl Latham, *The Communist Controversy in Washington*
(1966), which concludes that a significant amount of espionage had occurred. Latham has also edited a handy collection
of views on McCarthy, *The Meaning of McCarthyism* (1966).

Kennedy on the Eve

Arthur M. Schlesinger, Jr.

Time plays tricks with historical evaluations. In a brief ten years—a veritable blinking of the eye in man's history—the assessment of John Fitzgerald Kennedy has fluctuated wildly. During the 1960 presidential primaries, Kennedy aroused moderate enthusiasm. Longtime liberal Democrats had strong emotional attachments to the 1952 and 1956 candidate, Adlai E. Stevenson; conservative and Southern party members, although not united, were suspicious of Kennedy and his well-organized entourage. Even after the July convention the young politician hardly seemed to differ from his opponent, Richard M. Nixon: both were earnest and reputed to be political opportunists. A large hint of JFK's ability to excite people came with his famous television debates with Nixon in the closing weeks of the campaign. The inaugural address thrilled even more; Kennedy seemed to offer a fresh approach to politics. The renewal he promised sounded, to those who had ancient memories, like Woodrow Wilson pledging a national reconstruction almost a half-century before.

The post-inaugural bustle gave way to two crises, one immediate, the other prolonged; each adversely affected his reputation. The first was the Bay of Pigs invasion of Cuba. Kennedy's image as the cool, reasoning, and ef-

Source: Arthur M. Schlesinger, *A Thousand Days* (Boston: Houghton Mifflin Co., 1965), pp. 77–94, 99–113. Copyright © 1965 by Arthur M. Schlesinger. Reprinted by permission of the publisher.

ficient chief executive received a heavy blow. The failure of the new administration to scrutinize the entire abortive operation seemed to place the young President in the same category as his predecessor; the Bay of Pigs and the U-2 incident had embarrassingly similar features. The second crisis involved his legislative relationships. As the months of his presidency slipped by, Kennedy found that he could hardly move a nation until he could move a Congress. His legislative trophy case remained uncluttered during his presidency: for 1961, minor social security changes, an area redevelopment program, the Peace Corps, and a disarmament agency; for 1962, manpower training and highway building programs, a modest tax reform, and a more important foreign trade expansion act; for 1963, support for health services education, and Senate approval of a nuclear test ban treaty. The great promises of 1960 were unrealized: no civil rights legislation, no federal aid to education, no medical care legislation for the aged, and no major tax reform. His image was further tarnished.

There were redeeming notes, however. Although the Bay of Pigs was a fiasco, the President did assume total responsibility; people could chalk up the incident to his inexperience. His handling of the Cuban missile crisis during the autumn of 1962 elicited general approval, despite the grave concern felt about the possibilities of war. In fact, the stance of the administration on foreign affairs seemed sound: a firm, yet patient attitude toward the Soviet Union in regard to Cuba, Berlin, and nuclear testing. His firmness in facing down the steel industry in April 1962 when it attempted to raise prices ruffled some business feathers, but did convey the sense of being in charge. Lastly, his endorsement of the Justice Department's expanded civil rights activities helped offset to some degree the legislative failures in this area.

By November 1963, President Kennedy stood at a balance point. He spoke with eloquence about the gravity of world affairs and the opportunities for the United States to serve mankind. His oratory, like Woodrow Wilson's before him, stirred people abroad and at home: If

"Ich bin ein Berliner" electrified West German audiences, so his admonition (following his approval of the Test Ban Treaty) of "Let us . . . step back from the shadows of war and seek out the way of peace," heartened Americans. But in the realm of domestic reform the President had achieved little. His portrait was yet unfinished.

The assassin's bullet of November 22, 1963, has altered the image. Kennedy, struck down in his prime, has become a martyr. In the painful days following his death some of the things that had long been noted about his presidency took on added significance. He did represent the passing of the torch to a new generation of Americans. If it seemed that he had achieved so little, his real importance—some would say his greatness—lay in what he stood for: the long, painful, struggle for human rights and reason.

Yet in that symbolism there lay imbedded the very grounds for criticism. In the 1970's, some youths may well view JFK as proof of the failure of torch-passing, the failure of the democratic process itself. A decade has passed and much of the new frontier remains a frontier still. On another level, Kennedy seemed to hold out a hope that reasonable, efficient men of state could curb the unreason and violence of the post-1939 world. But it has been easy for some to see the Kennedy administrators as the sophisticated (therefore more dangerous) perpetrators and manipulators of a "military-industrial complex." The Southeast Asian war found, after all, its first major escalation not under the administration of a former five-star general, but at the hands of a civilian-dominated bureaucracy bemused with the technical promise of "paramilitary" warfare.

Nonetheless, the suggestion that Kennedy now commands an allegiance unmatched in his lifetime seems valid. Inside of six months of his murder, twenty books had been published, ranging from photographs to compilations of his wit; within two years the early ephemera had been supplanted by distinguished historical accounts. The finest work came from the pen of Arthur M. Schlesinger, Jr., a perceptive historian and "resident intellectual" at the White House during the Kennedy years. Schlesinger had been undaunted by the difficulties of writing contemporary history. He had observed that "the historian of the past is, in a sense, little more than the contemporary historian whose witnesses are dead—and therefore can write without fear of rebuttal."

Schlesinger's account, it goes without saying, is on the whole quite favorable to his subject. Still, Schlesinger is a master craftsman, and his biography of JFK may well stand in the future as the most perceptive and lucid account of the Kennedy Administration. James MacGregor Burns, himself a noted biographer of a noted President, has commented that, "a great President has found a great historian." The selection that follows permits the reader to judge for himself.

$\mathcal{M}$y first knowledge of John F. Kennedy went back to undergraduate days at Harvard twenty-five years before. His older brother, Joseph P. Kennedy, Jr., was one of my classmates, a confident, gregarious young man with a rollicking personality that swept all before it. He seemed destined to be a man of power, though one did not feel in him the inward and reflective quality one later found in his brothers John and Robert. But I never knew him well. He was a brave man and died in the war.

His younger brother John arrived in Cambridge as a freshman when Joe and I were in our third year. In those days the freshman class put on a smoker each spring; and the Freshman Smoker of 1937 shamed the older classes with its prodigies of talent imported from Broadway and Hollywood. One learned that young Jack Kennedy was responsible for this triumph. Even upper-classmen were impressed. I saw him from time to time in the Yard but do not recall that I ever exchanged a word with him. Joe and I finished Harvard in 1938, Jack two years later.

My next memory of Jack Kennedy goes back to London in the summer of 1944 when, as buzz-bombs roared overhead, I

read one day in *The New Yorker* John Hersey's quiet account
of his adventures in the Pacific. In 1946 I heard that he had
returned to Boston to run for Congress. In due course he won
the Democratic nomination for the House of Representatives
in the 11th district, which included Cambridge, and was
elected to the seat vacated by James M. Curley, who had once
again become mayor of Boston. Kennedy and I renewed, or
began, our acquaintance the following winter in Washington.
I saw him from time to time in these years before the Presidency, with increasing frequency toward the end of the fifties,
though I was not one of his intimates, if indeed he had real
intimates outside his family.

In these years I began to understand better the complexity
of mind and emotion which underlay that contained and
ironic exterior, but only a little better. Kennedy had to an
exceptional degree the gift of friendship and, in consequence,
a great diversity of friends; part of his gift was to give each
the sense that he alone had a clue to the mystery. The friends
came in layers—the Choate and Harvard friends, the friends
from the Navy, the social friends from Palm Beach and Newport, the Irish friends, the senatorial friends, the intellectual
friends—and each layer considered itself closest to the center.
But Kennedy kept the layers apart and included and baffled
them all. The ultimate reserve was a source of his fascination
and his power.

The Kennedy Family

How had it all come about? Part of the answer, of course,
lay in his upbringing. He was born into a family that was
large, warm and spirited. There is no point in idealizing the
Kennedys. Like any family, it had its share of tensions. Young
Joe Kennedy, the oldest son, was bigger and stronger than the
others; he was the leader of the children and occasionally, in
discharging his role, something of a bully. No doubt Jack
Kennedy was shoved around a good deal by his older brother.

But, more than most families, the Kennedys were bound together by a love which gave all the children a fundamental confidence. With its subtle and disparate solidarity, the family nourished a capacity for competition, for individuality and for loyalty.

Moreover, it was an Irish family. Little is more dangerous than to try to explain a man in terms of supposed ethnic traits. In most respects, Kennedy departed considerably from the Irish-American stereotype. He was reticent, patrician, bookish, urbane—much closer, indeed, to a young Lord Salisbury than to a young Al Smith or, for that matter, to a young John F. Fitzgerald. Yet the Irishness remained a vital element in his constitution. It came out in so many ways—in the quizzical wit, the eruptions of boisterous humor, the relish for politics, the love of language, the romantic sense of history, the admiration for physical daring, the toughness, the joy in living, the view of life as comedy and as tragedy.

And it gave him a particular slant on American society. Though the Kennedy family was well established politically and financially—Jack's grandfather had twice been mayor of Boston; his father was a Harvard graduate and a successful businessman—it was still marginal socially in Brahmin Boston; and its folk memories were those of a time, not too far distant, when to be Irish was to be poor and have gates slammed in one's face. Joseph P. Kennedy, a man of driving ambition, was determined to reverse all that. His passion was to break down the barriers and win full acceptance for himself and his family. Business success helped; he soon discovered that money encouraged people to forgive an Irish name, though this was less true in Boston than elsewhere. Money also enabled him to offer his sons the protective coloration of schooling at places like Choate, Milton and Harvard; it enabled him to open doors for them all their lives. But what was more important than money was the training he gave his children— a regimen of discipline tempered and transformed by affection.

Regarding money as a means and not as an end, Joe Kennedy forbade its discussion at the dinner table. Conversation turned, not on business, but on public affairs; no child could

doubt the order of priority. "I can hardly remember a meal-
time," Robert Kennedy said later, "when the conversation
was not dominated by what Franklin D. Roosevelt was doing
or what was happening around the world. . . . Since public
affairs had dominated so much of our actions and discussions,
public life seemed really an extension of family life." The
father confronted the children with large questions, encouraged them to have opinions of their own, demanded that their
opinions make sense, wrote them endless letters when he was
away (which was often), told them they had an obligation to
take part in public life and instilled convictions of purpose
and possibility. As John Kennedy put it one night at the
White House: "My father wasn't around as much as some
fathers when I was young; but, whether he was there or not,
he made his children feel that they were the most important
things in the world to him. He was so terribly interested in
everything we were doing. He held up standards for us, and
he was very tough when we failed to meet those standards.
The toughness was important. If it hadn't been for that,
Teddy might be just a playboy today. But my father cracked
down on him at a crucial time in his life, and this brought
out in Teddy the discipline and seriousness which will make
him an important political figure."

Young Jack kept up his side in the competitive world of the
Kennedys. But for all his vitality he had both a frailness and
a sensitivity which set him somewhat apart from the extro-
verted and gregarious family. He may even have been a little
lonely at times. He passed a surprising amount of his childhood sick in bed—with diphtheria, scarlet fever, acute ap-
pendicitis and chronic stomach trouble. He was the only one
in the family who liked to read; loneliness and sickness made
him read all the more. He spent hours in his room at River-
dale or Hyannis Port absorbed in history and biography—
King Arthur, *Scottish Chiefs*, *The White Company*, Cooper,
and later Churchill's *Marlborough* when he was in his teens.
History was full of heroes for him, and he reveled in the
stately cadences of historical prose. His memory of what he

read was photographic. Situations, scenes and quotations stuck in his mind for the rest of his life.

The interior life was a source of identity and of power. Already he was moving beyond his brother Joe, moving beyond his father, and developing distinctive standards and goals. The Kennedys were supposed never to finish second; but Jack could present a favorite quotation from Alan Seeger: "Whether I am on the winning or losing side is not the point with me. It is being on the side where my sympathies lie that matters." (He still, however, preferred to win.) Professor William G. Carleton of the University of Florida recalls an evening of discussion with the Kennedys at Palm Beach in April 1941: "It was clear to me that John had a far better historical and political mind than his father or his elder brother; indeed, that John's capacity for seeing current events in historical perspective and for projecting historical trends into the future was unusual." It used to be said that the older Kennedy 'made' his son Jack President and, if Joe, Jr., had only lived, would have 'made' him President first. I do not believe either of these things for a moment. I doubt whether young Joe, for all his charms and gifts, would have been President. And it was Jack Kennedy who, in the existential sense, first made himself and then made himself President. Out of some fierce, cool inner passion, he became a man in his own right who grew from but beyond the family in which he was born, which loved him so much and which he loved so much.

It is hard to judge how much his formal education mattered. He spent only one year at a Catholic school, Canterbury in Connecticut. He then went on to Choate, which he disliked heartily. During his Presidency his old school unveiled his portrait as Choate's most distinguished alumnus. He observed of the ceremony, "This is the most ironic celebration of which I have ever heard." He asked what use schools like Choate were and answered his own question in a message to his fellow alumni. "Those of us who have gone to Choate and comparable schools," he began, "represent really a very tiny minority." Private preparatory schools, he went on, would merit a place in American education only as they took in people of all classes and races; and those fortunate enough to go to such schools had to justify their special opportunities, preferably by entering the service of the nation. He named the Roosevelts, Harriman, Acheson, Douglas Dillon, Charles Bohlen and, among Choate alumni, Stevenson and Bowles, and suggested a trifle acidly that the careers of such men had done more than anything else to persuade the American democracy to accept the preparatory school "even when, or perhaps because, the men themselves do things which appear on occasion to disappoint a good many of their classmates."

Choate provided no intellectual excitement, and he finished only slightly above the middle of his class. His father sent him that summer to the London School of Economics, hoping to expose him to Harold Laski. Instead Kennedy exposed himself to jaundice and had to delay his entry into Princeton in the fall. Then a recurrence of jaundice knocked out the rest of his freshman year. With his Princeton friends advancing into the sophomore class, he yielded to his father's preference and shifted the next autumn to Harvard.

The English Experience

For a time Kennedy continued in his prep-school mood. He organized the Freshman Smoker, ruptured a disk in his back playing football, made the swimming squad and the *Crimson*, kept apart from the greaseballs in the Harvard Student Union and concentrated desultorily in the field of government.

In the meantime, a summer in Europe between his first and second Harvard years exposed him to wider horizons. With Lemoyne Billings, who had been his roommate at Choate and was now at Princeton, he spent a carefree two months wandering around the continent. His diary of the summer records a growing interest in public affairs. "The general impression," he noted after a few days in France, "seems to be that while they all like Roosevelt, his type of government would not succeed in a country like France which seems to lack the ability of seeing a problem as a whole. They don't like Blum as he takes away their money and gives it to someone else. That to a Frenchman is tres mauvais." He concluded the entry: "Looked around and finally got a fairly cheap room for the night (35 francs)."

A visit to St.-Jean-de-Luz on the Spanish border led him to reflect on the Spanish Civil War. He registered his own view as "rather governmental after reading Gunther [*Inside Europe*] even though St. Jean is rebel stronghold." However, a day of rebel atrocity stories, as he noted the next evening, "turns me a bit from government," and an afternoon at a bullfight "made me believe all the atrocity stories now as these southerners . . . are happiest at scenes of cruelty. They thought funniest sight was when horse ran out of the ring with his guts trailing."

On to Lourdes—"very interesting but things seemed to become reversed as Billings became quite ill after leaving." Carcassonne two days later: "an old medieval town in perfect condition—which is more than can be said for Billings." Then Milan: "Finished Gunther and have come to the decision that Facism [*sic*] is the thing for Germany and Italy, Communism for Russia and Democracy for America and England." In Rome he set down a list of questions:

> If the belligerent foreign troops were withdrawn, how much chance would Franco have?
>
> If Franco wins, what will be the extent of Mussolini's control, Hitler's? . . .
>
> Isn't the chance of war less as Britain gets stronger—or is a country like Italy liable to go to war when economic discontent is rife? . . .
>
> Gunther says "Facism, momentarily powerful, may be the convulsive last agonies of the capitalist cycle, in which case Facism will have been merely the prelude of Communism." Is this true?

These were still the thoughts of a sophomore; but later in the year his father became ambassador to Britain and Jack began spending his holidays whenever possible in London. This speeded his intellectual awakening. He was fascinated by English political society, with its casual combination of wit, knowledge and unconcern. The intelligent young Englishmen of his own age, like David Ormsby Gore, seemed more confident and sophisticated than his Harvard friends. He enjoyed the leisured weekends in the great country houses. It was history come alive for him, and it had a careless elegance he had not previously encountered.

This love of England found its expression later in the delight with which he read books like David Cecil's *The Young Melbourne*. It was especially a love for the Whig England of the early nineteenth century, rational and urbane. But it is too simple to suggest that Kennedy was no more than an American Melbourne. The manner captivated him a good deal more than the matter. Kennedy was enchanted by the Whig zest, versatility and nonchalance; he liked the idea of a society where politics invigorated but did not monopolize life. But Whiggism was a posture, not a purpose. It was too passive for a Kennedy. Where Melbourne was willing to yield to the popular voice, Kennedy hoped to guide and anticipate it. Melbourne was an accommodator; Kennedy wanted to be a leader. He infused the Whig style with Rooseveltian activism. He was socially a Whig but politically something else —probably, if a British analogue is required, a Tory Democrat. He liked the notion of aristocrats and commoners united against the selfishness of laissez faire. His mood in later years was often that of Coningsby: "I would make these slum-landlords skip." He had read Winston Churchill's life of his father and found as much historical sustenance, I believe, in Lord Randolph Churchill as in Lord Melbourne. (He did not meet Winston Churchill for another twenty years. He and Jacqueline had a house at Cannes in the late fifties with William Douglas-Home, the playwright, and his wife. One evening they dined with Churchill on the Onassis yacht. It was not altogether a success; Churchill, now an old man, had a little difficulty in distinguishing which of the group that came aboard the yacht was Jack Kennedy, and, when this was finally sorted out, the conversation was hard going. He had met his hero too late. But Churchill remained his greatest admiration.)

All this was still an inchoate stirring in between afternoons at Lady Cunard's, balls in Belgravia and weekends in the country. But London did give him a sense of the tone in which politics might be approached. It also gave him a rather appalling look at the way democracy responded to crisis. Kennedy was in and out of England in the months when Churchill was calling on his fellow countrymen with such slight effect to rouse themselves against the menace of Nazism. Harvard allowed him to spend the second term of the academic year of 1938–39 abroad, and he traveled through Eastern Europe to Russia, the Middle East and the Balkans, stopping in Berlin and Paris on his way back to Grosvenor Square. When he returned to Harvard in the fall of 1939, the question of British somnambulism before Hitler perplexed him more than ever. Professor Arthur Holcombe of the government department had already aroused an interest in the study of politics; and now, under the guidance of Professors Payson Wild and Bruce Hopper, he set to work on an honors essay analyzing British rearmament policy. After his graduation in 1940, the thesis was published.

Remembering that Churchill had called his collection of speeches *While England Slept,* Kennedy brashly called his own book *Why England Slept.* In retrospect, *Why England Slept* presents several points of interest. One is its tone—so aloof and clinical, so different from the Churchillian history he loved, so skeptical of the notion that the individual could affect events ("personalities," he wrote with regret about the American attitude toward history, "have always been more interesting to us than facts"). This detachment was all the more remarkable midst the flaring emotions of 1940. Though ostensibly writing to prepare America for its own crisis ("in studying the reasons why England slept, let us try to profit by them and save ourselves her anguish"), he remained agnostic about the choices confronting the American President. Kennedy did make the quiet suggestion that "a defeat of

the Allies may simply be one more step towards the ultimate
achievement—Germany over the world"; but, beyond this,
and doubtless out of deference to his father's and older
brother's isolationism, he stood aside in the book from the
great debate between the isolationists and the interventionists. (At Harvard, however, he wrote to the *Crimson* criticizing the isolationist views of his fellow editors.)

His purpose was to discover how much British unpreparedness could be attributed to the personal defects of British
politicians and how much to "the more general weakness of
democracy and capitalism"; and he found his answer not with
the leaders, but with the system. He declined to pursue guilty
men: "Leaders are responsible for their failures only in the
governing sector and cannot be held responsible for the nation as a whole. . . . I believe it is one of democracy's failings
that it seeks to make scapegoats for its own weaknesses." As
long as Britain was a democracy, the people could have
turned the leaders out if they disagreed with them. Nor did
he put much stock in the notion that a leader could change
the mind of the nation; after all, he remarked, Roosevelt
had been trying to awaken America since 1937 but Congress
was still cutting naval appropriations. The basic causes of
the British paralysis in his view were impersonal and institutional. "In regard to capitalism, we observe first that it was
obedience to its principles that contributed so largely to England's failure." Democracy, moreover, was "essentially peace-
loving" and therefore hostile to rearmament. Both capitalism
and democracy were geared for a world at peace; totalitarianism was geared for a world at war. A strong sense of the
competition between democracy and totalitarianism pervaded
the book—a competition in which, Kennedy believed, totalitarianism had significant short-run advantages, even though
democracy was superior *"for the long run."*

The War

As war came closer to America, Kennedy, having been rejected by the Army because of his back, succeeded in 1941 in persuading the Navy to let him in. After Pearl Harbor, he pulled every possible string to get sea duty, finally enrolling his father in the cause. In due course there followed the Pacific, PT-109, the Solomon Islands campaign, Talagi and Rendova, and the incredible few days in August 1943 when the Japanese destroyer *Amagiri* sliced his boat in half and plunged Kennedy and his crew into the waters of Ferguson Passage, now suddenly aflame with burning gasoline. Kennedy's calm bravery, his extraordinary feat in towing one of his crew to refuge by gripping the end of the life jacket belt in his teeth, his leadership, resourcefulness and cheer until rescue came—this was one of the authentic passages of heroism in the war, so well described in later accounts by John Hersey and Robert Donovan and so seldom mentioned by Kennedy himself. (In a Person to Person program with Edward R. Murrow in the late fifties, Kennedy called it "an interesting experience." Murrow responded: "Interesting. I should think that would be one of the great understatements." When during the Presidency Donovan proposed doing a book on PT-109, Kennedy tried his best to discourage him, saying that there was no story and that it would be a waste of his time. Donovan went ahead nevertheless and eventually decided that he would have to go out to the Solomons and re-swim Kennedy's course. Kennedy, who thought this utter madness, could not get over the idea of anyone's going to such trouble and expense.)

The incident in the Solomons embodied two of Kennedy's deeper preoccupations—with courage and with death. He hated discussing these matters in the abstract, but they were nonetheless enduring themes of his life. Robert Kennedy tells us that courage was the virtue his brother most admired. In the first instance, this meant physical courage—the courage of men under enemy fire, of men silently suffering pain, the courage of the sailor and the mountain climber and of men who stared down mobs or soared into outer space. And, when he entered politics, it came to mean moral courage—the courage to which he later dedicated his *Profiles,* the courage of "a man who does what he must—in spite of personal consequences, in spite of obstacles and dangers and pressures," the courage which, he said, "is the basis of all human morality."

Courage—and death. The two are related, because courage, if it is more than reckless bravado, involves the exquisite understanding that death may be its price. "The education of the average American child of the upper middle class," Norbert Wiener has written, "is such as to guard him solicitously against the awareness of death and doom." But this is less true of children brought up in an orthodox faith. Kennedy's religious upbringing, his illness, his reading about the death of kings—all must have joined to give him an early sense of human mortality. Then death became his intimate during the long hours in the black, streaming waters of Ferguson Passage. Exactly a year later, he was notified that his brother Joe had been killed on an air mission against Nazi submarine bases in western Europe. In another month his English brother-in-law, the Marquis of Hartington, the husband of his sister Kathleen, was killed in France.

In a looseleaf notebook of 1945, filled with fragments about Joe and Billy Hartington—Joe's posthumous citation, a *Washington Post* editorial on his death, Kathleen's letter about her husband's death and letters from Billy Hartington's fellow officers in the Coldstream Guards—he inserted two quotations describing the death of Raymond Asquith in France in 1915—one from Churchill's *Great Contemporaries*:

> The War which found the measure of so many men never got
> to the bottom of him, and, when the Grenadiers strode into the
> crash and thunder of the Somme, he went to his fate, cool,
> poised, resolute, matter-of-fact, debonair.

and another from a favorite book, John Buchan's *Pilgrim's Way*:

He loved his youth, and his youth has become eternal. Debonair
and brilliant and brave, he is now part of that immortal England which knows not age or weariness or defeat.

His wife later said, "The poignancy of men dying young
haunted him."

In Search of Self

Along with a deep sorrow over the battalions of wasted lives,
the war left him with an intense concern about the preven-
tion of such waste in the future. He went to San Francisco
in June 1945 as a special writer for the Hearst press to watch
the founding of the United Nations. For a young veteran,
with stabbing memories of violence and death, it was in a way
a disenchanting experience. But for a student of politics it
was an indispensable education.

"It would be very easy to write a letter to you that was
angry," he observed afterward to a PT-boat friend who had
sought his opinion of the conference. "When I think of how
much this war has cost us, of the deaths of Cy and Peter and
Orv and Gil and Demi and Joe and Billy and all of those
thousands and millions who have died with them—when I
think of all those gallant acts that I have seen or anyone
has seen who has been to the war—it would be a very easy
thing to feel disappointed and somewhat betrayed." The
conference, he continued, lacked moral force; not idealism
but self-interest brought the nations together. "You have seen
battlefields where sacrifice was the order of the day and to
compare that sacrifice to the timidity and selfishness of the
nations gathered at San Francisco must inevitably be dis-
illusioning."

Yet could the conference have achieved more? The hard
fact was that nations were not prepared to yield their sov-
ereignty to an international organization. He listened in the
corridors to the world government arguments of another

young veteran, Cord Meyer, about to start the World Federalists. "Admittedly world organization with common obedience to law would be solution," Kennedy scribbled in a notebook. "Not that easy. If there is not the feeling that war is the ultimate evil, a feeling strong enough to drive them together, then you can't work out this internationalist plan." "Things cannot be forced from the top," he told his PT-boat friend.

> The international relinquishing of sovereignty would have to spring from the people—it would have to be so strong that the elected delegates would be turned out of office if they failed to do it. . . . We must face the truth that the people have not been horrified by war to a sufficient extent to force them to go to any extent rather than have another war. . . . War will exist until that distant day when the conscientious objector enjoys the same reputation and prestige that the warrior does today.

These were the things to be considered "when you consider that Conference in San Francisco. You must measure its accomplishments against its possibilities. What [the] Conference accomplished is that it made war more difficult." He summed up his feelings about the UN in his notebook:

> *Danger of too great a build-up.*
> Mustn't expect too much.
> A truly just solution will leave every nation somewhat disappointed.
> There is no cure all.

This was his mood immediately after the war: don't expect too much: no cure-alls. The next year he wrote succinctly in the six-year report of the Harvard Class of 1940, "I joined the Navy in 1941, served in P.T. Boats in the Pacific and was retired in April, 1945, because of injuries." (The Class Secretary added a footnote: "Kennedy received the Navy and Marine Corps Medal.") Concluding a brief paragraph, Kennedy replied to a question asked all members of the class, "I am pessimistic about the future of the country."

He had expected to become a writer; but the San Francisco experience may have helped persuade him that it was better to sit at the conference table than to wait outside with the press. His brother's death also changed things. The family assumption had been that Joe, who had made his political debut as a delegate at the 1940 Democratic convention (where he cast his vote, as pledged, against Franklin Roosevelt), would be the Kennedy to enter politics. Though Ambassador Kennedy did not, as myth later had it, automatically promote his second son into the slot now so sadly vacant, Jack, like many young veterans, felt the need of doing something to help the world for which so many friends had died. Politics perhaps attracted him less as a means of saving this world than of keeping it from getting worse. In 1946 he returned to Boston to test the political air.

The return to Boston must have involved a form of what anthropologists call 'culture shock.' While born a Boston Irishman, he had never been a member of the Boston Irish community; and his life had carried him far away from his roots. Now, in the 11th Congressional District, he was back among his own people, yet not quite of them. He liked their toughness and their loyalty, but regretted their anti-intellectualism. Campaigning through the three-deckers of Charlestown and the North End, he fraternized for the first time with the men and women from whom the Kennedys and Fitzgeralds had sprung. In the dimly lit hall of one Charlestown tenement he encountered David Powers, a man of exceptional sweetness and fidelity, who beguiled him with his flow of stories, his knowledge of Irish Boston, and his capacity for affable relaxation. Kennedy, at first a little stiff and shy, soon began to relax himself, though, as the old Boston politician and raconteur Clem Norton (the model for Hennessy in Edwin O'Connor's *The Last Hurrah*) put it, he never quite acquired 'a street personality.'

In the fall of 1947 I returned to Massachusetts myself to teach history at Harvard. A note from Kennedy in January 1948 started "Dear Arthur" (and continued: "I have your letter of January 2nd, relative to your interest in conditions at the Harvard Square Post Office"); but my first distinct recollection is of a political meeting in Harvard Yard during the presidential election that October, where we sat together and chatted while he waited his turn to go to the platform. Thomas H. Eliot, who had represented Cambridge with distinction in the House until he was redistricted and beaten by Curley in the Democratic primary, was speaking. The position of the Yankee Democrat in Massachusetts was not easy; and Eliot appeared to be overcompensating for his suspicious origins by the warmth of his advocacy of Paul A. Dever, the Irish Catholic candidate for governor. Kennedy leaned over and said, "How can a man like Tom Eliot say such things about a man like Paul Dever?" Later my opinion of Dever was higher, and so too, I think, was Kennedy's. Eliot, who is now Chancellor of Washington University in St. Louis, may not have been so wrong as we thought. But at the time I was surprised and impressed by Kennedy's unorthodox reaction.

I should not have been so surprised. He had already shown his independence by his refusal to join his Massachusetts Democratic colleagues in the House in petitioning President Truman to pardon Curley, who, though still mayor of Boston, was by 1948 in Danbury prison for using the mails to defraud. (He was, it used to be said, the only mayor of Boston to serve two terms at once.) Occasional meetings with Kennedy in the next years strengthened the impression of a skeptical mind, a laconic tongue, enormous personal charm, an agreeable disdain for the rituals of Massachusetts politics and a detachment from the pieties of American liberalism. He still looked exceedingly young (actually he was six months older than I), but he was plainly purposeful and his own master.

In 1949, for some reason which now escapes me, perhaps because it might be a first step toward the governorship, I urged him to run for mayor of Boston. He replied, "I am interested in my work here in the House, and feel that there is much good that I can do from here." He was right, of course, to avoid the mayoralty trap; but it was soon evident that he was considering possibilities beyond the House. By 1950 he was making regular weekend visits to Massachusetts, speaking in places remote from his own district. He was plainly preparing to run for senator or governor in 1952. Which it would be depended on whether Paul Dever, now governor, chose to seek re-election or to challenge the incumbent Senator Henry Cabot Lodge, Jr. Kennedy's preference for the Senate was clear. As he said one day, gesturing at the State House, "I hate to think of myself up in that corner office deciding on sewer contracts."

Early in 1952 Senator Paul H. Douglas of Illinois delivered the Godkin Lectures at Harvard. The Douglases came for luncheon one winter Sunday along with Bernard De Voto, Joseph Alsop, the McGeorge Bundys and Kennedy. Douglas, who seemed to regard the young Congressman with paternal fondness, warned him sternly against trying for the Senate, especially if the Republicans should nominate Eisenhower. Why not accumulate seniority in the House? or would not the governorship be less risky? Kennedy listened quietly and said little. Doubtless he received much advice of this sort. But, almost as if he felt he had little time to lose, he had long since resolved to push ahead. When Dever announced in April that he planned to run again for the governorship, Kennedy promptly declared his candidacy for the Senate.

I was away from the state most of the fall, working on Adlai Stevenson's staff in Springfield, Illinois. When the Stevenson party was campaigning through Massachusetts in October, we were much impressed by the cool efficiency of the Kennedy operation and by Kennedy himself, slim, careless and purposeful against the sodden background of the old-time Boston politicians. He beat Lodge by 70,000 votes. In the gloom of Stevenson's defeat, his success was a consolation. Victory now sent him back to Washington as a junior member of the Democratic minority in the Senate.

War had been a hardening experience, and politics hardened him more. Massachusetts Democrats did not exist as a party in the usual sense of the word. They formed rather a collection of rival tongs, controlled by local chieftains and

presided over by an impotent state committee. Kennedy
carved out his own domain and pursued his own goals. He
showed himself determined, unrelenting and profane, able
to beat the pols on their own ground and in their own
language.

With his instinct for compartmentalization, he did not often
display this part of his life to friends in other layers. His
closest associate in these enterprises was his brother Robert,
who managed his campaign for the Senate in 1952. Though
Robert Kennedy was also a Harvard man, the Cambridge
liberals regarded him with marked distrust because of his
association with the McCarthy Committee; nor were his
expressed views on public policy reassuring. Early in 1954
he sent a letter to the *New York Times* which, among other
things, seemed to argue the Republican thesis about the iniq-
uity of the Yalta conference. I was moved to write a forceful
but perhaps condescending answer denouncing the letter as
"an astonishing mixture of distortion and error." Robert
Kennedy came back with a lively rejoinder. The last sentence
suggests the tone: "I do not wish to appear critical of Mr.
Schlesinger's scholarship for his polemics cover such a wide
variety of subjects that it is understandable that he is not
always able to read all of the documents he so vigorously
discusses." He sent me a copy along with a note to the effect
that he hoped his response would "clarify the record sufficiently for you to make the necessary public apology." I
replied in like spirit; but the *Times,* bored with the argument, did not bother to print the rebuttals and surrebuttals.
This exchange only amused Jack Kennedy, who later said,
"My sisters are very mad at you because of the letter you wrote
about Bobby."

In the 1956 campaign, Robert Kennedy joined the Stevenson party and accompanied the candidate in his trips around
the country. He said very little, and no one quite knew what
he was doing. (Actually he was learning how a national
campaign should—or should not—be run.) His presence was,
to my mind, a bit ominous; and I imagine he regarded mine
with equal enthusiasm. One day in October Stevenson ad-

dressed a meeting in West Virginia. He was due that night in New York; but fog and rain set in, and only one plane was available to fly the candidate north. Arrangements were made to send the rest of the party on to Pittsburgh by bus. When the buses finally appeared, we all tumbled in and groped for seats in the darkness. In a minute I turned to look at my seatmate and, to our joint annoyance, found Robert Kennedy. For the next several hours, we rode through the storm to Pittsburgh. Having no alternative, we fell into reluctant conversation. To my surprise he was pleasant, reasonable and amusing. Thereafter our relations were amiable and uncomplicated.

Next to his brother, Kennedy's chief lieutenant in Massachusetts was a Springfield public relations man who had once worked for Foster Furcolo, Lawrence O'Brien. O'Brien played a large role in organizing the 1952 campaign for the Senate and subsequently joined the senatorial staff. In 1956 the Kennedys engaged in a bitter fight with John McCormack for control of the Democratic State Committee. For that fracas Bobby added to the group a Harvard classmate and former football captain, Kenneth O'Donnell; in 1960 O'Donnell became John Kennedy's appointments secretary and a key figure in the campaign. O'Brien and O'Donnell were both astute, unruffled, soft-spoken and terse. Both had great humor: Larry's was friendly and genial, while Ken, who looked like one of the young IRA men in trenchcoats in John Ford's film of *The Informer*, had a grim, cryptic wit which could be devastating. Both were liberals in the New Deal tradition—more so at this time than the Kennedys. O'Brien had been an early Massachusetts member of Americans for Democratic Action. Once when Robert Kennedy brought O'Donnell home to dinner in their college days, O'Donnell defended Franklin Roosevelt with such vigor that Ambassador Kennedy, deeply angered, left the table. Nevertheless, both were realistic organization politicians slightly contemptuous of reformers and reform groups. They worked in perfect unison with the Kennedys, shared that common understanding which abbreviates communication to swift phrases and imperceptible changes in facial expression, and filled in a vital part of Kennedy's life. Dave Powers, less involved in politics, kept the whole group happy.

But the Irish Mafia did not possess Kennedy any more than anyone else did. They were his instruments in politics, as Ted Sorensen was his instrument on issues. He admired them all because he admired virtuosity in performance—"the ability," as he once put it, "to do things well, and to do them with precision and with modesty." The techniques by which people did things fascinated him, whether in politics or statecraft, writing or painting, sailing or touch football. He had an instinctive appreciation of excellence. He liked to cite Aristotle's definition of happiness: "The good of man is in the active exercise of his soul's faculties in conformity with excellence or virtue, or, if there be several human excellences or virtues, in conformity with the best and most perfect of them."

But, if there were several human excellences, faith in virtuosity per se could not be enough. Which would take precedence over the others? *Profiles in Courage* celebrated "grace under pressure" without regard to purpose; obviously Webster, Benton and Houston could not all have been right about the Compromise of 1850. The Kennedy of these years was still undefined. He was a Harvard man, a naval hero, an Irishman, a politician, a *bon vivant*, a man of unusual intelligence, charm, wit and ambition, "debonair and brilliant and brave," but his deeper meaning was still in process of crystallization.

. . . . .

Politics and Privacy

On issues he showed himself a practical and moderate liberal, who made quiet progress on questions of labor and social welfare without trying to force the pace faster than he thought the times permitted. During the first Eisenhower term there was much discussion within the Stevenson group about national policy. I circulated a memorandum suggesting that our inherited liberalism was dominated by the special experience of the depression, that prosperity raised problems of its own and that, where the New Deal had been necessarily concerned with the stark issues of subsistence and employment, the new period called for not a 'quantitative' but a 'qualitative' liberalism, dedicated to enriching the lives people lived. The problems of qualitative liberalism, the memorandum argued, "have to do with education, medical care, civil rights, housing, civil liberties, city planning . . . with the issues which make the difference between opportunity and defeat, between frustration and fulfillment, in the everyday life of the average person." Our country, the memorandum said, "is richer than ever before, and is getting even richer every moment—but is devoting a *decreasing* share of its wealth to the common welfare."

When I sent the memorandum to Kennedy, he replied a little pessimistically that "any attempts to put forward a very advanced program of social legislation would meet with the opposition of the [Democratic] leadership." This was partly because "many members of the Democratic party in the House and Senate are in agreement on the general lines of Eisenhower's middle-of-the-road program" and partly because of "the desire of the leadership to maintain a unified party on the assumption that the Democratic Party is the stronger political party of the two and that if Eisenhower does not run then victory will be almost assured for us."

He then moved on to the question of the Lodge-Gossett amendment, which proposed that in a presidential election each state's electoral votes be divided in the proportion of the popular vote. While this proposal had a democratic ring, its effect, Kennedy thought, would be to reduce the influence of the large, urbanized states and "increase the influence of the one party states in both Democratic and Republican ranks." Kennedy was far more perceptive than most historians and political scientists in seeing the defects of this amendment; his successful fight against it the next year marked his emergence as a significant figure in the Senate. He concluded his letter by mentioning "an article I am now working on in my spare time. It is on political courage. . . ."

These were his years of concentration on politics, and he soon showed the toughness, adroitness and intuition of a master. Yet while he considered politics—in another phrase he cherished from *Pilgrim's Way*—"the greatest and most honorable adventure," took pride in his political skills, delighted in political maneuver and combat and never forgot political effects for a single second, he stood apart, in some fundamental sense, from the political game. When David Ormsby Gore visited him in the hospital, Kennedy remarked that he was not sure he was cut out to be a politician; he saw the strength of opposing arguments too well; it would be easier if he had divine certitude that he was right. In his preliminary notes for *Profiles in Courage,* he wrote of Robert A. Taft, "He was partisan in the sense that Harry Truman was—they both had the happy gift of seeing things in bright shades. It is the politicians who see things in similar shades that have a depressing and worrisome time of it."

The total politician instinctively assumed a continuum between means and ends. But it was the tension between means and ends which fascinated and bothered Kennedy. His sickness provided an unaccustomed chance to reflect on such questions; and *Profiles in Courage* represented his most sustained attempt to penetrate the moral dilemmas of the political life. "Politics is a jungle," he wrote in his notes, "—torn between doing right thing & staying in office—between the local interest & the national interest—between the private good of the politician & the general good." In addition, "we have always insisted academically on an unusually high—even unattainable—standard in our political life. We consider it graft to make sure a park or road, etc., be placed near property of friends—but what do we think of admitting friends to the favored list for securities about to be offered to the less favored at a higher price? . . . Private enterprise system . . . makes OK private action which would be considered dishonest if public action."

How could people survive in the jungle? He thought the answer had something to do with that combination of toughness of fiber and courage which constituted character. In the cases of Taft and Walter George, for example, "it is not so much that they voted in a certain way that caused their influence because others voted the same way—or because of length of service—or because of areas of origin—though all had something to do with it. But mostly it was character—& the impression they gave—which all great and successful Parl. leaders have given—that they had something in their minds besides the next election. They were not cynical." He concluded: "Everyone admires courage & the greenest garlands are for those who possess it."

Gradually there evolved a sense of his own identity as a political man, compounded of his growing mastery of the political arts and, even more, of his growing understanding that, for better or worse, his public self had to be faithful to his private self. This second point may sound like something less than a blinding revelation. But it takes many politicians a long time to acquire it. Some never do, always hoping to persuade the voters that they are different from what they are. "No man, for any considerable period," Hawthorne once wrote, "can wear one face to himself, and another to the multitude, without finally getting bewildered as to which may be the true." Kennedy was prepared to settle for his own face—and no doubt was encouraged to do so by his own cool evaluation of the alternatives. One day his father asked him why he wanted to take on the appalling burden of the Presidency. "These things have always been done by men," Kennedy said, "and they can be done by men now." As he looked around him, the others who yearned to assume the burden did not seem to him conspicuously better qualified than himself.

The process of internal definition went on in other ways, and Jacqueline Kennedy made her own contribution to it. She must at first have been overwhelmed by the life into which marriage plunged her. Politics had been for her corny old men shouting on the Fourth of July, at least until the advent of Stevenson; his was the first political voice to whom she listened. And, once in this new world, she found it hard to get used to the ground rules. Her husband sometimes came home irritated by the action of a fellow politician. Jacqueline, concluding that this man was an enemy, would glare across the room when she met him. Then Jack would speak agreeably about him, and she would exclaim, "Are you saying nice things about X? I've been hating him for three weeks." Her husband would reply, "No, no, that was three weeks ago. Now he has done Y." He would tell her that in politics you rarely had friends or foes, only colleagues, and that you should never get in so deep a quarrel as to lose all chance of conciliation; you might need to work with the other fellow later.

The teeming world of the Kennedys was another problem. Jacqueline had to fight to preserve her own identity in this family of active parents-in-law, athletic, teasing brothers-in-law, energetic, competent sisters-in-law. There often seemed no point in trying to compete in politics, any more than in touch football; and she sometimes carried her self-defense to inordinate extremes, as when she would pretend a total ignorance about politics or impose a social ban on politicians. Like all marriages, this one may have had its early strains. Their life together was almost nomadic, shuttling back and forth from Washington to Boston, from Newport to Palm Beach, living often with parents-in-law. They did not really have a house of their own until they had been married four years and their first child was born. Jacqueline often feared that she was a political liability and that everyone considered her a snob from Newport who had bouffant hair and French clothes and hated politics. Some of Kennedy's supporters did feel this way in 1960, but he never mentioned it to her and never asked her to change. He was never worried; he loved her as she was. More and more she embodied something of increasing value for him—a surcease from daily business, a standard of excellence, a symbol of privacy, a style of life.

This was partly because she proved able to extend his knowledge and sensibility. Before they were married, he had her translate and summarize ten or a dozen French books about Indochina; she was then living in the Auchincloss house in Virginia and labored late into hot summer nights to finish the assignment. When she read aloud passages from de Gaulle's *Memoires,* especially the introductory evocation of his image of France, he seized the idea for his own speeches about America. Whatever concerned her interested him, and often he would soon know more about it than she did. But perhaps her greatest influence was to confirm his feelings about the importance of living his life according to the values he honored most. He was determined not to let his public role stunt or stifle his inner existence. At Hyannis Port in August 1960, after the succession of party leaders had paid their respects to their new candidate for President, Kennedy drew one day at lunch a distinction between the totally absorbed professional, for whom politics was the whole of life, and those who enjoyed the game and art of politics but preserved a measure of detachment from it. Jacqueline remarked of some of their visitors that their private faces were completely suppressed by the public face. She had asked one political wife, "What have you been doing since the convention?" expecting her to say, "Oh dear, I've just been resting up since that madhouse" or something of the sort. Instead the reply came: "I've been writing letters to all those good people who were so helpful to my husband." "It was," Jackie said, "as if they were on television all the time."

Kennedy's determination to defend his privacy was crucial; for it permitted the inner self, so voracious for experience and for knowledge, so intent on reason and result, so admiring of grace and elegance, to ripen into free and confident maturity—and to renew and replenish the public self. By holding part of himself back from politics, he opened himself to fresh ideas and purpose. I do not mean to imply that he ever condescended to politics. His highest hope was to inspire the young with a lofty sense of the political mission. But politics was not the be-all and end-all; and because, with his wife's complicity, he declined to yield himself entirely to it, he was able to charge it with creativity.

The Kennedy Mind: I

Kennedy was called an intellectual very seldom before 1960 and very often thereafter—a phenomenon which deserves explanation.

One cannot be sure what an intellectual is; but let us define it as a person whose primary habitat is the realm of ideas. In this sense, exceedingly few political leaders are authentic intellectuals, because the primary habitat of the political leader is the world of power. Yet the world of power itself has its intellectual and anti-intellectual sides. Some political leaders find exhilaration in ideas and in the company of those whose trade it is to deal with them. Others are rendered uneasy by ideas and uncomfortable by intellectuals.

Kennedy belonged supremely to the first class. He was a man of action who could pass easily over to the realm of ideas and confront intellectuals with perfect confidence in his capacity to hold his own. His mind was not prophetic, impassioned, mystical, ontological, utopian or ideological. It was less exuberant than Theodore Roosevelt's, less scholarly than Wilson's, less adventurous than Franklin Roosevelt's. But it had its own salient qualities—it was objective, practical, ironic, skeptical, unfettered and insatiable.

It was marked first of all, as he had noted to Jacqueline, by inexhaustible curiosity. Kennedy always wanted to know how things worked. Vague answers never contented him. This curiosity was fed by conversation but even more by reading. His childhood consolation had become an adult compulsion. He was now a fanatical reader, 1200 words a minute, not only at the normal times and places but at meals, in the bathtub, sometimes even when walking. Dressing in the morning, he would prop open a book on his bureau and read while he put on his shirt and tied his necktie. He read mostly history and biography, American and English. The first book he ever gave Jacqueline was the life of a Texan, Marquis James's biography of Sam Houston, *The Raven*. In addition to *Pilgrim's Way, Marlborough* and *Melbourne,* he particularly liked Herbert Agar's *The Price of Union,* Samuel Flagg Bemis's *John Quincy Adams,* Allan Nevins's *The Emergence of Lincoln,* Margaret Coit's *Calhoun* and Duff Cooper's *Talleyrand.* He read poetry only occasionally—Shakespeare and Byron are quoted in the looseleaf notebook he kept in 1945–46— and by this time fiction hardly at all. His wife does not remember him reading novels except for two or three Ian Fleming thrillers, though Kennedy himself listed *The Red and the Black* among his favorite books and, at some point in his life, had read most of Hemingway and a smattering of contemporary fiction—at least *The Deer Park, The Fires of Spring* and *The Ninth Wave.* His supposed addiction to James Bond was partly a publicity gag, like Franklin Roosevelt's supposed affection for "Home on the Range." Kennedy seldom read for distraction. He did not want to waste a single second.

He read partly for information, partly for comparison, partly for insight, partly for the sheer joy of felicitous statement. He delighted particularly in quotations which distilled the essence of an argument. He is, so far as I know, the only politician who ever quoted Madame de Staël on Meet the Press. Some quotations he carried verbatim in his mind. Others he noted down. The looseleaf notebook of 1945–46 contained propositions from Aeschylus ("In war, truth is the first casualty"), Isocrates ("Where there are a number of laws drawn up with great exactitude, it is a proof that the city is badly administered; for the inhabitants are compelled to frame laws in great numbers as a barrier against offenses"), Dante ("The hottest places in Hell are reserved for those who, in a period of moral crisis, maintain their neutrality"), Falkland ("When it is not necessary to change it is necessary not to change"), Burke ("Our patience will achieve more than our force"), Jefferson ("Widespread poverty and concentrated wealth cannot long endure side by side in a democracy"), de Maistre ("In all political systems there are relationships which it is wiser to leave undefined"), Jackson ("Individuals must give up a share of liberty to preserve the rest"), Webster ("A general equality of condition is the true basis, most certainly, of democracy"), Mill ("One person with a belief is a social power equal to ninety-nine who have only interest"), Lincoln ("Public opinion is everything. With it nothing can fail, without it nothing can succeed"), Huck Finn on *Pilgrim's Progress* ("The statements are interesting—but steep"), Chesterton ("Don't ever take a fence down until you know the reason why it was put up"), Brandeis ("Unless our financial leaders are capable of progress, the institutions which they are trying to conserve will lose their foundation"), Colonel House ("The best politics is to do the right thing"), Churchill ("The whole history of the world is summed up in the fact that, when nations are strong, they are not always just, and when they wish to be just, they are often no longer strong. . . . Let us have this blessed union of power and justice"), Lippmann ("The political art deals with matters peculiar to politics, with a complex of material circumstances, of historic deposit, of human passion, for which the problems of business or engineering do not provide an analogy"), Hindu proverbs ("I had no shoes—and I murmured until I met a man who had no feet"), Joseph P. Kennedy ("More men die of jealousy than cancer") and even John F. Kennedy:

> To be a positive force for the public good in politics one must have three things; a solid moral code governing his public actions, a broad knowledge of our institutions and traditions and a specific background in the technical problems of government, and lastly he must have political appeal—the gift of winning public confidence and support.

There emerges from such quotations the impression of a moderate and dispassionate mind, committed to the arts of government, persuaded of the inevitability of change but distrustful of comprehensive plans and grandiose abstractions, skeptical of excess but admiring of purpose, determined above all to be effective.

His intelligence was fundamentally secular, or so it seemed to me. Of course, this was not entirely true. As Mary McCarthy wrote in her *Memories of a Catholic Girlhood*, "If you are born and brought up a Catholic, you have absorbed a great deal of world history and the history of ideas before you are twelve, and it is like learning a language early; the effect is indelible." Though Kennedy spent only one year of his life in a Catholic school, he assimilated a good deal of the structure of the faith, encouraged probably by his mother and sisters. He often adopted the Catholic side in historical controversy, as in the case of Mary Queen of Scots; and he showed a certain weakness for Catholic words of art, like 'prudence,' and a certain aversion toward bad words for Catholics, like 'liberal.' Nor could one doubt his devotion to his Church or the occasional solace he found in mass.

Yet he remains, as John Cogley has suggested, the first President who was a Roman Catholic rather than the first Roman Catholic President. Intellectual Catholicism in American politics has ordinarily taken two divergent forms, of which Senator Thomas J. Dodd of Connecticut and Senator Eugene McCarthy of Minnesota were contemporary representatives. Kennedy was different from either. Unlike Dodd, he lived far away from the world of the Holy Name Societies, Knights of Columbus and communion breakfasts. He discussed the princes of the American Church with the same irreverent candor with which he discussed the bosses of the Democratic party. When a dispatch from Rome during the 1960 campaign suggested Vatican doubts about his views of the proper relationship between church and state, Kennedy said, "Now I understand why Henry VIII set up his own church." His attitude toward life showed no traces of the black-and-white moralism, the pietistic rhetoric, the clericalism, the anti-intellectualism, the prudery, the fear of Protestant society, which had historically characterized parts of the Irish Catholic community in America. On the other hand, he did not, like Eugene McCarthy, seek to rescue Catholic doctrine from fundamentalism and demonstrate its relevance to the

modern world. Catholic intellectuals recognized his indifference to the scholastic tradition, and some disdained him for
it.

Kennedy's religion was humane rather than doctrinal. He
was a Catholic as Franklin Roosevelt was an Episcopalian—
because he was born into the faith, lived in it and expected
to die in it. One evening at the White House he argued with
considerable particularity that nine of the ten commandments were derived from nature and almost seemed to imply
that all religion was so derived. He had little knowledge of
or interest in the Catholic dogmatic tradition. He once wrote
Cogley, "It is hard for a Harvard man to answer questions
in theology. I imagine my answers will cause heartburn at
Fordham and B. C. [Boston College]." One can find little
organic intellectual connection between his faith and his
politics. His social thought hardly resulted from a determination to appy the principles of *Rerum Novarum* to American
life. He felt an immense sense of fellowship with Pope John
XXIII, but this was based more on the Pope's practical character and policies than on theological considerations. Some
of his Protestant advisers probably knew the encyclicals better
than he did. Once during the 1960 campaign I handed him a
speech draft with the comment that it was perhaps too
Catholic. He said with a smile, "You Unitarians"—meaning
Sorensen and myself—"keep writing Catholic speeches. I
guess I am the only Protestant around here."

Still, his basic attitude was wholly compatible with the
sophisticated theology of Jesuits like Father John Courtney
Murray, whom he greatly admired. In the notebook he kept
during his sickness, he wrote down some lines from Barbara
Ward: "What disturbs the Communist rulers is not the phraseology of religion, the lip-service that may be paid to it, or
the speeches and declarations made in its favor. . . . Religion
which is a mere adjunct of individual purpose is a religion
that even the Soviets can tolerate. What they fear is a religion
that transcends frontiers and can challenge the purpose and
performance of the nation-state." This was not in the mid-

fifties the typical attitude of American Catholics; but, if Kennedy was not a typical American Catholic, his example helped create the progressive and questing American Catholicism of the sixties. Above all, he showed that there need be no conflict between Catholicism and modernity, no bar to full Catholic participation in American society.

His detachment from traditional American Catholicism was part of the set of detachments—detachment from middle-class parochialism, detachment from the business ethos, detachment from ritualistic liberalism—which gave his perceptions their peculiar coolness, freshness and freedom, and which also led those expecting commitments of a more familiar sort to condemn him as uncommitted. In fact, he was intensely committed to a vision of America and the world, and committed with equal intensity to the use of reason and power to achieve that vision. This became apparent after he was President; and this accounts in part for the sudden realization that, far from being just a young man in a hurry, a hustler for personal authority, a Processed Politician, he was, as politicians go, an intellectual and one so peculiarly modern that it took orthodox intellectuals a little time before they began to understand him.

Another reason for the change in the intellectuals' theory of Kennedy was their gradual recognition of his desire to bring the world of power and the world of ideas together in alliance—or rather, as he himself saw it, to restore the collaboration between the two worlds which had marked the early republic. He was fascinated by the Founding Fathers and liked to harass historians by demanding that they explain how a small and underdeveloped nation could have produced men of such genius. He was particularly fascinated by the way the generation of the Founders united the instinct for ideas and the instinct for responsibility. "Our nation's first great politicians," he wrote, "—those who presided at its birth in 1776 and at its christening in 1787—included among their ranks most of the nation's first great writers and scholars." But today the gap between the intellectual and politician seems to be growing. . . . today this link is all but gone. Where are the scholar-statesmen? The American politician of today is fearful, if not scornful, of entering the literary world with the courage of a Beveridge. And the American author and scholar of today is reluctant, if not disdainful, about entering the political world with the enthusiasm of a Woodrow Wilson.

His summons to the scholar-statesman went largely unnoticed by the intellectual community in the fifties, perhaps because he chose such improbable forums as *Vogue* and a Harvard Commencement. Only when he began as President to put his proposition into practice did the intellectual community take a fresh look at him.

The Kennedy Mind: II

The character of his reading and quoting emphasizes, I think, the historical grain of his intelligence. Kennedy was in many respects an historian manqué. The historical mind can be analytical, or it can be romantic. The best historians are both, Kennedy among them. *Why England Slept,* with its emphasis on impersonal forces, expressed one side; *Profiles in Courage,* with its emphasis on heroes, expressed the other. But, even in his most romantic mood, Kennedy never adopted a good-guys *vs.* bad-guys theory of history. He may have been a Whig, but he was not a Whig historian. He had both the imagination and the objectivity which enabled him to see the point in lost causes, even in enemy fanaticisms. In a review of Liddell Hart's *Deterrent or Defense* in 1960, he praised the author's credo: "Keep strong, if possible. In any case, keep cool. Have unlimited patience. Never corner an opponent, and always assist him to save his face. Put yourself in his shoes—so as to see things through his eyes. Avoid self-right-eousness like the devil—nothing is so self-blinding." Liddell Hart was addressing these remarks to statesmen; they work just as well for historians.

Kennedy rarely lost sight of other people's motives and problems. For all the presumed coolness on the surface, he had an instinctive tendency to put himself into the skins of others. Once during the 1960 campaign, Kennedy, returning to New York City on a Sunday night from a visit with Mrs. Roosevelt in Hyde Park, dropped in at Voisin's for dinner with a couple of friends. At a neighboring table, a man obviously drunk, began in a low but penetrating voice to direct a stream of unprintable comment at him. Kennedy's companions raised their own voices in the hope that he would not hear, but to no avail. Finally one made a motion to call the headwaiter. Kennedy laid a hand on his sleeve and said, "No, don't bother. Think how the fellow's wife must be feeling." His friend looked and saw her flushed with embarrassment. He later reacted with comparable dispassion to de Gaulle and Khrushchev.

He liked to quote Lincoln: "There are few things wholly evil or wholly good. Almost everything, especially of Government policy, is an inseparable compound of the two, so that our best judgment of the preponderance between them is continually demanded." When something had enough steam behind it to move people and make an impression on history, it must have some rational explanation, and Kennedy wanted to know what that rational explanation was. The response of the fifties that it was all a struggle between good and evil never satisfied him.

But it was not a case of *tout comprendre, tout pardonner.* Though he saw the human struggle, not as a moralist, but as an historian, even as an ironist, irony was never permitted to sever the nerve of action. His mind was forever critical; but his thinking always retained the cutting edge of decision. When he was told something, he wanted to know what he could do about it. He was pragmatic in the sense that he tested the meaning of a proposition by its consequences; he was also pragmatic in the sense of being free from metaphysics. In his response, too, to the notion of a pluralist universe, Kennedy was a pragmatist—if one may make sensible use of this word, which came into political vogue in the first years of the Kennedy administration and then was oddly revived in the first years of the Johnson administration with the implication that the Kennedy years had not, after all, been pragmatic but were somehow ideological. They were not ideological, though they could perhaps be termed intellectual.

The historical mind is rarely ideological—and, when it becomes so, it is at the expense of history. Whether analytical or romantic, it is committed to existence, not to essence. Kennedy was bored by abstractions. He never took ideology very seriously, certainly not as a means of interpreting history and even not as part of the material of history. If he did not go the distance with de Gaulle in reducing everything to national tradition and national interest, he tended to give greater weight in thinking about world affairs to national than to ideological motives. Like de Gaulle, but unlike the ideological interpreters of the cold war, he was not surprised by the split between Russia and China.

If historic conflicts infrequently pitted total good against total evil, then they infrequently concluded in total victory or total defeat. Seeing the past with an historian's eyes, Kennedy knew that ideals and institutions were stubborn, and that change took place more often by accommodation than by annihilation. His cult of courage was in this sense ethical rather than political; he saw the courage of "unyielding devotion to absolute principle" as the moral fulfillment of the individual rather than as necessarily the best way of running a government. Indeed, he took pains to emphasize in *Profiles* that politicians could also demonstrate courage "through their acceptance of compromise, through their advocacy of conciliation, through their willingness to replace conflict with co-operation." Senators who go down to defeat in vain defense of a single principle "will not be on hand to fight for that or any other principle in the future." One felt here an echo of St. Thomas: "Prudence applies principles to particular issues; consequently it does not establish moral purpose, but contrives the means thereto."

The application of principle requires both moral and intellectual insight. Kennedy had an unusual capacity to weigh the complexities of judgment—in part because of the complexities of his own perceptions. The contrast in *Profiles* between the courage of compromise and the courage of principle expressed, for example, a tension deep within Kennedy—a tension between the circumspection of his political instinct and the radicalism of his intellectual impulse; so too the contrast between the historical determinism, the deprecation of the individual and the passive view of leadership implied in *Why England Slept* and the demand in *Profiles* that the politician be prepared, on the great occasions, to "meet the challenge of courage, whatever may be the sacrifices he faces if he follows his conscience." All this expressed the interior strain between Kennedy's sense of human limitation and his sense of hope, between his skepticism about man and his readiness to say, "Man can be as big as he wants. No problem of human destiny is beyond human beings."

All these things, coexisting within him, enabled others to find in him what qualities they wanted. They could choose one side of him or the other and claim him, according to taste, as a conservative, because of his sober sense of the frailty of man, the power of institutions and the frustrations of history, or as a progressive, because of his vigorous confidence in reason, action and the future. Yet within Kennedy himself these tensions achieved reunion and reconciliation. He saw history in its massive movements as shaped by forces beyond man's control. But he felt that there were still problems which man could resolve; and in any case, whether man could resolve these problems or not, the obligation was to carry on the struggle of existence. It was in essence, Richard Goodwin later suggested, the Greek view where the hero must poise himself against the gods and, even with knowledge of the futility of the fight, press on to the end of his life until he meets his tragic fate.

For Further Reading

John F. Kennedy has been well served by memoirists besides Schlesinger. The President's highly trusted speechwriter and counsel has written a sober yet loving portrait of JFK: Theodore C. Sorenson, *Kennedy* (1965). An earlier analysis by Sorenson of executive problems is still valuable, *Decision-Making in the White House* (1963). Pierre Salinger, *With Kennedy* (1966) rounds out the "inside" views, this from the White House press secretary. The 1960 election campaign is brilliantly described in Theodore H. White, *The Making of the President 1960* (1962). Political surveys and analyses of the 1960's are Theodore J. Lowi, *The End of Liberalism* (1969); James MacGregor Burns, *The Deadlock of Democracy* (1963); and Hugh Sidey, *John F. Kennedy, President* (1964). Although ostensibly a campaign biography, Burns's *John Kennedy: A Political Profile* (1960) is quite good. Three admiring early accounts are William Manchester, *Portrait of a President* (1962); Tom Wicker, *Kennedy Without Tears* (1964); and Pierre Salinger and Sander Vanocur, eds., *A Tribute to John F. Kennedy* (1964). Manchester's controversial *The Death of a President* (1967) is by far the best account of the tragic events in Dallas.

Kennedy's economic policies and business relations are analyzed by Seymour E. Harris, *Economics of the Kennedy Years and a Look Ahead* (1964); by Grant McConnell, *Steel and the Presidency* (1963); and by Roy Hoopes, *The Steel Crisis* (1963). The record on civil rights is critically assayed in Alexander M. Bickel, *Politics and the Warren Court* (1966). On defense policies see William W. Kaufman, *The McNamara Strategy* (1964); and Maxwell D. Taylor, *Responsibility and Response* (1967).

Foreign affairs have, as usual, dominated the interest of scholars and commentators. In addition to the general works by Spanier, Lukacs, Rees, Hammond, Halle, and Steel cited earlier in this volume, see the fascinating analysis by Roger

Hilsman, *To Move a Nation* (1967). On the test ban treaty see William B. Bader, *The United States and the Spread of Nuclear Weapons* (1968). The Berlin crisis is covered by Jean Edward Smith, *The Defense of Berlin* (1963); while Elie Abel, *The Missile Crisis* (1966), details the 1962 Cuban difficulties. For a revisionist's view of the same crisis see David Horowitz, *The Free World Colossus* (1965). William D. Rogers, *The Twilight Struggle* (1967) finds the Alliance for Progress a slight success; but Simon G. Hanson, in "The Alliance for Progress," *Inter-American Economic Affairs,* 22 (1968) proclaims it a failure. The accounts of the Southeast Asian conflict are numerous. Best for the background are Victor Bator, *Vietnam* (1965); David Halberstam, *The Making of a Quagmire* (1964); Robert Shaplen, *Lost Revolution* (1965); George M. Kahn and John W. Lewis, *The United States in Vietnam* (1967); and Arthur M. Schlesinger, Jr., *The Bitter Heritage* (1966).

A thorough bibliography, within the limits of its time span, may be found in James Tracy Crown, *The Kennedy Literature* (1968). A fine collection of appraisals of Kennedy is Aida DiPace Donald, ed., *John F. Kennedy and the New Frontier* (1966).

Economic Abundance and the American Character

David M. Potter

*T*wo hundred years ago, Hector St. John Crevecoeur asked, "What then is the American, this new man?" The question still obsesses Americans, not merely on the level suggested by Crevecoeur, but on another as well. The former involves an attempt to define the qualities that peculiarly inhere in American nationality. This is what Crevecoeur had in mind. The second level deals with loyalty, patriotism, and "Americanism." And while the selection that follows deals primarily with the first, some attention must here be paid to the second.

It is natural that a nation composed of peoples with no common ethnic roots should be especially concerned with its self-identity. Lacking ethnic homogeneity, neighbors do not always share the same values, perceive the same dangers, and rise collectively to meet challenges. At times of great social stress this uncertainty becomes acute.

The absence of ethnic commonality may help to explain aspects of American behavior. Racism—the attribution, both studied and subconscious, by one group of inferiority to another, based on physical characteristics—is an elaborate and complex American reality, a reality only recently widely acknowledged by white Americans

Source: David M. Potter, *People of Plenty* (Chicago: The University of Chicago Press, 1954), pp. 166–208. Copyright © 1954 by the University of Chicago. Reprinted by permission of the publisher.

themselves. To assign it one cause would be simplistic. Yet white racism is as old as our society and by all accounts durable. Although the relationship is admittedly unclear, could there not be a causal link between America's ethnic heterogeneity and white racism? Or, to put it another way, has not ethnic diversity intensified racism? In an ever mobile, changing society "whiteness" may have become a surrogate, both instinctively and quite consciously, for the absent ethnic homogeneity. Most Americans were neither Celts, Franks, Angles, Saxons, nor Romans; most were, however, white. Lest this notion be deemed too farfetched, consider two historical examples among many. First, the rationale behind early nineteenth-century schemes to colonize Negroes was that slaves and free blacks could be repatriated to Africa; that is, they were not Americans. And second, the various late-nineteenth century Japanese and Chinese exclusion acts also assumed that the yellow-skinned Orientals were not Americans. The mere fact of their skin color made their loyalty to America questionable.

The attempt to define nationality by skin color (as Roger B. Taney in effect did in the Dred Scott case) is but one manifestation of Americans' nervousness over their identity. In the twentieth century this concern has increased, largely due to the United States' growing awareness of the world beyond its boundaries. To be sure, there have always been statesmen, scholars, and other assorted rascals who have looked outward from American shores. Business entrepreneurs, especially following the calamitous depressions of 1873 and 1893, have long seen new international dimensions to American life. Still, for the great majority of citizens this outward-looking orientation, as opposed to one focusing on internal matters, has developed only over the past three-quarters of a century.

The chief by-products of this internationalism, unfortunately, have been wars. These conflicts only heightened the endless process of national definition. During World War I the government fostered an Americanism campaign that ended after the 1918 armistice in the Red Scare. During the interbellum years, the two major veterans' organizations, the American Legion and the Veterans of Foreign Wars, devoted a good portion of their energies to trying to define Americanism. Although they only defined what was not American, they kept the issue alive—even burning—as they spearheaded a patriotic drive to rewrite textbooks. World War II did not bring with it all the excesses of the earlier conflict largely because President Roosevelt and his administration actively worked to avert witch-hunting. But good intentions can last only so long. By the 1950's the proof of Americanism once again became an issue in the McCarthy era. College students may well have chuckled at spoofs that asked "Are you now, or have you ever been, a Valentine?" but the serious side could be seen in Congress's attachment to its House Committee on Un-American Activities. Since the escalation of the Southeast Asian war in the early 1960's, another wave of national defining has begun. This time it has taken the form of rallying to the flag: The Old Glory bumper sticker, "Love it or Leave it," has become a common sight on American roadways.

As indicated earlier, Crevecoeur's question works on another level as well, that of determining those characteristics that set the American apart from other men. Most of the numerous analysts who have dealt with this aspect of the question have followed Crevecoeur's lead and assumed that the American *is* different. The most significant and lasting work has been done by Frederick Jackson Turner. As noted in Volume III of this series, Turner singled out the natural American environment, the frontier, in order to explain why and how the American differed from Europeans. Turner's conclusion that the early American was characteristically individualistic, innovative, adaptive, and idealistic has been shared by many observers.

But Turner's idealistic conclusions are at variance with other observations that stress American materialism. Alexis de Tocqueville, America's most celebrated visitor, noted over a century ago that Americans had a "passion" for well-being: "I know of no country, indeed, where the love of money has taken stronger hold on the affections of men." Tocqueville also concluded that Americans preferred equality to liberty. Though a friendly critic, he emphasized the hardly flattering American tendency toward conformity and acquisitiveness.

An exciting attempt to reconcile the seeming contradictions of our national character has been made by historian David M. Potter. Potter opens his inquiry into the nature of the American character by deciding that the then-available studies by historians offer little assistance. Instead, behavioral scientists such as anthropologist Margaret Mead, psychologist Karen Horney, and sociologist David Riesman provide the most substantial insights, viz., that national character is ever-changing since environment and institutions are altered over periods of time. These and other scholars have impelled Potter to concentrate much more specifically on the ways in which the American natural and man-made environments impinge upon individuals and how, in reaction, those individuals behave. Thus, in the selection that follows, Potter maintains that advertising as an institution (a major part of our social environment) is the chief transmitter of the values of a consumer culture and thus directly affects the behavior (hence the character) of Americans. Potter ultimately concludes that economic abundance in countless ways (for example, the shift from breast to bottle feeding of infants and the consequent impact on the mother-child relationship) has shaped, and continues to shape, the American character.

The Institution of Abundance: Advertising

*F*or millions of people throughout the world, during the last three centuries, America has symbolized plenty. This profusion of wealth, this abundance of goods, has borne a significance that far transcends the field of economics. American democracy, in the broad sense, was made possible to begin with by a condition of economic surplus, and the constant incidence of this abundance has differentiated American democracy from the democracy of other, less richly endowed countries.

Abundance, then, must be reckoned a major force in our history. But one may question whether any force can be regarded as possessing major historic importance unless it has developed its own characteristic institution. Democracy, for instance, produces the institution of popular government— the whole complex of parties, elections, representative bodies, constitutions, and the like. Religion manifests itself in the church, with a canon law, a clergy, and a whole ecclesiastical system. Science and learning find institutional embodiment in universities, with all their libraries, laboratories, faculties, and other apparatus of scholarship. If abundance can legitimately be regarded as a great historical force, what institution is especially identified with it? Does any such institution exist?

In *The Great Frontier,* Walter Prescott Webb contends that the four-hundred-year boom beginning with the age of discovery profoundly altered all the institutions of Western civilization, and especially that it led to the emergence of laissez faire capitalism. He maintains this view most ably and with great insight, and it would be hard to deny that, in the large sense in which he deals with the subject, laissez faire capitalism is an institution of abundance. It is, however, a modification, profound to be sure, of an earlier capitalism and is not a wholly new institution. If we seek an institution that was brought into being by abundance, without previous existence in any form, and, moreover, an institution which is peculiarly identified with American abundance rather than with abundance throughout Western Civilization, we will find it, I believe, in modern American advertising.

Advertising as such is by no means a neglected subject. The excesses of advertising and of advertising men have been a favorite theme for a full quorum of modern satirists, cynics, and Jeremiahs. From the patent-medicine exposés in the early years of the century to the latest version of *The Hucksters,* advertising men have incurred fairly constant attack—their unscrupulous natures and their stomach ulcers being equally celebrated. Since advertising lends itself both to aesthetic

criticism and to moral criticism and since humanity is ever
ready with views in each of these areas, the flow of opinion has
been copious.

But advertising as an institution has suffered almost total
neglect. One might read fairly widely in the literature which
treats of public opinion, popular culture, and the mass media
in the United States without ever learning that advertising now
compares with such long-standing institutions as the school
and the church in the magnitude of its social influence. It
dominates the media, it has vast power in the shaping of popular standards, and it is really one of the very limited group of
institutions which exercise social control. Yet analysts of society have largely ignored it. Historians seldom do more than
glance at it in their studies of social history, and, when they
do, they usually focus attention upon some picturesque or titil-
lating aspect, such as the way in which advertising has reflected
or encouraged a new frankness about such previously tabooed
subjects as ladies' underwear. Histories of American periodicals
and even of the mass media deal with advertising as if it were
a side issue. Students of the radio and of the mass-circulation
magazines frequently condemn advertising for its conspicuous
role, as if it were a mere interloper in a separate, pre-existing,
self-contained aesthetic world of actors, musicians, authors,
and script-writers; they hardly recognize that advertising created modern American radio and television, transformed the
modern newspaper, evoked the modern slick periodical, and
remains the vital essence of each of them at the present time.
Marconi may have invented the wireless and Henry Luce may
have invented the news magazine, but it is advertising that has
made both wireless and news magazines what they are in
America today. It is as impossible to understand a modern
popular writer without understanding advertising as it would
be to understand a medieval troubadour without understanding the cult of chivalry, or a nineteenth-century revivalist without understanding evangelical religion.

Before undertaking the consideration of advertising as an
institution of social control—an instrument comparable to the
school and the church in the extent of its influence upon so-

ciety—perhaps it would be well to begin by observing something of the institution's growth to its present physical magnitude and financial strength.

A century ago advertising was a very minor form of economic activity, involving relatively small sums of money and
playing only a negligible part in the distribution of goods or
the formation of consumer habits. It was practiced principally
by retail distributors who offered items without the mention of
brands. Producers, who regarded the distributors as their market and who had as yet no concept of trying to reach the ultimate consumer, did not advertise at all and did not attempt
to signalize their product by a distinctive name or label.
Advertising ran heavily toward short prosaic notices like the
want ads of today, in which the tone was didactic rather than
hortatory or inspirational, and the content was factual. But
patent medicines, even at that time, were a conspicuous exception.

Publishers usually assumed that advertisements ought to be
of this nature, and, to protect the position of the small advertiser, some of them refused to accept notices using any type
larger than agate. But, to apply the *New Yorker*'s phrase historically, there has always been an ad man, and some of the
ad men of the mid-century began to use great numbers of
agate-sized letters, arranging them in the shape of large letters,
just as the members of a college band are sometimes arranged
in formation to spell out the initials of the alma mater. Publishers also correctly assumed that any considerable number of
small, compact advertisements would lend a deadly monotony
to the printed page, and some of them accordingly limited
rather narrowly the amount of advertising that they would
accept. In 1874, for instance, *The Youth's Companion* restricted the quantity of its advertising. As late as the 1870's,
when the Howe Sewing Machine Company offered $18,000 for
the back cover of *Harper's*, it was somewhat astonished to meet
with a polite but firm refusal.

But those days are gone forever, and no other phenomenon
of eighty years ago is now more remote. By 1880 advertising
had increased threefold since the Civil War period. By 1900 it

stood at $95,000,000 a year, which marked a tenfold increase over the amount in 1865. By 1919 it exceeded half a billion dollars, and by 1929 it reached $1,120,000,000. After 1929 it declined because of the Depression, but by 1951 it had again surpassed all previous levels and stood at $6,548,000,000 a year.

This immense financial growth reflects a number of vast and far-reaching changes. To begin with, the physical appearance of advertising underwent a complete transformation. The small box-insert ad gave way increasingly to larger spreads, and at last the full-page advertisement became the dominant form. Daniel Starch has shown, for instance, that in the 1860's and 1870's the average advertisement in the *Boston Evening Transcript* and the *New York Tribune* was about four column-inches, but by 1918 it was four times this size. In magazines, advertisers in the 1880's used half-page spaces two and a half times as often as they used full pages; by 1920 they did so only one-third as often. Before 1890 full-page entries constituted only a fifth of the advertising in magazines; but by 1920 they accounted for nearly half, and today the proportion must easily exceed half. Also, black and white gave way increasingly to color. As early as 1868 the *Galaxy* adopted the practice of using colored inserts, and, though this proved a little too far in advance of the times, it ultimately became standard practice among all large-circulation magazines.

Along with these changes in form went significant changes in the economic interests which advertised. For the first time producers began to perceive the possibilities in general advertising. At an earlier time they had addressed advertising by mail or on other limited bases to the distributors whom they hoped to induce to handle their goods, but they had left it to the distributor to deal with the ultimate consumer. As I have previously observed, they had apparently never conceived of the possibility of manufacturing their product under a distinctive brand name, or of using general advertising to create a consumer demand for their brand and thus of exerting pressure upon the distributor to keep their products in stock. But in the 1880's four pioneer producers began regularly to advertise their brands on a large scale. Significantly, perhaps, three of these were soaps: Sapolio, Pear's, and Ivory; the fourth was Royal Baking Powder. All of them achieved a large growth which was indisputably the result of advertising, and by doing so they demonstrated a truth which other producers were quick to grasp. As early as 1905, *Printer's Ink* proclaimed this new gospel when it declared: "This is a golden age in trade marks— a time when almost any maker of a worthy product can lay down the lines of a demand that will not only grow with years beyond anything that has ever been known before, but will become, in some degree, a monopoly. . . . Everywhere . . . there are opportunities to take the lead in advertising—to replace dozens of mongrel, unknown, unacknowledged makes of a fabric, a dress essential, a food, with a standard trade-marked brand, backed by the national advertising that in itself has come to be a guarantee of worth with the public."

As producers recognized the possibilities of this golden age, their advertising grew until it became primary: almost all so-called "national advertising" in magazines and over large networks is advertising by producers—while advertising by distributors, mostly in newspapers and over local broadcasting stations, has become secondary. The historian of the N. W. Ayer and Son Advertising Agency reports that "in the 'seventies and 'eighties, those who advertised through the Ayer firm were largely retailers and others who sold directly to the public. By 1890 most of these had ceased to use the Ayer agency, and its principal work was the advertising of manufacturers who sold through dealers and retailers but preferred to get control over their ultimate market."

Concurrently, the nature of the appeal which advertising employed was transformed. Producers were no longer trying merely to use advertising as a coupling device between existing market demand and their own supply; rather, they were trying to create a demand. Since the function of advertising had become one of exerting influence rather than one of providing information, the older factual, prosy notice which focused upon the specifications of the commodity now gave way to a more lyrical type of appeal which focused instead upon the desires of the consumer. This change was foreshadowed as early as 1903 by Walter Dill Scott, in an article on "The Psychology of Advertising," which formulated the basic law of the subject so clearly that he deserves to be regarded as the Archimedes, if not the Nostradamus, of the advertising world: "How many advertisers," he asked, "describe a piano so vividly that the reader can hear it? How many food products are so described that the reader can taste the food? . . . How many describe an undergarment so that the reader can feel the pleasant contact with his body? Many advertisers seem never to have thought of this, and make no attempt at such a description." That was in 1903. Today many advertisers seem to have thought of nothing else, and certainly all of them understand that advertising operates more to create wants in the minds of people than to capitalize on wants that are already active.

Inevitably a question arises: Why did this immense growth of advertising take place? To this query each of us might offer responses of his own, but perhaps the most carefully considered answer, at least in terms of economics, is provided by Neil H. Borden in his extremely thorough study of *The Economic Effects of Advertising* (1942). Borden explains this growth partly in terms of the widening economic gap between producers and consumers and the consequently increased need for a medium of communication, and he attributes the growth of large-scale national advertising, with its color, large spreads, and other expensive features, to the growth of big corporations able to pay for such publicity. But in addition to these explanations he adds another very essential one: "The quest for product differentiation became intensified as the industrial system became more mature, and as manufacturers had capacity to produce far beyond existing demand."

In other words, advertising is not badly needed in an economy of scarcity, because total demand is usually equal to or in excess of total supply, and every producer can normally sell as much as he produces. It is when potential supply outstrips demand—that is, when abundance prevails—that advertising begins to fulfill a really essential economic function. In this situation the producer knows that the limitation upon his operations and upon his growth no longer lies, as it lay historically, in his productive capacity, for he can always produce as much as the market will absorb; the limitation has shifted to the market, and it is selling capacity which controls his growth. Moreover, every other producer of the same kind of article is also in position to expand output indefinitely, and this means that the advertiser must distinguish his product, if not on essential grounds, then on trivial ones, and that he must drive home this distinction by employing a brand name and by keeping this name always before the public. In a situation of limited supply the scarcity of his product will assure his place in the market, but in a situation of indefinitely expandable supply his brand is his only means of assuring himself of such a place.

Let us consider this, however, not merely from the standpoint of the enterpriser but in terms of society as a whole. At once the vital nature of the change will be apparent: the most critical point in the functioning of society shifts from production to consumption, and, as it does so, the culture must be reoriented to convert the producer's culture into a consumer's culture. In a society of scarcity, or even of modern abundance, the productive capacity has barely sufficed to supply the goods which people already desire and which they regard as essential to an adequate standard of living. Hence the social imperative has fallen upon increases in production. But in a society of abundance, the productive capacity can supply new kinds of goods faster than society in the mass learns to crave these goods or to regard them as necessities. If this new capacity is to be used, the imperative must fall upon consumption, and the society must be adjusted to a new set of drives and values in which consumption is paramount.

The implications of the consumer orientation have received consideration from a number of writers, including David Riesman, who, in *The Lonely Crowd,* has described the consumer personality with notable insight. Among such writers, Percival and Paul Goodman, in their study *Communitas,* have, with brilliance and irony, pictured the life of a consumer society in the future. They begin by showing how, when unplanned production entered a phase of violent fluctuations in the 1920's, government responded with a New Deal which embodied a whole series of devices for the planning and stabilization of production. However, they observe, "there is no corresponding planning of consumption. . . . But hand in hand with a planned expanding production, there must be a planned expanding demand. . . . To leave the demand to the improvisations of advertisers is exactly on a par with the unplanned production of 1929." In order to plan an expansion of demand, they suggest, society requires an analysis of "Efficient Consumption," comparable to, though reversing, Veblen's concept of "Efficient Production." When Veblen set up laboriousness, interest in technique, and other productive virtues of the engineers in contradistinction to the restrictive qualities or practices of the capitalists, he was still thinking in terms of a need for more goods. "But," they continue, "the fact is that for at least two decades now it has been not scarcity of production which has kept men in political subjection (ironically enough, it has partly been the insecurity of so-called 'overproduction'); economically, it has been precisely the weakness, rather than the strength, of the consumption attitudes of emulation, ostentation, and sheer wastefulness which have depressed the productivity which is the economist's ideal. Only the instincts unleashed by war have sufficed, under modern conditions, to bring economic salvation.

"Then let us reverse the analysis and suggest how, even in peacetime, men can be as efficiently wasteful as possible. The city which we design on this principle is not only a theoretical solution for the economics which seem to have become official but also springs from the existent moral demands of the people who have crowded into such metropoles as New York."

In the society of consumption, as the Goodmans visualize it, production is only a means to the end of consumption, and therefore satisfaction in the work disappears. The workman accordingly focuses all his demands upon suitable working conditions, short hours, and high wages, so that he may hasten away with sufficient time, wealth, and energy to seek the goals of the consumer. This quest can be carried on "only in a great city. And the chief drive toward such goods is not individual but social. It is imitation and emulation which result in the lively demand. At first, perhaps, it is 'mass comforts' which satisfy cityfolk—these belong to the imitation of each other; but in the end it is luxuries; for these belong to emulation, to what Veblen used to call the 'imputation of superiority.' . . . All this can take place only in a great city. . . . The heart of the city of expanding effective demand is the department store. . . . Here all things are available according to desire— and are on display in order to suggest the desire. The streets are corridors of the department store; for the work of the people must not be quarantined from its cultural meaning."

In their description of the department-store metropolis, the Goodmans have pictured an unlovely utopia, but the utopia, nonetheless, of a consumer society. I have quoted them at some length because of the clarity with which they show the intrinsic nature of a pure consumer culture. But consumer societies, like all other kinds, seem to fall short of their utopias, and we revert to the question how the citizen, in our mixed production-consumption society, can be educated to perform his role as a consumer, especially as a consumer of goods for which he feels no impulse of need. Clearly he must be educated, and the only institution which we have for instilling new needs, for training people to act as consumers, for altering men's values, and thus for hastening their adjustment to potential abundance is advertising. That is why it seems to me valid to regard advertising as distinctively the institution of abundance.

If it is correct to regard advertising in this way, we must recognize at once that we are dealing with a force that is not merely economic. We are dealing, as I have already suggested, with one of the very limited group of institutions which can properly be called "instruments of social control." These institutions guide the life of the individual by conceiving of him in a distinctive way and encouraging him to conform as far as possible to the concept. For instance, the church, representing the force of religion, conceives of man as an immortal soul; our schools and colleges, representing the force of learning, conceive of him as a being whose behavior is guided by reason; our business and industry, representing the force of the economic free-enterprise system, conceive of him as a productive agent who can create goods or render services that are useful to mankind. Advertising, of course, is committed to none of these views and entertains them only incidentally. Representing as it does the force of a vast productive mechanism seeking outlets for an overwhelming flow of goods, it conceives of man as a consumer. Each institution is distinctive, again, in the qualities to which it appeals and in the character of the reward which it offers: the church appeals to the spirit or conscience of the individual and offers the rewards of salvation and peace of mind; learning appeals to the reason of man and offers the hope of a perfected society from which evils have been eliminated by the application of wisdom; free enterprise appeals to the energies and the capacities of man and offers the rewards of property, personal attainment, and satisfaction in the job. Advertising appeals primarily to the desires, the wants—cultivated or natural—of the individual, and it sometimes offers as its goal a power to command the envy of others by outstripping them in the consumption of goods and services.

To pursue this parallel a step further, one may add that the traditional institutions have tried to improve man and to develop in him qualities of social value, though, of course, these values have not always been broadly conceived. The church has sought to inculcate virtue and consideration of others—the golden rule; the schools have made it their business to stimulate ability and to impart skills; the free-enterprise system has constantly stressed the importance of hard work and the sinfulness of unproductive occupations. And at least two of these institutions, the church and the school, have been very self-conscious about their roles as guardians of the social values and have conducted themselves with a considerable degree of social responsibility.

In contrast with these, advertising has in its dynamics no motivation to seek the improvement of the individual or to impart qualities of social usefulness, unless conformity to material values may be so characterized. And, though it wields an immense social influence, comparable to the influence of religion and learning, it has no social goals and no social responsibility for what it does with its influence, so long as it refrains from palpable violations of truth and decency. It is this lack of institutional responsibility, this lack of inherent social purpose to balance social power, which, I would argue, is a basic cause for concern about the role of advertising. Occasional deceptions, breaches of taste, and deviations from sound ethical conduct are in a sense superficial and are not necessarily intrinsic. Equally, the high-minded types of advertising which we see more regularly than we sometimes realize are also extraneous to an analysis of the basic nature of advertising. What is basic is that advertising, as such, with all its vast power to influence values and conduct, cannot ever lose sight of the fact that it ultimately regards man as a consumer and defines its own mission as one of stimulating him to consume or to desire to consume.

If one can justifiably say that advertising has joined the charmed circle of institutions which fix the values and standards of society and that it has done this without being linked to any of the socially defined objectives which usually guide such institutions in the use of their power, then it becomes necessary to consider with special care the extent and nature of its influence—how far it extends and in what way it makes itself felt.

To do this, it may be well to begin with the budget, for the activity of all major institutions—great churches, great governments, great universities—can be measured in part by what they spend, and, though such measurements are no substitute for qualitative evaluation, they are significant. In political history the importance of the power of the purse is proverbial. I have already said that the amount spent for advertising in the United States in 1951 was $6,548,000,000. Perhaps this may be a little more meaningful if I add that the amount is equivalent to $199 per year for every separate family in the United States. Compare this with what the nation paid for primary and secondary public education in 1949, which amounted to a total expenditure of $5,010,000,000. This means that, for every household, we paid $152. Our national outlay for the education of citizens, therefore, amounted to substantially less than our expenditure for the education of consumers. It would also be interesting to compare the financial strength of advertising and of religion, but, since the churches do not publicize records of their financial operations, I can only remark that there were 180,000 gainfully employed clergymen in the United States in 1950, and most of them were men of very modest incomes. For every clergyman supported by any church, advertising spent $36,000.

Perhaps more explicit comparisons may serve to reinforce this point of the relative magnitude of advertising activities. I will mention two: In 1949–50 the operating expenses of Yale University were $15,000,000; in 1948 the expenses, for newspaper advertising only, of two major distilleries, Schenley and National Distillers, were more than half of this amount, or $7,800,000. In 1944 the major political parties spent $23,000,-000 to win the public to the support of Mr. Roosevelt or of Governor Dewey; in 1948, Procter and Gamble, Colgate-Palmolive-Peet, and Lever Brothers spent more than $23,000,000 to win the public to the support of one or another of their products.

With expenditures of this order of magnitude, advertising clearly thrusts with immense impact upon the mass media and, through them, upon the public. The obvious and direct impact is, of course, through the quantity of space it occupies in the newspapers and magazines and the amount of time it occupies in radio and television broadcasts. Either in space or in time the totals are impressive, and, if advertising had no influence upon the information in newspapers, the stories in magazines, and the programs in radio and television, it would still be a force worthy of major consideration because of the influence of the advertising matter itself. But it does have a profound influence upon the media, and for students of American opinion and American life it is important that this influence should be understood.

To appreciate this influence, let us consider the position of most magazines a century ago, as contrasted with their position today. At that time the only financial support which a magazine could expect was from its readers. This meant that, if a

person did not care to read, the magazine had no means of
appealing to him and no objective in doing so. If editors worried about circulation, it was because they needed more revenue from subscriptions, and if they had enough subscriptions
to support them on a modest scale of operations, they could
safely proceed on a basis of keeping their standards high and
their circulation limited. They did not worry very much about
advertising, for the reason that there was not much advertising
to worry about. At the time of the Civil War, for instance, it is
estimated that the total income from advertising received by
all newspapers and periodicals averaged about 25 cents per
capita yearly for the population at that time.

Today, of course, these conditions have ceased to apply.
Newspapers and magazines no longer look to their subscribers
as the major source of revenue. As long ago as 1935 the revenue
of all newspapers in the country was $760,000,000, of which
$500,000,000 came from advertising and $260,000,000 from subscriptions. At the same time, the magazines of the United States
enjoyed a revenue of $144,000,000 from subscriptions and
$186,000,000 from advertising. That is, approximately two out
of every three newspaper dollars came from advertising, and
more than one out of every two magazine dollars came from
the same source. The subscriber had been reduced to a sad
position: whereas at one time periodicals had fished for subscribers, they now fished for advertisers and used subscribers as
bait. Since that time, newspaper advertising has increased more
than threefold, to the total of $2,226,000,000, and magazine
advertising has risen to $562,000,000, from which we may infer
that the subscriber is now, more than ever before, a secondary
figure. If I may express the same point in a different way, the
situation is this: In 1935 American families paid an average of
$6.60 a year to receive newspapers, but advertisers paid an
average of $12.70 to have newspapers sent to each family, and
in 1951 advertising was paying $56 a year to have newspapers
delivered to each family. Clearly that was far more than the
household itself could possibly be expected to pay. Similarly,
with magazines, while subscribers in 1935 were paying $3.60 a
year to receive them, advertisers were paying $4.70 to have

them sent, and by 1951 American advertising had increased enough to pay $14 per family per year as its stake in the magazines on the living-room table of the American home. In many cases, as of magazines with large advertising sections, the real situation is that the advertiser buys the magazine for the "purchaser," and what the purchaser pays as the "price" of the magazine is really only a kind of qualifying fee to prove that he is a bona fide potential consumer and not a mere deadhead on whom this handsome advertising spread would be wasted.

If this were merely a matter of some magazines being published for consumers and other magazines being published for readers, with the public retaining a choice between the two, the result would not have been quite so sweeping; but the effect of this change has been to threaten with extinction the magazine that is published first and foremost for its readers.

The threat operates in this way: the magazine with large advertising revenue can afford to pay its contributors more, and therefore it can secure better contributors than the magazine which enjoys very little revenue of this kind. In a sense, the advertiser is prepared to buy better authors for the reader than the reader is prepared to buy for himself. But this means automatically that any magazine which wishes to secure or retain the best writers must get advertising. But to get advertising it must also get mass circulation. To get mass circulation it must publish material with a mass appeal. Also, it must keep its subscription costs low, which in turn makes it more dependent than ever upon advertising revenue. At this point a fixed cycle is virtually inescapable: millions of readers are essential to secure a large revenue from advertising, advertising is essential to enable the magazine to sell at a price that will secure millions of readers—therefore, the content of the magazine must be addressed to the millions. Thus the best writers, those who have proved able to write for the most discriminating readers, are put to work writing for consumers who may not be readers at all.

But it is even more significant to realize that other media are far more completely part of the institutional apparatus of advertising than are periodicals. Magazines and newspapers are still paid for in part by the consumer; but radio and television programs are paid for almost wholly by advertisers. In 1951 it was estimated that there were 100,000,000 radios in the United States, and radio advertising was estimated at $690,000,000. That is, advertisers were annually spending $6.90 to provide each set with programs, while the programs received by the 15,000,000 television sets were being subsidized at the rate of $32 a set.

What this means, in functional terms, it seems to me, is that the newspaper feature, the magazine article, the radio program, do not attain the dignity of being ends in themselves; they are rather means to an end: that end, of course, is to catch the reader's attention so that he will then read the advertisement or hear the commercial, and to hold his interest until these essential messages have been delivered. The program or the article becomes a kind of advertisement in itself—becomes the "pitch," in the telling language of the circus barker. Its function is to induce people to accept the commercial, just as the commercial's function is to induce them to accept the product.

A year or two ago an English critic complained of American periodical writing that it "fixes the attention but does not engage the mind." If this is true, it is not because of any intrinsic vacuity on the part of American writers but because the most important financial supporters of such writing are paying for it to do exactly what is alleged. "To fix the attention but not to engage the mind" is a precise statement of the advertiser's formula.

In saying this, I do not mean at all to suggest that advertisers are personally hostile to thoughtful writing or that they consciously desire to encourage writing which has a low intellectual content. On the contrary, it should be recognized that some of the advertising associations have shown themselves soberly aware of the power they wield and acutely desirous of using it for the public good. But it is the nature of advertising that it must aim for a mass appeal, and it is the nature of the mass media that they must present any item—an idea or a fact or a point of view—in such a way that it will attract the maximum number of readers. To do this, of course, they must suppress any controversial or esoteric aspects of the item and must express it in terms of the least common denominator. But these terms are usually emotional ones rather than rational ones, for the emotional impulses of a large group of people are much more uniform throughout the group than are the mental processes of various individuals in the same group. Walter Lippmann expressed this idea very precisely a good many years ago, in his *The Phantom Public.* He was speaking of political action, but his words nevertheless apply to all communication which involves masses of people. "Since the general opinions of large numbers of persons," he said, "are almost certain to be a vague and confusing medley, action cannot be taken until these opinions have been factored down, canalized, compressed, and made uniform. The making of one general will out of a multitude of general wishes . . . consists essentially in the use of symbols which assemble emotions after they have been detached from their ideas. . . . The process, therefore, by which general opinions are brought to coöperation consists of an intensification of feeling and a degradation of significance."

Mr. Donald Slesinger, speaking at the University of Chicago some years ago, made a very similar observation in a context which included other matters besides politics. "Since common experience is essential to communication," he said, "the greater the number to be [simultaneously] reached, the simpler the communication must be."

These factors of simplification, of intensifying the feeling while degrading the significance, and of fixing the attention of the mass audience are all related to one basic condition of the media, namely, that they are concerned not with finding an audience to hear their message but rather with finding a message to hold their audience. The prime requisite of the message is that it must not diminish the audience either by antagonizing or by leaving out anyone. Moreover, since the actual personnel and tastes of a vast, amorphous, and "invisible" audience cannot possibly be known, the result is, in effect, to set up an axiom that the message must not say anything that, in the opinion of a cautious proprietor, might *possibly* offend or leave out some of those who might *possibly* form part of the audi-

ence. For such an axiom there are several implicit corollaries of
far-reaching importance. First, a message must not deal with
subjects of special or out-of-the-way interest, since such subjects
by definition have no appeal for the majority of the audience.
Second, it must not deal with any subject at a high level of maturity, since many people are immature, chronologically or
otherwise, and a mature level is one which, by definition, leaves
such people out. Third, it must not deal with matters which
are controversial or even unpleasant or distressing, since such
matters may, by definition, antagonize or offend some members
of the audience.

If I may examine each of these corollaries briefly, we are confronted first with the fact that many perfectly inoffensive and
noncontroversial subjects are excluded from the media simply
because these subjects appeal to only a limited number of people. Being directed to the millions, the media must necessarily
avoid consideration of subjects which interest only the thousands or the hundreds. This implies a danger to freedom of expression, but not the precise danger against which the guardians of our liberties are usually warning us. They fear that
large publishers and advertisers, wielding autocratic power,
will ruthlessly suppress minority ideas. The dynamics of the
mass market, however, would seem to indicate that freedom
of expression has less to fear from the control which large advertisers exercise than from the control which these advertisers
permit the mass market to exercise. In the mass media we have
little evidence of censorship in the sense of deliberate, planned
suppression imposed by moral edict but much evidence of
censorship in the sense of operative suppression of a great
range of subjects—a suppression imposed by public indifference or, more precisely, by the belief of those who control the
media, that the public would be indifferent.

For instance, as Slesinger remarked, motion pictures cannot
concern themselves with topics that interest only a minority of
people. To borrow his illustration, there is no group which
would regard treatment of the themes of horticulture or
antique-collecting as objectionable, yet, in fact, motion pictures
are in effect barred from using these themes, because "the part

of the audience that was interested in horticulture might very well be completely bored by the collection of antiques. But both the gardeners and the antique-collectors can readily get together on a kiss in the dark."

Closely related to the exclusion of special subjects is the avoidance of advanced or mature treatment of the subjects which are accepted. Paul F. Lazarsfeld has investigated this aspect of the matter as it manifests itself in connection with radio and has stated his conclusions very pointedly. He speaks of the appearance of a new type of "radio consumer" in many cultural areas. "Radio," he said, writing in 1941, "has helped to bring to the attention of the American people the important events in Europe and thus has contributed to the generally increased interest in news. However, it has been shown in special studies that this new type of news-consumer created by radio has a more hazy knowledge and a less acute interest in those events than the traditional and smaller groups of people with long-established news interests. A similar audience has been developed in the field of serious music. There is no doubt that the broadcasting of good music over hundreds of stations in this country has enlarged the number of those who like it. Still, a more detailed study of their tastes and attitudes has shown that the musical world of these new music lovers is different, if not inferior, to that of the musical elite of past decades and as judged by classical standards."

In a democracy no one should disparage the value of any activity which serves to raise the level of popular taste, but it is still legitimate to count the cost of such a gain. Particularly in connection with news broadcasting and in connection with popular articles on public affairs, it seems to me that we can easily see the application of Walter Lippmann's formula, "the intensification of feeling and the degradation of significance."

Finally, there is the avoidance of the controversial or distressing. This manifests itself not only in connection with obvious matters such as labor unionization, race relations, or the like, but more fundamentally in the creation of a stereotype of society from which all questions of social significance are carefully screened out. Lazarsfeld has made this point, also, very strikingly with radio "soap operas" as his illustration. These programs, numbering nearly three hundred a day ten years ago, are eagerly awaited throughout the nation by millions of women who might certainly be expected "to pattern their own behavior upon the solutions for domestic problems that appear in the serials." But, in fact, Lazarsfeld found that the programs carefully refrained from exercising any such influence: "The settings are middle class—conforming to the environment of the listeners. In forty-five serials carefully followed up for three weeks, not one character was found who came from the laboring class. Inasmuch as they are upper-class characters, they are used to lend glamour to the middle-class settings rather than to play a role of their own. All problems are of an individualistic nature. It is not social forces but the virtues and vices of the central characters that move the events along. People lose jobs not for economic reasons but because their fellow-men lie or are envious. A simple black and white technique avoids any insoluble conflicts. Even the everyday activities of the characters are patterned according to what the listeners presumably do themselves; reading, for instance, is something which is rarely done in these plays. No other effect than the reinforcement of already existing attitudes can be expected from such programs."

In a sense—a negative sense—the desire to offend no one involves an attitude of what may be called "tolerance." As David Riesman tellingly remarks, the writer or broadcaster, addressing himself to the amorphous audience, does not know how the virus of indignation may be received, and he must therefore "be preoccupied with the antibodies of tolerance." But, clearly, this tolerance is, as the phrase implies, one of mental asepsis rather than one of mental nourishment. It deals with ideas not by weighing them but by diluting them. Tolerance once implied that the advocates of an idea might be heard without prejudice and judged on their merits, but this toleration merely implies that, since society will refrain from exercising the power to judge them, it will relieve itself of responsibility to hear them. It involves not impartiality of judgment but simply default of judgment.

In the realm of politics, of course, antagonistic points of view do continue to receive a hearing, and the continued presence of vigorously partisan editorials and radio addresses by men in political life may seem to disprove all that I have just been saying; but the significant fact is that the political sector is the only one where the indulgence, or even the recognition, of vigorously maintained viewpoints is permitted. Many social questions, many of the profound problems of American life, lie beyond the pale.

In this discussion of the importance of advertising, the purpose has been to explore its effects upon the noneconomic phases of our culture. For that reason I have refrained from introducing some significant points in connection with the changes wrought by advertising in the economy. For instance, it is important that advertising tends less to provide the consumer with what he wants than to make him like what he gets. In this connection Richard B. Tennant, in his recent book on the American cigarette industry, shows that the American Tobacco Company, in the second decade of this century, produced at least eight different brands of cigarettes, designed to meet the diverse demands of varying smoking tastes and different purses; but after 1925 it began to concentrate its advertising upon Lucky Strikes and after 1927 began to dispose of its minor brands to other companies, though it did later develop Herbert Tareytons and Pall Malls. Also, it is important that advertising tends to minimize information and maximize appeal, with the result that producers tend less to differentiate their products physically, in terms of quality, or economically, in terms of price, than to differentiate them psychologically in terms of slogan, package, or prestige. "How many advertisers," asked Walter Dill Scott in 1903, "describe an undergarment so that the reader can feel the pleasant contact with the body?" Surely this is one question to which time has given us a definite answer.

But the most important effects of this powerful institution are not upon the economics of our distributive system; they are upon the values of our society. If the economic effect is to make the purchaser like what he buys, the social effect is, in a parallel but broader sense, to make the individual like what he gets—to enforce already existing attitudes, to diminish the range and variety of choices, and, in terms of abundance, to exalt the materialistic virtues of consumption.

Certainly it marks a profound social change that this new institution for shaping human standards should be directed, not, as are the school and the church, to the inculcation of beliefs or attitudes that are held to be of social value, but rather to the stimulation or even the exploitation of materialistic drives and emulative anxieties and then to the validation, the sanctioning, and the standardization of these drives and anxieties as accepted criteria of social value. Such a transformation, brought about by the need to stimulate desire for the goods which an abundant economy has to offer and which a scarcity economy would never have produced, offers strong justification for the view that advertising should be recognized as an important social influence and as our newest major institution—an institution peculiarly identified with one of the most pervasive forces in American life, the force of economic abundance.

Abundance and the Formation of Character

As this analysis draws toward a close, any student of the behavioral sciences who has read this far may quite possibly feel that he has been imposed upon. As far back as chapter 2, I was rash enough to suggest that history and the behavioral sciences might have something to offer, each to the other, in the study of man. In that chapter it was asserted that history has a function in explaining the determinants of culture; the value of history in interpreting national character was asserted, and emphasis was even placed upon the statement of Hans Gerth and C. Wright Mills that "the structural and historical features of modern society must be connected with the most intimate features of man's self."

But then, so the complaint might run, this relation between

the public and the private aspects of American life was not really developed. The author, being a student of history, did as might be expected. After superficial lip service to an arresting idea—the idea of working along an important but neglected interdisciplinary frontier—he relapsed into a comfortable historical perspective from which he could examine the kind of topics which historians customarily examine: the quest for equality, the ideal of democracy, the concept of an American mission to redeem the world, the experience of the frontier, and the impact of advertising. What possible value can such discussions have for a behavioral scientist who is trying to find out about the formation of personality or character in an individual infant? This infant—any infant—is the child of specific parents. He lives in a specific place and is exposed not only to his parents but to kinspeople and neighbors and, by the third or fourth year of life, to other small fry whom the psychologist will designate as his "peers." The behavioral scientist wants to know how the circumstances and traits of all these people control their attitudes and behavior toward the infant; in what way they manifest these attitudes and project their own values, their tensions, their orientation, upon the child; and by what process he receives these projections from the outside and internalizes them as part of the character within his own personality. This is what the behavioral scientist means when he talks about the formation of personality or of character. Certainly, therefore, the question arises: What pertinence can such topics as "mobility," "equality," "democracy," "the frontier," or "advertising" have in the kind of investigation that he conducts?

The present chapter seeks to face this question honestly, by attempting to show in direct terms how these generalized and impersonal factors, pertaining to the economy of abundance, do impinge upon the primary conditions in the infancy of an American child. If worth-while links between history and the behavioral sciences really exist, the only conclusive way to establish them will be by showing them fully in this way. But, before proceeding to this attempt, it seems valid to recognize that the general historical factors already discussed and the specific life-experiences which seem critical to the behavioral scientist are not as disparate as they might appear.

Ever since the time of Freud, behavioral scientists have steadily been broadening their conception of the range of external experience which goes into the formation of personality. Freud himself dealt heavily in biological drives and instinctual impulses which were inherent in the individual and did not have to be accounted for by any experience with the external world. Subsequently, however, psychoanalysts like Erich Fromm and Karen Horney recognized that many manifestations which Freud had regarded as universal were, in fact, limited to specific cultures. In the course of time, these revisionists fought and won the battle for recognition of the principle that culture determines personality. But even after this victory many seemed anxious to confine themselves to the narrowest possible segment of the culture. It was generally agreed that "the effects of environmental forces in moulding the personality are, in general, the more profound, the earlier in the life history of the individual they are brought to bear." This premise gave to investigators a sound basis for assigning a very high priority to parent-child relationships and the experiences of infancy, and this priority seems to be altogether valid. But there has been an especially marked tendency in very recent studies to accord more recognition to the broad range of the cultural experience. It was because of this tendency that Haring, in his comparison between the characters of the Japanese of Amami Oshima and the Japanese of Japan proper, makes such an emphatic point of the fact that police tyranny and not infant training seems to be the critical factor in causing the divergence. The same reason led T. W. Adorno, in 1950, to assert the necessity for taking general social and economic conditions into account: "The major influences upon personality development arise in the course of child training as carried forward in a setting of family life. What happens here is profoundly influenced by economic and social factors. It is not only that each family in trying to rear its children proceeds according to the ways of the social, ethnic, and religious groups in which it has membership, but crude economic factors affect directly the parents' behavior toward the child. This means that broad changes in social conditions and institutions will have a direct bearing upon the kinds of personalities that develop within a society."

One of the most striking expressions of this demand for a broader recognition of the whole gamut of experience has been voiced by Hans Gerth and C. Wright Mills (*Character and Social Structure* [New York: Harcourt, Brace & Co., 1953]), and, though it was quoted previously in chapter 2, it is perhaps of sufficient importance to justify repetition. Their position is that they are not even prepared to concede that the experiences of infancy are crucial without submitting the whole question to intensive study: "We cannot . . . rest content with the assumption that the kinship order, with its tensions of early love and authority, is necessarily the basic and lasting factor in the formation of personality; and that other orders of society are projective systems from this, until we have studied the selection and continued formation of personality in the economic and religious and political institutions of various social structures. The father may not be the *primary* authority, but rather the replica of the power relations of society, and of course, the unwitting transmitter of larger authorities to his spouse and children."

In the light of these statements and others like them and in view also of the factors currently being examined by students of personality, it is now evident that social psychology is steadily reaching out more widely to bring the major tendencies of the political, economic, and social spheres within the range of its analysis. Topics such as "advertising," or "the frontier," or "the democratic ideal" no longer seem so remote from the study of personality as they once appeared.

Also, these topics are not so far removed from "the most intimate features of man's self" as a literal approach to them might indicate. It is true that historical discussion of such topics is usually couched in general or collective terms, so that one thinks of democracy in connection with public decisions; of advertising in connection with the mass media; or of the frontier in connection with the temporary absence of public institutions and services such as law, organized religion, and organized medicine. But all these clearly have their bearings upon the individual in his personal capacity. American ideas of equality, for instance, apply not only politically between fellow-citizens but also within the family, where relations between husband and wife or even between parent and child do not reflect the principle of authority nearly so much as in most countries which share the Western tradition. The frontier exercised many imperatives upon the individual, for it determined rigorously the role which he had to fill: he had to be capable of performing a very wide variety of functions without relying upon anyone else, and he had to exercise his own judgment in deciding when to perform them. From his early youth this was what society required of him. Also, it expected him to show a considerable measure of hardihood, and to do this from childhood, especially if he were a boy. To take the example of advertising, this also trains the individual for a role—the role of a consumer—and it profoundly modifies his system of values, for it articulates the rationale of material values for him in the same way in which the church articulates a rationale of spiritual values.

In the same way, almost all public and general forces can be found operating in the private and individual sphere. Hence it is not at all far-fetched to argue that even a discussion of the general aspect of one of these forces is full of implicit indications which touch the personal lives and the conditioning and response of individuals. Many such indications are intended in the preceding chapters. But, if the utility of the historical approach in an understanding of the factors of personality formation is to be adequately proved, something more than an indirect or implicit relationship must be established. The questions recur: What, if anything, does the factor of abundance have to do with the process of personality formation (in so far as this process is understood) in the United States? How does the process differ from that in countries where the measure of abundance is not so great?

To these questions, I believe, some highly explicit answers are possible. Let us therefore be entirely concrete. Let us consider the situation of a six-month-old American infant, who is not yet aware that he is a citizen, a taxpayer, and a consumer.

This individual is, to all appearances, just a very young specimen of *Homo sapiens,* with certain needs for protection, care, shelter, and nourishment which may be regarded as the universal biological needs of human infancy rather than specific cultural needs. It would be difficult to prove that the culture has as yet differentiated him from other infants, and, though he is an American, few would argue that he has acquired an American character. Yet abundance and the circumstances arising from abundance have already dictated a whole range of basic conditions which, from his birth, are constantly at work upon this child and which will contribute in the most intimate and basic way to the formation of his character.

To begin with, abundance has already revolutionized the typical mode of his nourishment by providing for him to be fed upon cow's milk rather than upon his mother's milk, taken from the bottle rather than from the breast. Abundance contributes vitally to this transformation, because bottle feeding requires fairly elaborate facilities of refrigeration, heating, sterilization, and temperature control, which only an advanced technology can offer and only an economy of abundance can make widely available. I will not attempt here to resolve the debated question as to the psychological effects, for both mother and child, of bottle feeding as contrasted with breast feeding in infant nurture. But it is clear that the changeover to bottle feeding has encroached somewhat upon the intimacy of the bond between mother and child. The nature of this bond is, of course, one of the most crucial factors in the formation of character. Bottle feeding also must tend to emphasize the separateness of the infant as an individual, and thus it makes, for the first time, a point which the entire culture reiterates constantly throughout the life of the average American. In addition to the psychic influences which may be involved in the manner of taking the food, it is also a matter of capital importance that the bottle-fed baby is, on the whole, better nourished than the breast-fed infant and therefore likely to grow more rapidly, to be more vigorous, and to suffer fewer ailments, with whatever effects these physical conditions may have upon his personality.

It may be argued also that abundance has provided a characteristic mode of housing for the infant and that this mode further emphasizes his separateness as an individual. In societies of scarcity, dwelling units are few and hard to come by, with the result that high proportions of newly married young people make their homes in the parental ménage, thus forming part of an "extended" family, as it is called. Moreover, scarcity provides a low ratio of rooms to individuals, with the consequence that whole families may expect as a matter of course to have but one room for sleeping, where children will go to bed in intimate propinquity to their parents. But abundance prescribes a different regime. By making it economically possible for newly married couples to maintain separate households of their own, it has almost destroyed the extended family as an institution in America and has ordained that the child shall be reared in a "nuclear" family, so-called, where his only intimate associates are his parents and his siblings, with even the latter far fewer now than in families of the past. The housing arrangements of this new-style family are suggested by census data for 1950. In that year there were 45,983,000 dwelling units to accommodate the 38,310,000 families in the United States, and, though the median number of persons in the dwelling unit was 3.1, the median number of rooms in the dwelling unit was 4.6. Eighty-four per cent of all dwelling units reported less than one person per room. By providing the ordinary family with more than one room for sleeping, the economy thus produces a situation in which the child will sleep either in a room alone or in a room shared with his brothers or sisters. Even without allowing for the cases in which children may have separate rooms, these conditions mean that a very substantial percentage of children now sleep in a room alone, for, with the declining birth rate, we have reached a point at which an increasing proportion of families have one child or two children rather than the larger number which was at one time typical. For instance, in the most recent group of mothers who had completed their childbearing phase, according to the census,

19.5 per cent had had one child and 23.4 had had two. Thus almost half of all families with offspring did not have more than two children throughout their duration. In the case of the first group, all the children were "only" children throughout their childhood, and in the second group half of the children were "only" children until the second child was born. To state this in another, and perhaps a more forcible, way, it has been shown that among American women who arrived at age thirty-four during the year 1949 and who had borne children up to that time, 26.7 per cent had borne only one child, and 34.5 per cent had borne only two. If these tendencies persist, it would mean that, among families where there are children, hardly one in three will have more than two children.

The census has, of course, not got around to finding out how the new-style family, in its new-style dwelling unit, adjusts the life-practice to the space situation. But it is significant that America's most widely circulated book on the care of infants advises that "it is preferable that he [the infant] not sleep in his parents' room after he is about 12 months old," offers the opinion that "it's fine for each [child] to have a room of his own, if that's possible," and makes the sweeping assertion that "it's a sensible rule not to take a child into the parents' bed for any reason." It seems clear beyond dispute that the household space provided by the economy of abundance has been used to emphasize the separateness, the apartness, if not the isolation, of the American child.

Not only the nourishment and housing, but also the clothing of the American infant are controlled by American abundance. For one of the most sweeping consequences of our abundance is that, in contrast to other peoples who keep their bodies warm primarily by wearing clothes, Americans keep their bodies warm primarily by a far more expensive and even wasteful method: namely, by heating the buildings in which they are sheltered. Every American who has been abroad knows how much lighter is the clothing—especially the underclothing—of Americans than of people in countries like England and France, where the winters are far less severe than ours, and every American who can remember the conditions of a few decades ago knows how much lighter our clothing is than that of our grandparents. These changes have occurred because clothing is no longer the principal device for securing warmth. The oil furnace has not only displaced the open fireplace; it has also displaced the woolen undergarment and the vest.

This is a matter of considerable significance for adults but of far greater importance to infants, for adults discipline themselves to wear warm garments, submitting, for instance, to woolen underwear more or less voluntarily. But the infant knows no such discipline, and his garments or bedclothes must be kept upon him by forcible means. Hence primitive people, living in outdoor conditions, swaddle the child most rigorously, virtually binding him into his clothes, and breaking him to them almost as a horse is broken to the harness. Civilized peoples mitigate the rigor but still use huge pins or clips to frustrate the baby's efforts to kick off the blankets and free his limbs. In a state of nature, cold means confinement and warmth means freedom, so far as young humans are concerned. But abundance has given the American infant physical freedom by giving him physical warmth in cold weather.

In this connection it may be surmised that abundance has also given him a permissive system of toilet training. If our forebears imposed such training upon the child and we now wait for him to take the initiative in these matters himself, it is not wholly because the former held a grim Calvinistic doctrine of child-rearing that is philosophically contrary to ours. The fact was that the circumstances gave them little choice. A mother who was taking care of several babies, keeping them clean, making their clothes, washing their diapers in her own washtub, and doing this, as often as not, while another baby was on the way, had little choice but to hasten their fitness to toilet themselves. Today, on the contrary, the disposable diaper, the diaper service, and most of all the washing machine, not to mention the fact that one baby seldom presses upon the heels of another, make it far easier for the mother to indulge the child in a regime under which he will impose his own toilet controls in his own good time.

Thus the economy of plenty has influenced the feeding of

the infant, his regime, and the physical setting within which he lives. These material conditions alone might be regarded as having some bearing upon the formation of his character, but the impact of abundance by no means ends at this point. In so far as it has an influence in determining what specific individuals shall initiate the infant into the ways of man and shall provide him with his formative impressions of the meaning of being a person, it must be regarded as even more vital. When it influences the nature of the relationships between these individuals and the infant, it must be recognized as reaching to the very essence of the process of character formation.

The central figures in the dramatis personae of the American infant's universe are still his parents, and in this respect, of course, there is nothing peculiar either to the American child or to the child of abundance. But abundance has at least provided him with parents who are in certain respects unlike the parents of children born in other countries or born fifty years ago. To begin with, it has given him young parents, for the median age of fathers at the birth of the first child in American marriages (as of 1940) was 25.3 years, and the median age of mothers was 22.6 years. This median age was substantially lower than it had been in the United States in 1890 for both fathers and mothers. Moreover, as the size of families has been reduced and the wife no longer continues to bear a succession of children throughout the period of her fertility, the median age of mothers at the birth of the last child has declined from 32 years (1890) to 27 years (1940). The age of the parents at the birth of both the first child and the last child is far lower than in the case of couples in most European countries. There can be little doubt that abundance has caused this differential, in the case of the first-born by making it economically possible for a high proportion of the population to meet the expenses of homemaking at a fairly early age. In the case of the last-born, it would also appear that one major reason for the earlier cessation of child-bearing is a determination by parents to enjoy a high standard of living themselves and to limit their offspring to a number for whom they can maintain a similar standard.

By the very fact of their youth, these parents are more likely to remain alive until the child reaches maturity, thus giving him a better prospect of being reared by his own mother and father. This prospect is further reinforced by increases in the life-span, so that probably no child in history has ever enjoyed so strong a likelihood that his parents will survive to rear him. Abundance has produced this situation by providing optimum conditions for prolonging life. But, on the other hand, abundance has also contributed much to produce an economy in which the mother is no longer markedly dependent upon the father, and this change in the economic relation between the sexes has probably done much to remove obstacles to divorce. The results are all too familiar. During the decade 1940–49 there were 25.8 divorces for every 100 marriages in the United States, which ratio, if projected over a longer period, would mean that one marriage out of four would end in divorce. But our concern here is with a six-month-old child, and the problem is to know whether this factor of divorce involves childless couples predominantly or whether it is likely to touch him. The answer is indicated by the fact that, of all divorces granted in 1948, no less than 42 per cent were to couples with children under eighteen, and a very large proportion of these children were of much younger ages. Hence one might say that the economy of abundance has provided the child with younger parents who chose their role of parenthood deliberately and who are more likely than parents in the past to live until he is grown, but who are substantially less likely to preserve the unbroken family as the environment within which he shall be reared.

In addition to altering the characteristics of the child's parents, it has also altered the quantitative relationship between him and his parents. It has done this, first of all, by offering the father such lucrative opportunities through work outside the home that the old agricultural economy in which children worked alongside their fathers is now obsolete. Yet, on the other hand, the father's new employment gives so much more leisure than his former work that the child may, in fact, receive considerably more of his father's attention. But the most vital transformation is in the case of the mother. In the economy of scarcity which controlled the modes of life that were traditional for many centuries, an upper-class child was reared by a nurse, and all others were normally reared by their mothers. The scarcity economy could not support many nonproductive members, and these mothers, though not "employed," were most decidedly hard workers, busily engaged in cooking, washing, sewing, weaving, preserving, caring for the henhouse, the garden, and perhaps the cow, and in general carrying on the domestic economy of a large family. Somehow they also attended to the needs of a numerous brood of children, but the mother was in no sense a full-time attendant upon any one child. Today, however, the economy of abundance very nearly exempts a very large number of mothers from the requirement of economic productivity in order that they may give an unprecedented share of their time to the care of the one or two young children who are now the usual number in an American family. Within the home, the wide range of labor-saving devices and the assignment of many functions, such as laundering, to service industries have produced this result. Outside the home, employment of women in the labor force has steadily increased, but the incidence of employment falls upon unmarried women, wives without children, and wives with grown children. In fact, married women without children are two and one-half times as likely to be employed as those with children. Thus what amounts to a new dispensation has been established for the child. If he belongs to the upper class, his mother has replaced his nurse as his full-time attendant. The differences in character formation that might result from this change alone could easily be immense. To mention but one possibility, the presence of the nurse must inevitably have made the child somewhat aware of his class status, whereas the presence of the mother would be less likely to have this effect. If the child does not belong to the upper class, mother and child now impinge upon each other in a relationship whose intensity is of an entirely different magnitude from that which prevailed in the past. The mother has fewer physical distractions in the care of the child, but she is more likely to be restive in her maternal role because it takes her away from attractive employment with which it cannot be reconciled.

If abundance has thus altered the relationship of the child with his parent, it has even more drastically altered the rest of his social milieu, for it has changed the identity of the rest of the personnel who induct him into human society. In the extended family of the past, a great array of kinspeople filled his cosmos and guided him to maturity. By nature, he particularly needed association with children of his own age (his "peers," as they are called), and he particularly responded to the values asserted by these peers. Such peers were very often his brothers and sisters, and, since they were all members of his own family, all came under parental control. This is to say that, in a sense, the parents controlled the peer group, and the peer group controlled the child. The point is worth making because we frequently encounter the assertion that parental control of the child has been replaced by peer-group control; but it is arguable that what is really the case is that children were always deeply influenced by the peer group and that parents have now lost their former measure of control over this group, since it is no longer a familial group. Today the nursery school replaces the large family as a peer group, and the social associations, even of young children, undergo the same shift from focused contact with family to diffused contact with a miscellany of people, which John Galsworthy depicted for grown people in the three novels of the *Forsyte Saga*. Again, the effects upon character may very well be extensive.

Abundance, then, has played a critical part in revolutionizing both the physical circumstances and the human associations which surround the American infant and child. These changes alone would warrant the hypothesis that abundance has profoundly affected the formation of character for such a child. But to extend this inquiry one step further, it may be worth while to consider how these altered conditions actually impinge upon the individual. Here, of course, is an almost unlimited field for investigation, and I shall only attempt to indicate certain crucial points at which abundance projects conditions that are basic in the life of the child.

One of these points concerns the cohesive force which holds the family together. The family is the one institution which touches all members of society most intimately, and it is perhaps the only social institution which touches young children directly. The sources from which the family draws its strength are, therefore, of basic importance. In the past, these sources were, it would seem, primarily economic. For agrarian society, marriage distinctively involved a division of labor. Where economic opportunity was narrowly restricted, the necessity for considering economic ways and means in connection with marriage led to the arrangement of matches by parents and to the institution of the dowry. The emotional bonds of affection, while always important, were not deemed paramount, and the ideal of romantic love played little or no part in the lives of ordinary people. Where it existed at all, it was as an upper-class luxury. (The very term "courtship" implies this upper-class orientation.) This must inevitably have meant that the partners in the majority of marriages demanded less from one another emotionally than do the partners of romantic love and that the emotional factor was less important to the stability of the marriage. Abundance, however, has played its part in changing this picture. On the American frontier, where capital for dowries was as rare as opportunity for prosperous marriage was plentiful, the dowry became obsolete. Later still, when abundance began to diminish the economic duties imposed upon the housewife, the function of marriage as a division of labor ceased to seem paramount, and the romantic or emotional factor assumed increasing importance. Abundance brought the luxury of romantic love within the reach of all, and, as it did so, emotional harmony became the principal criterion of success in a marriage, while lack of such harmony became a major threat to the existence of the marriage. The statistics of divorce give us a measure of the loss of durability in marriage, but they give us no measure of the factors of instability in the marriages which endure and no measure of the increased focus upon emotional satisfactions in such marriages. The children of enduring marriages, as well as the children of divorce, must inevitably feel the impact of this increased emphasis upon emotional factors, must inevitably sense the difference in the foundations of the institution which holds their universe in place.

In the rearing of a child, it would be difficult to imagine any factors more vital than the distinction between a permissive and an authoritarian regime or more vital than the age at which economic responsibility is imposed. In both these matters the modern American child lives under a very different dispensation from children in the past. We commonly think of these changes as results of our more enlightened or progressive or humanitarian ideas. We may even think of them as results of developments in the specific field of child psychology, as if the changes were simply a matter of our understanding these matters better than our grandparents. But the fact is that the authoritarian discipline of the child, within the authoritarian family, was but an aspect of the authoritarian social system that was linked with the economy of scarcity. Such a regime could never have been significantly relaxed within the family so long as it remained diagnostic in the society. Nor could it have remained unmodified within the family, once society began to abandon it in other spheres.

Inevitably, the qualities which the parents inculcate in a child will depend upon the roles which they occupy themselves. For the ordinary man the economy of scarcity has offered one role, as Simon N. Patten observed many years ago, and the economy of abundance has offered another. Abundance offers "work calling urgently for workmen"; scarcity found the "worker seeking humbly any kind of toil." As a suppliant to his superiors, the worker under scarcity accepted the principle of authority; he accepted his own subordination and the obligation to cultivate the qualities appropriate to his subordination, such as submissiveness, obedience, and deference. Such a man naturally transferred the principle of authority into his own family and, through this principle, instilled into his children the qualities appropriate to people of their kind—submissiveness, obedience, and deference. Many copybook maxims still exist to remind us of the firmness of childhood discipline, while the difference between European and American children—one of the most clearly recognizable of all national differences—serves to emphasize the extent to which Americans have now departed from this firmness.

This new and far more permissive attitude toward children has arisen, significantly, in an economy of abundance, where work has called urgently for the workman. In this situation, no longer a suppliant, the workman found submissiveness no longer a necessity and therefore no longer a virtue. The principle of authority lost some of its majesty, and he was less likely to regard it as the only true criterion of domestic order. In short, he ceased to impose it upon his children. Finding that the most valuable trait in himself was a capacity for independent decision and self-reliant conduct in dealing with the diverse opportunities which abundance offered him, he tended to encourage this quality in his children. The irresponsibility of childhood still called for a measure of authority on one side and obedience on the other, but this became a means to an end and not an end in itself. On the whole, permissive training, to develop independent ability, even though it involves a certain sacrifice of obedience and discipline, is the characteristic mode of child-rearing in the one country which most distinctively enjoys an economy of abundance. Here, in a concrete way, one finds something approaching proof for Gerth and Mills's suggestion that the relation of father and child may have its importance not as a primary factor but rather as a "replica of the power relations of society."

If scarcity required men to "seek humbly any kind of toil," it seldom permitted women to seek employment outside the home at all. Consequently, the woman was economically dependent upon, and, accordingly, subordinate to, her husband or her father. Her subordination reinforced the principle of authority within the home. But the same transition which altered the role of the male worker has altered her status as well, for abundance "calling urgently for workmen" makes no distinctions of gender, and, by extending economic indepen-

dence to women, has enabled them to assume the role of partners rather than of subordinates within the family. Once the
relation of voluntarism and equality is introduced between
husband and wife, it is, of course, far more readily extended to
the relation between parent and child.

If abundance has fostered a more permissive regime for the
child, amid circumstances of democratic equality within the
family, it has no less certainly altered the entire process of imposing economic responsibility upon the child, hence the process of preparing the child for such responsibility. In the
economy of scarcity, as I have remarked above, society could
not afford to support any substantial quota of nonproductive
members. Consequently, the child went to work when he was as
yet young. He attended primary school for a much shorter
school year than the child of today; only a minority attended
high school; and only the favored few attended college. Even
during the brief years of schooling, the child worked, in the
home, on the farm, or even in the factory. But today the
economy of abundance can afford to maintain a substantial
proportion of the population in nonproductive status, and it
assigns this role, sometimes against their will, to its younger
and its elder members. It protracts the years of schooling, and
it defers responsibilities for an unusually long span. It even
enforces laws setting minimal ages for leaving school, for going
to work, for consenting to sexual intercourse, or for marrying.
It extends the jurisdiction of juvenile courts to the eighteenth
or the twentieth year of age.

Such exemption from economic responsibility might seem
to imply a long and blissful youth free from strain for the
child. But the delays in reaching economic maturity are not
matched by comparable delays in other phases of growing up.
On the contrary, there are many respects in which the child
matures earlier. Physically, the child at the lower social level
will actually arrive at adolescence a year or so younger than his
counterpart a generation ago, because of improvement in
standards of health and nutrition. Culturally, the child is made
aware of the allurements of sex at an earlier age, partly by
his familiarity with the movies, television, and popular mag-

azines, and partly by the practice of "dating" in the early teens. By the standards of his peer group, he is encouraged to demand expensive and mature recreations, similar to those of adults, at a fairly early age. By reason of the desire of his parents that he should excel in the mobility race and give proof during his youth of the qualities which will make him a winner in later life, he is exposed to the stimuli of competition before he leaves the nursery. Thus there is a kind of imbalance between the postponement of responsibility and the quickening of social maturity which may have contributed to make American adolescence a more difficult age than human biology alone would cause it to be. Here, again, there are broad implications for the formation of character, and here, again, abundance is at work on both sides of the equation, for it contributes as much to the hastening of social maturity as it does to the prolongation of economic immaturity.

Some of these aspects of the rearing of children in the United States are as distinctively American, when compared with other countries, as any Yankee traits that have ever been attributed to the American people. In the multiplicity which always complicates social analysis, such aspects of child-rearing might be linked with a number of factors in American life. But one of the more evident and more significant links, it would seem certain, is with the factor of abundance. Such a tie is especially pertinent in this discussion, where the intention of the whole book has been to relate the study of character, as the historian would approach it, to the same subject as it is viewed by the behavioral scientist. In this chapter, especially, the attempt has been made to throw a bridge between the general historical force of economic abundance and the specific behavioral pattern of people's lives. Historical forces are too often considered only in their public and over-all effects, while private lives are interpreted without sufficient reference to the historical determinants which shape them. But no major force at work in society can possibly make itself felt at one of these levels without also having its impact at the other level. In view of this fact, the study of national character should not stand apart, as it has in the past, from the study of the process of character formation in the individual. In view of this fact, also, the effect of economic abundance is especially pertinent. For economic abundance is a factor whose presence and whose force may be clearly and precisely recognized in the most personal and intimate phases of the development of personality in the child. Yet, at the same time, the presence and the force of this factor are recognizable with equal certainty in the whole broad, general range of American experience, American ideals, and American institutions. At both levels, it has exercised a pervasive influence in the shaping of the American character.

For Further Reading

In addition to *People of Plenty,* Potter has written two shorter pieces on the American character and on nationalism: "The Quest for the National Character," in John Higham, ed., *The Reconstruction of American History* (1962); and "The Historian's Use of Nationalism and Vice Versa," *American Historical Review* 67 (July 1962), pp. 942–50. An able summary is Hans Kohn, *American Nationalism* (1957). Margaret Mead, *And Keep Your Powder Dry* (1942), and David Riesman and Nathan Glazer, *The Lonely Crowd* (rev. ed., 1961), works which greatly influenced Potter, are still very valuable for the student of the American past. A good collection of articles and an excellent annotated bibliography can be found in Michael McGiffert, ed., *The Character of Americans* (1964). An especially noteworthy analysis is Walter P. Metzger, "Generalizations About National Character," in Louis R. Gottschalk, ed., *Generalizations in the Writing of History* (1963), chap. 6.

There are few outstanding interpretative essays on the nature of the American experience. Apart from Frederick Jackson Turner and Charles Austin Beard, the ones that have influenced professionals the most—not infrequently in a negative way—seem to be Louis Hartz, *The Liberal Tradition in America* (1955); Richard Hofstadter, *The American Political Tradition* (1948); Henry Nash Smith, *Virgin Land* (1950); and

William Appleman Williams, *The Contours of American History* (1961). Other fine essays are Max Lerner, *America As a Civilization* (1957); Jacques Barzun, *God's Country and Mine* (1954); Geoffrey Gorer, *The American People* (1948); Denis W. Brogan, *The American Character* (1956); and Oscar Handlin, *Race and Nationality in American Life* (1957).